Bush's Wars

Bush's Wars

TERRY H. ANDERSON

OXFORD
UNIVERSITY PRESS

OXFORD
UNIVERSITY PRESS

Oxford University Press, Inc., publishes works that further
Oxford University's objective of excellence
in research, scholarship, and education.

Oxford   New York
Auckland   Cape Town   Dar es Salaam   Hong Kong   Karachi
Kuala Lumpur   Madrid   Melbourne   Mexico City   Nairobi
New Delhi   Shanghai   Taipei   Toronto

With offices in
Argentina   Austria   Brazil   Chile   Czech Republic   France   Greece
Guatemala   Hungary   Italy   Japan   Poland   Portugal   Singapore
South Korea   Switzerland   Thailand   Turkey   Ukraine   Vietnam

Copyright © 2011 by Terry H. Anderson

Published by Oxford University Press, Inc.
198 Madison Avenue, New York, NY 10016

www.oup.com

Oxford is a registered trademark of Oxford University Press

Library of Congress Cataloging-in-Publication Data
Anderson, Terry H.
Bush's wars / Terry H. Anderson.
   p.   cm.
Includes bibliographical references and index.
ISBN 978-0-19-974752-8 (hardback : acid-free paper) 1. United States—Foreign rela-
tions—2001–2009. 2. United States—Foreign relations—2009–3. War on Terrorism, 2001–2009—
Causes. 4. War on Terrorism, 2001–2009—Influence. 5. Afghan War, 2001—Causes. 6. Afghan War,
2001—Influence. 7. Iraq War, 2003—Causes. 8. Iraq War, 2003—Influence. I. Title.
E902.A5745   2011
973.931—dc22

9 8 7 6 5 4 3 2 1

Printed in the United States of America
on acid-free paper

To veterans of the wars in Afghanistan and Iraq,

and to my veteran, Rose

Contents

Preface

"You can't possibly figure out the history of the Bush presidency—until I'm dead."
—George W. Bush to his biographer Robert Draper,
December 12, 2006

On September 11, 2001, nineteen terrorists commandeered four passenger airplanes, slammed into the World Trade Center and Pentagon, killing over 2,700, and changed the future of the United States. Shortly after those attacks, President George W. Bush turned to his political adviser Karl Rove and said, "I am here for a reason, and this is how we're going to be judged." During the next 20 months the president declared his "War on Terror," ordered the attack on Afghanistan, and invaded Iraq.

Bush's Wars examines the administration's approach toward terrorism, Afghanistan, and especially Iraq—the most significant event of the first decade of the third millennium.

"Bush misled the nation into an unnecessary war," stated one of my Democratic colleagues as civil war raged in that country in 2006. "No," a Republican friend stated, "Iraq was noble intentions gone wrong." The conversation reflects the two basic interpretations of how and why the United States became involved in a war in Iraq. Critics have claimed that President Bush was interested in deposing Saddam as soon as he came into office, and he and his subordinates misled, even lied to, the American people in order to initiate a war in Iraq. This side argues that the tragedy of September 11, 2001, simply opened the door for the president to claim that Saddam Hussein was involved in the attack and was manufacturing weapons of mass destruction (WMDs) for himself and terrorists to use against the United States and the West. The president's supporters and policymakers in the administration disagree. The "president had an honest, well-grounded rationale, one that was not undermined by our failure to find WMD stockpiles in Iraq," wrote the former undersecretary of defense Douglas Feith. "President Bush ultimately decided that the risks of getting drawn into a renewed war on Saddam's terms were unacceptable. Weighing America's vulnerabilities against Saddam's record of aggression, he decided that it would be too dangerous to allow Saddam to choose the time and place of his next war with us."[1]

Many have written books on aspects of the War on Terror, Afghanistan, and Iraq. Many insiders in Baghdad and Washington, along with former administration officials, have published volumes, including Ali Allawi, Hans Blix, L. Paul Bremer, Richard Clarke, Larry Diamond, Michael DeLong, Tyler Drumheller, Charles Duelfer, Douglas Feith, Tommy Franks, Bob Graham, Chuck Hagel, Scott McClellan, Karl Rove, Ricardo Sanchez, James Stephenson, George Tenet, Joseph Wilson, and Valerie Plame Wilson. Journalists have interviewed thousands in America, Afghanistan, and Iraq, resulting in books by James Bamford, Rajiv Chandrasekaran, David Corn, James Fallows, Dexter Filkins, David Finkel, Michael Gordon, Seymour Hersh, Michael Isikoff, Sandra Mackey, James Mann, Jane Mayer, George Packer, Martha Raddatz, Thomas Ricks, Nir Rosen, Ron Suskind, Bob Woodward, and Michael Yon. Furthermore, the U.S. government has produced *The 9/11 Report* on the attack, the Duefler and Kay Reports on Iraq's WMDs, the Robb-Silberman Report on intelligence, while an increasing number of veterans have penned their accounts of combat in Iraq and Afghanistan, including Gary Berntsen, Colby Buzzell, Donovan Campbell, John Crawford, Andrew Exum, Paul Rieckhoff, Rob Schultheis, and Gary Schroen.

This small library of books has been very helpful, but this volume is different—it is the first history of Bush's Wars.

In order to understand how and why the Bush administration became involved in the War on Terror, the conflict in Afghanistan, and the war in Iraq, the reader needs sufficient background. Thus, I have included two introductory chapters. Introduction East, "The Improbable Country and the Graveyard of Empires," briefly traces the origins and problems of establishing the nations of Iraq and Afghanistan. It examines the rise of Islam, the British origins of modern Iraq, and the problems Sunni kings had governing a mostly Shiite nation, which the author Sandra Mackey labeled "The Improbable Country." It surveys main themes and events in Iraq up to the Baathist regime in the 1970s, and it also examines the origins and development of Afghanistan, various conquests of that region, which for centuries has been labeled the "Graveyard of Empires." Finally, it discusses the evolving British and Russian influence in Afghanistan into the 1970s.

The Introduction West, "The United States, Saddam, and al Qaeda, 1970s–2000," is more detailed. It introduces Saddam Hussein, his rise to and consolidation of power, and it surveys his attacks first on Iran in 1980 and then on Kuwait a decade later, along with the American response, Desert Storm. The chapter also inspects U.S. relations with Iran and the American response to the Soviet invasion and occupation of Afghanistan during the 1980s. The next decade the United States witnessed a new threat—Islamic terrorism and the rise of al Qaeda—and the chapter examines President Bill Clinton's response.

The book then focuses on the main topic—the Bush administration. Chapter 1 examines the president's first eleven months in office. "Bush, bin Laden, and the Pinnacle of World Sympathy" begins with the 2000 presidential campaign and shifts to the new administration's interest in Saddam as the threat from al Qaeda grew. It describes the tragedy of September 11, 2001, and the administration's response—the War on Terror and Operation Enduring Freedom against the Taliban in Afghanistan. It ends with U.S. and Northern Alliance troops routing the Taliban government in Afghanistan during the long, traumatic autumn of 2001, a time that was the pinnacle of world sympathy and support for the stricken United States. Chapter 2 begins with the president's "Axis of Evil" speech in January 2002 and traces the administration's rush to war with Iraq until the beginning of combat operations in March 2003. It focuses on how the administration attempted to convince a wary nation that a conflict in Iraq was in the national interest. Chapter 3, "Operation Iraqi Freedom," examines the quick "victory" of U.S. forces and the postwar problems faced by the American administrators Jay Garner and L. Paul Bremer. It investigates Bremer's Coalition Provisional Authority and its attempts to rule a nation while Lieutenant General Ricardo Sanchez and the U.S. military were facing a rising insurgency, one that was beginning to rage by autumn 2003. The next chapter, "Bush's War," investigates the conflict from the Ramadan Offensive in autumn 2003 to the end of the Bush administration. It examines how Secretary of Defense Donald Rumsfeld and his generals tried to fight the insurgency and why they failed as Iraq plunged toward civil war. The next secretary of defense, Robert Gates, along with Lieutenant General David Petraeus and his colleagues, changed the strategy, resulting in the 2007–08 "surge" and counterinsurgency, which significantly decreased the violence in Iraq. All the while, and as the administration concentrated on securing the Improbable Country, the Taliban reemerged in the Graveyard of Empires.

I end the book with two short chapters: the Epilogue, which briefly investigates the War on Terror, Afghanistan, and Iraq during the administration of President Barack Obama, up to August 2010, when the last combat troops left Iraq, and "Concluding Remarks and Legacies."

As I wrote this book, I continued teaching and assigned an article I published about how the nation became involved in the war in Iraq. Most of my students were shocked that they lived through this era yet knew so little about the conflict. They are not alone; surveys reveal that citizens in this electronic age are unaware of the facts or often are inaccurate in their assumptions about the War on Terror and conflicts in Afghanistan and Iraq. In that sense, as a colleague said to me, "by writing this book you are doing a public service." I hope so, for now is time to examine the origins, developments, main events, and legacies of Bush's Wars.

Finally, a statement on style and a caveat to readers. Over the years, Western authors have spelled Islamic names many ways, and I have tried to use the most common usage. Also, in a book this size, I have had to focus on the narrative and delete many connecting but peripheral topics. Thus, this book excludes interesting topics such as the Pentagon's involvement in the stories of Jessica Lynch and Pat Tillman, the former New York City police commissioner Bernard Kerik's failed attempts to train Iraqi police, Patrick Fitzgerald's inquiry into the outing of CIA agent Valerie Plame Wilson and the judicial proceedings of I. Lewis "Scooter" Libby, the relatives of the September 11 victims and the development of the 9/11 Commission, many government commissions that investigated the Bush administration and Iraq after the invasion, and many military campaigns in Afghanistan and Iraq. Indeed, authors have written large books on many of these topics, so this volume would have had to be many times its size. The aim of this volume is not to be encyclopedic but to efficiently examine the history of Bush's Wars.

Thus, this book is an attempt to "figure out," in Bush's words, the history of the defining policies of his presidency—and to do it years before his death.

TA
College Station, Texas
December 8, 2010

Acknowledgments

Many journalists and war correspondents have held thousands of interviews that have been published or have resulted in many fine books about a certain aspect of Bush's Wars. Although I cite them in endnotes, they deserve a special thanks for providing interviews that helped me write this book: Tom Bullock, Rajiv Chandrasekaran, David Corn, James Fallows, David Finkel, Dexter Filkins, Anne Garrels, Michael Isikoff, Sandra Mackey, Nil Rosen, George Packer, and especially Tom Ricks. I also want to thank NPR and PBS. Their fine journalists have interviewed thousands of participants and have aired them in programs and posted full interviews on their website. For military operations, I would like to thank the U.S. Army Combat Studies Institute, the Combined Arms Center, and the Contemporary Operations Study Team, who held extensive interviews with military personnel and published them in many books, including *On Point* and *A Different Kind of War*.

At Texas A&M I have the pleasure of working with fine colleagues who have discussed parts of this project: Dale Baum, Troy Bickham, Jim Bradford, Chip Dawson, Chester Dunning, Jeff Engel, Andy Kirkendall, John Lenihan, Jason Parker, and Brian Linn, who along with Arnie Krammer, suggested the title.

The Texas A&M University Association of Former Students again generously funded a semester leave, which allowed me to finish the manuscript on time.

The Oxford University Press team was superb. Dave McBride listened to my plans, encouraged me, supplied a fine contract, and sent the manuscript to readers. Dave also edited the manuscript, asked tough questions, and forced many positive changes. Alexandra Dauler kept the process moving smoothly and Sylvia Cannizzaro performed thoughtful copyediting.

I would also like to thank other readers. George Herring read the first half of the manuscript, supplying his usual valuable comments. Leor Halevi tried to keep me accurate concerning the Islamic world (his specialty), and Peter L. Hahn saved me from some errors in the first chapters. Two USMC combat vets at Texas A&M read chapters and supplied comments that helped keep me, a USN Vietnam vet, in line with the land-based military. Vietnam vet Colonel Bill Collopy (ret.) read chapter 3, and Iraq and Afghanistan vet Colonel Gerald "Jerry" L. Smith read chapters 3 and 4. I also was fortunate that the former ambassador to Iraq, and current dean of the Bush School at Texas A&M, Ryan Crocker, read chapter 3 and saved me from errors concerning the initial occupation.

Two favorite people read the entire manuscript and edited it before submission. In spring 2009, Alex Gandy was the finest senior in my undergraduate course U.S. 1945 to the Present—I hired her. She was a delight to work with, giving me her generation's perspective and asking probing questions, forcing numerous changes that improved this manuscript. My wife Rose Eder reads everything that I publish, and while working on this book she was my companion climbing Kilimanjaro, scuba diving with whale sharks in the Galapagos, watching leatherbacks lay eggs in Raja Ampat, exploring steaks and wines in Argentina, and catching trout and salmon in Alaska. She's ready for the next adventure.

Two friends helped me in other important ways. After months of straining over the computer, Janet Jones, masseuse extraordinaire, soothed my neck and back, released nerve aggravation, and put a smile back on my face. My "bro" Dan Eder provided continual commentary on my project and tried unsuccessfully to have me name this book "Between Iraq and a Hard Place."

In the acknowledgments it is customary to inform the reader that the author takes full responsibility for any and all errors. Normally, I would do that, but in an astonishing act of unparalleled generosity my brothers SK and JD, my tennis partners David Ogden and Joe Golsan, and the incredible poetry girls Kathi Appelt, Dinny Linn, and Rose, all have offered to be the "fall guys." They will answer for all mistakes—at least that's what I remember after a few cold brews. What buddies!

Finally, this book is dedicated to the veterans of the wars in Afghanistan and Iraq, and to my wife—she knows why.

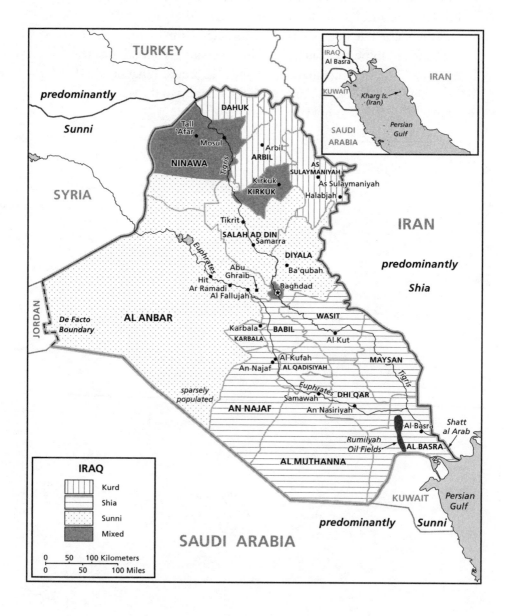

TURKEY

predominantly

Sunni

SYRIA

JORDAN

DAHUK

Tall 'Afar

Mosul

Arbil

NINAWA **ARBIL**

Kirkuk

KIRKUK

AS SULAYMANIYAH

As Sulaymaniyah

Halabjah

Tigris

Tikrit

SALAH AD DIN

Samarra

DIYALA

Euphrates

Ba'qubah

Abu Ghraib

Hit

Ar Ramadi

Al Fallujah

Baghdad

AL ANBAR

De Facto Boundary

WASIT

Karbala

BABIL

KARBALA

Al Kut

Al Kufah

An Najaf

AL QADISIYAH

MAYSAN

sparsely populated

Euphrates

DHI QAR

Samawah

AN NAJAF

An Nasiriyah

Tigris

Al Basra

Shatt al Arab

Rumilyah Oil Fields

AL BASRA

AL MUTHANNA

KUWAIT

Persian Gulf

predominantly **Sunni**

SAUDI ARABIA

predominantly

Shia

IRAN

IRAQ

Al Basra

KUWAIT

SAUDI ARABIA

Kharg Is. (Iran)

Persian Gulf

IRAN

IRAQ

	Kurd
	Shia
	Sunni
	Mixed

0   50   100 Kilometers

0   50   100 Miles

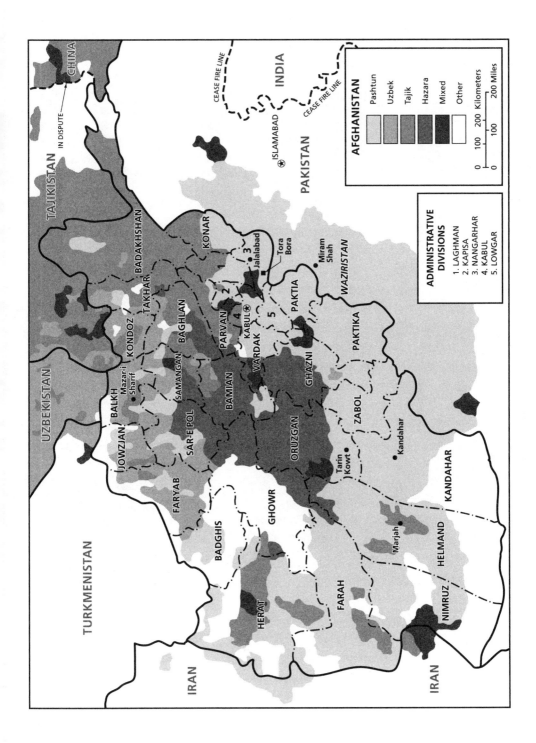

Bush's Wars

Introduction East

*The Improbable Country and
the Graveyard of Empires*

Alexander the Great conquered the area in 334 BC, and his men named it Mesopotamia, the land "between rivers." The waters of the Tigris and Euphrates made a fertile valley that had been home to ancient kingdoms—Sumer, Akkad, Babylon, Assyria. Alexander died the next year in Babylon, and over the next two centuries the Greek presence in the area declined as they were confronted by the Persians, who in turn were challenged by the Romans. For over 500 years the area was the battleground between the imperial armies of Rome and Persia, and the heirs to the conflict were Byzantium, or the Eastern Roman Empire, with its capital at Constantinople, and the Persian Sasanid Empire in Ctesiphon on the Tigris River. Eventually, years of fighting weakened both the Byzantines and Persians, and in 632 they were confronted in the land between rivers by the armies of Islam.

Those armies had spread out from Medina and Mecca and had conquered the Arabian Peninsula by that year, the date when the Prophet Muhammad died. His followers looked for a caliph, a successor to lead the emerging Islam community. "No event in history has divided Islam more profoundly and durably than the succession to Muhammad," wrote one scholar, for during the next decades it resulted in a great schism between two main groups of Muslims: the Shiites (or Shia) and Sunnis.

The term "Shia" derives from shortening "Shiat Ali," partisans of Ali ibn Abi Talib, who was Muhammad's cousin and son-in-law; Ali had married the Prophet's daughter, Fatima. The Shia believed the Prophet had designated Ali, so to them Ali was next in the order of succession after Muhammad. Sunnis disagreed; they felt that the community of followers had chosen Abu Bakr, Muhammad's father-in-law, to lead the new religion. Abu Bakr became the first caliph, but he died a couple years later, and the community appointed others to the caliphate. Eventually, Ali became caliph, but in 661 he was assassinated and so became one of the first martyrs of Islam. Supposedly, Ali was buried in Najaf in southern Mesopotamia; the Imam Ali Mosque there became Islam's third holiest shrine, after the Prophet's Mosque in Medina and the Grand Mosque in Mecca. Since, Shiites generally have believed that martyrdom is a road to heaven. They also believed that since the Prophet eventually had many wives and children, only his descendants could be Islamic leaders, imams or ayatollahs, meaning "signs of God." These descendant-leaders were almost infallible in the hierarchy of Shia Islam. One grandson of Muhammad, the youngest son of Ali, Husayn bin Ali, led his troops against other early believers and died at the Battle of Karbala, south of Baghdad. He became a martyr after his death in 1680, and Shiites make an annual pilgrimage to his shrine at Karbala. Eventually, Shiites moved into Persia and established trade routes from India to Najaf and Karbala, which became important centers for their commerce, education, and religion, while Basra became an important Shiite port.

Sunnis followed a different path. Their name came from "sunna," "the tradition of the Prophet." They supported no formal clergy, formed independent mosques, and believed that any learned man could rise to leadership within the faith. Their scholars developed numerous schools of law and traditions, and eventually Sunnis became the largest group on the Arabian peninsula and throughout the Middle East. In Mesopotamia, they settled in the central area in and around Baghdad.

While Sunnis and Shiites have argued—and battled—over the origins of Islam for centuries, there was little debate about their conquest. At the time of the Prophet's death the Islamic armies were moving into Mesopotamia and during the next 30 years they conquered lands from Persia to Egypt. During the next decades they invaded

Afghanistan and North Africa, and in the next centuries Islam spread from the Iberian Peninsula to the Balkans to Southeast Asia.

Islamic expansion concerned Christian popes and kings. Arabs had taken over Palestine in the seventh century, but for the most part they allowed Christians to make pilgrimages to the Holy Land. Yet in the eleventh century Moslem armies were moving toward Constantinople (modern Istanbul, Turkey), capital of the Christian Byzantine Empire, while Christian princes on the Iberian Peninsula were trying to push Islam out of what today is modern Spain and Portugal. In 1095, at the Council of Clermont, France, Pope Urban II preached that it was time to take back Jerusalem and the first Christian city, Antioch. The pontiff declared that those who died in this endeavor would have remission for their sins, opening the gates to heaven. That resulted in numerous volunteers, who began the first crusade in 1098. Christian armies landed in the Holy Land and began the siege of Antioch, which they captured; the next year they took Jerusalem. In both towns the crusaders destroyed mosques and temples, massacred both Jewish and Moslem civilians, and committed atrocities, even cannibalism. The Christians held the areas for about 50 years, the Moslems counterattacked, and in 1147 French and German armies marched to Jerusalem, the second crusade. That was followed by another Islamic advance in 1187, when the sultan of Egypt recaptured Jerusalem, sparking the third crusade. This was the Kings' Crusade, led by King Philip II of France, the Holy Roman Emperor Frederick I, and Richard the Lionhearted of England. As usual, the brutality was excessive; although Richard promised he would leave civilians unharmed if the city of Acre surrendered, he had his soldiers massacre everyone.

And so it was. For centuries Europeans attacked the Middle East in numerous crusades—assaulting Islam—and searing hatred of the West into Moslem minds. But there was no lasting victory, for the armies of Islam always counterattacked. In 1453 Sunni Turks captured Constantinople, causing the collapse of the Byzantine Empire and the establishment of Istanbul as headquarters of the new Ottoman Empire. At its greatest expanse their Islamic empire reached from southern Spain to Sicily and into Hungary, from Morocco to Mesopotamia, and north to Mosul, a city on the edge of land occupied by the Kurds, people of Persian descent who spoke their own language and practiced Sunni Islam.

The Ottoman Empire did not extend to Persia, which proved impossible to conquer and which, beginning in the sixteenth century, launched numerous invasions into Mesopotamia. The Sunni Ottomans fought the Shiite Persians for 300 years. In 1508 Persians seized parts of Mesopotamia, desecrated Sunni religious sites, and repressed local Sunnis. The Ottomans returned in 1534, capturing Baghdad and massacring Shiite soldiers and clerics. Persians invaded in 1623, took Baghdad, and slaughtered the Sunni inhabitants. Fifteen years later, the Ottomans retook the city and murdered almost 2,000 Shiites in their shrine cities of Najaf and Karbala. Peace reigned for almost a century, until 1733, when the Persians again invaded, laid siege to Baghdad, and starved to death 100,000 inhabitants, mostly Sunnis. A century later, the Ottomans attacked Karbala, massacring 30,000 Persian Shiites. That was the final act of massive bloodletting, but memories of these conflicts burned deep into the minds of both Islamic sects.

Ottoman rulers realized the distrust between the Sunni and Shia, so in areas of mixed faiths and race, they divided up subjects by *millet*, a community of people sharing the same religion, and in *wilayets*, or provinces, of which three eventually became Iraq: Baghdad (Sunni), Basra (Shiite), and Mosul (Kurds). Within the *wilayets* not all people were equal. Because they were Sunnis themselves, Ottomans gave the top political and social positions in Mesopotamia to Sunnis, leaving the scraps to Shiites, Kurds, Jews, and Christians. Generally, Sunnis dominated the government, courts, and educational system. During the eighteenth and nineteenth centuries many nomadic tribes in the south converted to Shiism, making that the largest sect in contemporary Iraq.

That was the tenuous status quo in Mesopotamia when World War I erupted in Europe. The Allied Powers of Britain, France, Russia, and eventually Italy faced off against the Central Powers of Germany, Austria-Hungary, and the Ottoman Empire. Just three months after the guns of August 1914 the British landed an expeditionary force of Indian soldiers near Basra and moved up Mesopotamia to meet the Ottoman army near Baghdad. While some thought that was a military diversion from the main battlefields of Europe, the reason was obvious to educated Englishmen. Throughout the nineteenth century Britain had aimed to protect the jewel of its empire, India, and to do that it had gained control of the vital waterway, the Suez Canal. Moreover, in 1908 oil had been discovered in Persia, which stimulated interest on the Continent as they manufactured automobiles, trucks, tanks, and airplanes, and were shifting their coal-burning navies to petroleum. The British, Dutch, and Germans wanted to secure oil concessions in the *wilayets* of Mesopotamia, especially Mosul, and in March 1914 the Ottomans signed an agreement that granted the concession to the Turkish Oil Company, a company in which the British controlled the majority of shares.

The British invasion, however, proved difficult, and soon the expeditionary force was bogged down, unable to dislodge the Ottoman forces. Needing assistance, the British dispatched T. E. Lawrence, a military intelligence officer, to organize Arab tribes into a fighting force, and eventually "Lawrence of Arabia" and his Arab troops weakened the Ottomans. To get the Arabs to fight on their side, the British formed alliances with them and the Kurds—and double-crossed both. The British promised the Kurds independence and the Arabs ownership of land in the Kurdish north, including the large oil reserve in Mosul. In fact, the British and the French negotiated the Sykes-Picot Agreement, totally ignoring Arab desires and designating that after the war London and Paris would control the remnants of the Ottoman Empire.

By the end of the war the British had taken Baghdad and driven north into Mosul, extending their occupation into southern Kurdistan. Exhausted by the conflict and corruption, the Ottoman Empire, now called the "sick man of Europe," finally died as the victors met and signed the Treaty of Versailles. In the Middle East, France got the mandate for Syria, which included the future Lebanon, and Britain, which already controlled Egypt, received mandates for what eventually became Palestine, Jordan, and Iraq.

"Our armies do not come into your cities and lands as conquerors or enemies, but as liberators," declared Lieutenant General Stanley Maude, commander of the British expeditionary force, after he entered Baghdad in 1917. Yet shortly thereafter, the British liberators refused to evacuate, convincing most inhabitants that the new British rulers simply had replaced the Ottomans.

The British occupation created distrust, resentment, and eventually revolt. The English used their own colonialists to replace Sunni civil servants and officers, who became unemployed; Shiite clergy hated being occupied by Christians; Kurds felt betrayed. In 1919 a Kurdish sheik proclaimed himself "King of Kurdistan," prompting the British army to advance north and crush the rebellion with bombardments—and poison gas—which first had been used in battle during World War I. Kurdistan never became a nation, and those people were incorporated into Turkey, Iran, and Iraq. In the south, Arabs grew restless with the occupation, called for Arab nationalism, and revolted in 1920. The rebels deployed over 130,000 men against the occupiers, and it took the British army six months to regain control, losing over 2,000 troops and killing some 10,000 Iraqis.

The revolts, however, had an impact on the British. They realized that the occupation of the Middle East was very expensive, and in order to decide what to do in the area they held a conference in Cairo. The new colonial secretary, Winston Churchill, chaired the meeting. Also in attendance were Sir Percy Cox, the diplomat in charge of Mesopotamia; Lawrence of Arabia, who was a celebrity because of a best-selling biography about him; and Gertrude Bell, an amazing English woman who had been searching for artifacts in Mesopotamia for years and was fluent in Arabic. At Cairo, the British decided on a new name for their mandate—Iraq—a name that had been used since ancient times to denote the lands of the lower Tigris and Euphrates basin, and they established a monarchy for Iraq.

The British faced numerous problems in the postwar Middle East, and the first was national borders. Some areas were obvious. The Egyptians had lived by the Nile and had built an empire whose history spanned back over 3,000 years to Ramses II, and the Persians had occupied the land that became Iran for 2,500 years since Cyrus the Great. Certain tribes, families, and religious groups had dominated other areas, such as the Hashimites, "family of the Prophet," in what became Saudi Arabia and Jordan. But other areas lacked definition, so where would new nations be created? The British administration drew boundaries for Iraq, and much of that task fell to Sir Percy Cox and the "Daughter of the Desert," Gertrude Bell, the appointed oriental secretary in Baghdad. Borders of most of the emerging states were primarily based on European claims to oil reserves, with little regard to tribal, ethnic, or religious differences. That was particularly true in Iraq, where Cox and Bell separated the port of Kuwait, a bay that had been ruled by the Sabah family but also had been a district in the Basra Province under the Ottomans.

In 1899, the family had asked for British protection, which was given, so the Sabahs no longer felt part of the Ottoman Empire (despite remaining in it formally), to the chagrin of their northern Arab neighbors. Bell made Kuwait a small British protectorate, and that shrunk the Iraqi coast and made trade more difficult from Basra since it had to go down the Shatt al-Arab waterway instead of directly out of Kuwait Bay on the Persian Gulf. Bell also concocted a diamond-shaped neutral zone between Iraq and the new Kingdom of Saudi Arabia, which eventually created tension over future oil reserves. More importantly, the British had little understanding of the potential for conflict when they combined the two main Islamic groups, Shiite and Sunni, into Iraq.

The British could relate much more easily to the Sunnis, who were only about 20 percent of the population of Iraq. "The truth is I'm becoming a Sunni myself," Gertrude Bell wrote to her father. They "are staunch and they are guided . . . by reason." To her, the Shiites were unpredictable, for they could be swayed by "some ignorant fanatic" religious leader "to think differently" and rebel against the British Empire. Thus, the English established a Sunni king, and to help them control the oil reserves, pro-British monarchies also appeared in Jordan and Syria.

Iraq was "a creature of its fragmented past," wrote the Middle East journalist Sandra Mackey. "It was a contrived political entity with no natural center of gravity." Sunni Baghdad looked west toward other Sunni lands; Shiite southern provinces looked east toward Iran; and the Kurdish north, isolated from the Arab nation, looked inward. The population divided along the lines of land and wealth, tribal groupings, and, of course, religion. Mackey labeled Iraq "The Improbable Country."[1]

The British also had a role in inventing what became Afghanistan. Alexander the Great arrived with his army about 330 BC. "We are dealing with savage beast," the Greek leader supposedly told his army, "which lapse of time only can tame, when they are caught and caged, because their own nature cannot tame them." The Hellenic campaign was difficult. Tribesmen and horse warriors fought ruthlessly, resulting in a bloody war of attrition. In seven years the army failed to subdue the area; the Greeks' tenuous grip collapsed after Alexander's death in 323 BC.

After the demise of the Greeks, several kingdoms fought for control of the area—the Seleucids, Bactria, Mauryan—and during the first century AD the Buddhist Kushans moved in and spread their religion and culture. They built monasteries, stupas, and the enormous Buddha statues in Bamiyan along the Silk Road, a caravan route linking the markets of China and Mesopotamia. The "Central Asian roundabout," the British historian Arnold Toynbee called Afghanistan, since trade and migration "routes converge from the Tigris-Euphrates Basin via the Iranian Plateau, from India through the passes over the Hindu Kush, from the Far East via the Tarim Basin, and from the adjacent Eurasian Steppe."

A series of empires invaded the land during the next fourteen centuries. In 652 AD, the Arab armies arrived from Persia and began the long process of displacing Buddhism and establishing Islam. Gengis Khan and his Mongol army swept through the area in 1220, devastating the land and eventually creating an empire that stretched from China to the Caucasus. The Mongol conqueror Timur (or Tamerlane) began his Afghan conquest in 1383, followed by an attack from Persia when Emperor Babur captured Kabul in 1504 and established the Mughal Empire. In the seventeenth and eighteenth centuries the Pashtun tribes increased their power and eventually the area was populated mostly with Pashtuns in the south, Tajiks in the north, and some Uzbeks and Hazaras in the northwest; all but the Hazaras practiced Sunni Islam.

Most of these conquests were brutal, and the invading armies eventually realized that Afghans were a fiercely independent people who resisted foreign conquest and eventually overcame their invaders; for centuries the rugged terrain had been called the Graveyard of Empires.

The British learned that the hard way. In an attempt to shore up their colony of India, and blunt possible Russian influence, the British invaded Afghanistan in 1839 and attempted to establish a puppet regime in Kabul. Three years later, angry mobs were attacking the foreigners, and the remaining British army of 4,500 and its followers of 12,000 were forced to flee Kabul and begin a perilous retreat to Jalalabad in what is now Pakistan. Under constant ambush in frigid cold and heavy snow, only one British soldier, wounded and on a dying horse, arrived in Jalalabad. In the next decades, the Russian Empire expanded along the Amu Darya, or Amu River, to the northern mountains of Afghanistan and sent diplomats to Kabul. That provoked the British. In 1878, some 34,000 British troops launched another invasion, which was almost as disastrous as the first because of numerous tribal revolts and insurgencies. But after a year of violence, the Afghans were exhausted and temporarily subdued and their land was placed under British diplomatic influence. That meant that the British, not the Afghans or Pakistanis, drew the borders of eastern Afghanistan. In 1893, Sir Henry Mortimer Durand demarcated the border between British India, which would become Pakistan, and Afghanistan. As in Iraq, the British did not draw the border based on ethnic or tribal allegiances, but on their own imperial ambitions. They divided the Pashtun people in order to enlarge colonial India, with the result that 40 percent of Afghanistan's current population is Pashtun and almost 20 percent of Pakistan's; in fact, more Pashtuns reside in contemporary northwest Pakistan than in Afghanistan.

During World War I, the British and Russians kept ample pressure on the Afghan government until the czarist regime collapsed in 1917. That, along with another insurgency and turmoil in Kabul, prompted a third British invasion. Within a year, the British Empire relented, and in 1919 London and Kabul signed a treaty recognizing the independence of Afghanistan.

After the treaty, Amanullah Khan, a Pashtun, became king. But after visiting Europe he returned to advocate Western reforms and was overthrown in 1929 by Habibullah Kalakani, a Tajik, who only lasted months until members of the Pashtun Musahiban family founded a dynasty that lasted five decades. Progress was slow and uneven in the country, and by 1970 there were increasing concerns that the king was out of touch with his people. In July 1973, the former prime minister Muhammad Daoud Khan staged a coup with the backing of the Afghan Army and proclaimed a republic with himself as president.

The United States showed little interest in the nation until Daoud tried to improve ties with the Soviet Union. Americans had already fought communist expansion in Korea from 1950 to 1953 and had been doing the same during the 1960s in Southeast Asia, so in the 1970s the CIA grew more concerned about Daoud's relations with the Soviets and the growing Afghan communist parties. Daoud attempted to impose more centralized control as the USSR became Afghanistan's main trading partner and supplier of military hardware.

But by the late 1970s, Daoud also began looking for closer ties with Arab nations and the West, which angered the USSR and the emerging communist People's Democratic Party of Afghanistan. In 1978, after the assassination of a prominent leftist leader, 15,000 joined the funeral procession and rioted. Daoud arrested Marxist leaders, provoking the military to stage a bloody coup d'état. Daoud was murdered, and tribes, communist, and Islamic groups fought for power. With Soviet backing, Nur Mohammad Taraki emerged and signed Decree No. 1, which proclaimed a new nation called the Democratic Republic of Afghanistan. He introduced Marxist policies that conflicted with Islamic beliefs and sharia law, and signed a friendship treaty with the USSR, which resulted in more military equipment heading to Kabul. That alarmed the United States. The "Soviets were on the march," recalled one CIA official. In 1979 Taraki was murdered, which eventually brought Babrak Karmal to power, but the fragile nation slid further into rebellion. Its army was in mutiny or desertion, and the Karmal government was near collapse, prompting the Russian invasion that stunned the West. "It'll be over in three or four weeks," the Soviet leader Leonid Brezhnev said to a colleague.

Iraq also was fragile from the 1920s to the 1970s. In the earlier decade, the British established a weak parliament and gave the monarchy not to an Iraqi but to a foreigner. They imported a Sunni leader from the Hashemite family of Saudi Arabia. King Faisal briefly had been the ruler of Syria before the British placed him on the throne in Baghdad. Many locals considered him an outsider and favored a leader from Basra, but the British expelled him to one of their colonies, Ceylon. The English then rigged a plebiscite in which Faisal won 96 percent of the vote, successfully withholding democracy from the majority Shiites.

Thankful for the throne, the king responded appropriately to the British. One of his first actions was to enter into a treaty guaranteeing that Baghdad would consult with London on virtually all foreign policy decisions and most domestic issues. It also placed English advisers throughout the new Iraqi government. The king allowed the reconfiguration of the Turkish Oil Company into the Iraq Petroleum Company (IPC), which guaranteed that the company and the nation's oil reserves would be owned by British, Dutch, French, and American corporations.

King Faisal faced numerous problems and relied on advice and protection from the British. The Persian government refused to recognize Iraq, claiming Najaf and Karbala as "holy places of Persia." As a result, the British had to negotiate a border agreement that gave those Shiite holy cities to Iraqi Sunni rule. The British also trained Faisal's army and made Sunnis most of the officers and Shiites the enlisted men. That led to oppression of the Shiites, and they responded with sporadic attacks on British troops, resulting in high expenses for the empire. "I hate Iraq," Colonial Secretary Churchill confessed in 1926. "I wish we had never gone to the place." By 1930, Faisal was demanding more autonomy and the British signed the Anglo-Iraqi Treaty. It promised independence in two years but safeguarded London's petroleum interest and oversight of the Iraq army. It also granted the British two military bases, one fifty miles west of Baghdad and the other near Basra.

Iraq was not a good training ground for a constitutional monarchy. Faisal died in 1933, and his son Ghazi I became the king. He had been educated in Britain but disliked the British and at age 21 was more interested in enjoying his own pleasures than in ruling the nascent country. In 1936, a general and his men revolted, killed the defense minister, and created a new government, but they left the playboy king on the throne. The general lasted only a year before he was assassinated. A year later Ghazi dissolved the parliament and in 1939 began ann-ouncing plans to invade Kuwait—where oil had been discovered the previous year. That increased nationalistic fervor in Iraq, but before the king could reunite Kuwait with Iraq he sped his new Buick convert-ible on a midnight ride down a road and into a tree, dying an hour later. His son, Faisal II, assumed the throne, but since he was a young child, the real power was held by his uncle, the regent Abdul al-Ilah and his premier Nuri al-Said.

The two men ruled the country as Europe became embroiled in World War II. Germany occupied France, and Britain fought for its sur-vival. To maintain their oil supply, Britain landed troops in Basra with-out Iraqi consent, which prompted some skirmishes with renegades in the local army. London also made contradictory promises in the Middle East, pledging Iraq more independence after the war and promising the Palestinians and the Jews a future homeland in the same area—Palestine. Iraq remained in turmoil during the war, with soaring infla-tion, food shortages that led to starvation, tribal conflict, and scattered rebellions in Kurdistan. "There are few countries which . . . present more security problems than Iraq," noted a British report in 1945. "It has tribal and minority problems. The maintenance of security with so many pol-itical causes would tax the ingenuity of a sophisticated country, how much more so of Iraq."

After the war Abdul al-Ilah and al-Said kept a tight reign on the government, even though Faisal II had returned after being educated in England. "He was by training as nearly a British product as it is possible for a foreigner to be," declared a British military officer stationed in Iraq. Faisal II was 18 in 1953 as he ascended to the throne, pledging to be a constitutional monarch who would safeguard democratic principles. In reality, al-Ilah and al-Said controlled the press and politics while the economy sunk into a series of recessions. Agriculture and oil were the mainstays, but drought reduced crops and led to starvation, and the vast majority of the oil revenue filled the coffers of British, French, and American corporations. To Iraqis, it was just another expression of foreign domination and Western imperialism, stimulating Arab nationalism.

Yet before that nationalism could catch fire, the Grand Alliance that had won World War II was breaking down. What followed was the cold war. Throughout the 1950s the United States and Britain became increasingly concerned about the spread of Soviet communism in the Middle East. To prevent that, the Anglo-Americans provided military aid to Iraq and helped form the Arab League. Iraq, Jordan, Lebanon, Syria, Egypt, Saudi Arabia, and Yemen would supposedly contain communism, and in 1955 the British convinced Iraq to join its old enemies Iran and Turkey in the Baghdad Pact, a defense agreement that also included Pakistan. That satisfied American and British aims but irritated Arab nationalists, who saw the pact as yet another demonstration of Western domination.

Two other events fed the fire of Arab nationalism in the 1950s. In 1952 a group of army officers overthrew Egypt's King Farouk and established a new leader, Gamel Abdel Nasser. Soon, he was boosting the pan-Arab movement throughout the Middle East, a movement that had been reignited by the 1948 war for Palestine and the establishment of the Jewish state, Israel. Nasser condemned the Baghdad Pact, urged neutrality in the cold war, and advocated a revolt against the British-backed King Faisal II, a "lackey of Western imperialism." Then, Nasser stunned the West by nationalizing the Suez Canal. In response, in 1956 the British, French, and Israelis invaded Egypt. The Iraq government protested the invasion, but actually King Faisal II supported the British. That put him at odds with most of his subjects who supported the Egyptians over the Western invaders and Jews. The United Nations eventually intervened and the invaders withdrew, but more Iraqis questioned their king and premier Nuri al-Said.

Among the doubters were the so-called Free Officers within the Iraqi army. In 1958, Iraq formed a federation with Jordan in an attempt to slow the spread of Nasser's pan-Arab nationalism. Al-Said ordered the Iraqi army to Jordan in July, but General Abdul Karim Qassim refused, declaring that his Iraqi troops would not get involved in a potential conflict with other Arabs, and that sparked the revolt of the Free Officers. The secret army group blocked the main roads, took over the train, radio, and telegraph stations, and surrounded the palace. They captured the young king, and after promising to let him leave the country safely, executed him and his uncle, the former regent Abdul al-Ilah, killing off the most powerful members of the Hashemite dynasty. The other power broker, al-Said, was caught the next day attempting to escape Baghdad dressed as a woman. Citizens cut up his body and dragged the remains through the streets.

Watching the bloody coup from Washington, President Dwight Eisenhower said to his National Security Council, "If you go and live with these Arabs, you will find that they simply cannot understand our ideas of freedom or human dignity. They have lived so long under dictatorships of one form or another, how can we expect them to run successfully a free government?"

General Qassim had no interest in a free government but did want to reform Iraq. First, his administration distanced itself from the British. They renamed the country the Republic of Iraq, closed the British military bases, withdrew from the Baghdad Pact, declared neutrality in the cold war, and created alliances with and started buying arms from communist nations, including the Soviet Union—all actions that alarmed the West. Qassim also withdrew from Britain's sterling block; Iraq's currency was no longer tied to the British Commonwealth. He began domestic reforms, reducing the hours in the working day, increasing salaries for low and mid-level bureaucrats, and enforcing social security for the aged. He passed a progressive law for women, which demanded equal rights in inheritance, and, in contrast to Islamic law, restricted the rights of men to divorce wives. He continued to make Iraq a more secular regime and appointed a woman to direct a government ministry, a first in the Arab world. He improved the educational and health systems and attempted to revive the economy, instituting a land reform program, encouraging industrialization, and building housing.

Qassim's revolution also included the oil industry. Since Western corporations controlled Iraq's oil revenues through the Iraq Petroleum Company, only about 5 percent of oil income remained in Baghdad. The general demanded a 50–50 share in profits, employment of Iraqi workers instead of foreigners, and eventually the ownership of 90 percent of oil concessions in all areas that had not yet been drilled in Iraq. The Western owners were outraged. They contacted the Eisenhower and later the John F. Kennedy administrations, and the CIA began to encourage Iraqi military officers to stage a coup. Qassim charged forward and passed Public Law 80, which would strip the IPC of 99 percent of its concessions, increasing revenue for Iraq; the new law was to begin in 1963. He also began negotiating with other Arab nations, and in 1960 the five most important producers—Saudi Arabia, Iran, Iraq, Kuwait, and Venezuela—formed the Organization of Petroleum Exporting Countries (OPEC), which during the cold war had major implications for the West. "Middle East oil," said U.S. Secretary of the Treasury Robert Anderson, was "as essential to mutual security as atomic warheads."

The next year, 1961, the British withdrew from Kuwait and it became an independent nation. Five days later, Qassim declared Kuwait a part of Iraq and threatened an invasion, which prompted a quick return of British forces. The British, United Nations, and the Arab League protested Iraq's claim, and Qassim broke diplomatic relations with many Arab nations. Sensing weakness, the Kurds rebelled, forcing Qassim to send his army to the north, where he became involved in a protracted struggle.

The Free Officers had ended the monarchy but had failed to unite Iraq. The Iraqi nationalists, often aligned with socialists or communists, remained at odds with Arab nationalists, who either wanted to form an alliance or become more integrated with other Arab nations. Wracked by power struggles, a new political movement began to take hold in Iraq—the Baathists.

After World War II two Syrians formed the Baath Party, named from a term that means "rebirth" or "insurrection" in Arabic. Their motto was their aim: "One Arab nation with an eternal mission." Pan-Arabs with a socialist bent, they advocated modernizing the economy and ending Western dominance in the Middle East. During the early

1950s the party was active in Iraq, and appealed to the young, educated elites, both Shiites and Sunnis, though the latter led the party in Iraq.

Qassim's hold on power became increasingly tenuous during his five-year rule. The Free Officers had expected Iraq to move closer to the Pan-Arabism expounded by Egypt's Nasser, but Qassim made an alliance with the communists which in March 1959 sparked another Free Officer revolt in Mosul. Qassim suppressed it with a vicious assault, resulting in many deaths and stimulating the pro-Arab Baathists to plan their own coup. In October a few Baathists, including the young party member Saddam Hussein, attempted to assassinate the ruler, opening fire on his motorcade as it drove through the streets of Baghdad and wounding the general. His guards returned fire, injuring the assailants, including Saddam, and rushed their leader to the hospital. Qassim recovered and then attempted to crush the Baath Party. Later, the Kurds attacked Mosul, and again, Qassim dispatched his loyal troops to crush the revolt and execute the rebel leaders.

By 1963 the Baathists again had decided the time was ripe to assassinate Qassim. The Kennedy administration also was becoming increasingly alarmed. Worried that Iraq was slipping toward communism, the CIA supported the plot. In February, just days before Public Law 80 was to go into effect, the Baathists staged their uprising. They neutralized most of the army and attacked the headquarters for two days before Qassim finally surrendered. The assailants gave him a hearing, held a trial, and executed him, all within one hour. His bullet-riddled body was shown nightly on Iraqi TV. The killing continued; between February and October the Baathists rounded up communists and suspected opponents and murdered ten thousand, many of them slaughtered in the streets of Baghdad.[2]

The first Baath regime, however, only lasted nine months. Although the Kennedy administration sent the new government arms, and American corporations such as Bechtel and Mobil began doing business in Iraq, the Baathists had no background in governing and bickered constantly as party ideologues alienated the military. Baathists won control of the cities by expanding the National Guard from less than 5,000 to 40,000 in three months, and placing their politicians in local offices, but soon the guard was challenging the army and fighting erupted. Army General Abd al-Salam Arif, a former ally of Qassim, ordered his troops to attack the guard, which they disarmed and dispersed. Arif took control in November 1963 and proclaimed himself president and commander in chief. Arif stabilized Iraq but only momentarily. He removed the remaining Baathists from power and introduced nationalization laws that gave the state ownership of most large industries. He negotiated with the Kurds and brokered a cease-fire. But in 1966, as he was traveling in his helicopter, a sandstorm caused a crash, killing him. The cabinet elected his brother Abd al-Rahman Arif president, and the regime hobbled along until June 1967 and the Arab-Israeli war.

The Six Day War was the Waterloo of Islamic pride and Arab nationalism. It was a stunning defeat, resulting in significant gains for the Jewish State: Egypt lost the Sinai; Jordan lost Jerusalem; Syria lost the Golan Heights. Israel won the West Bank, which since has been an open sore to Moslems.

Iraq lost nothing, but the disaster made the second Arif regime look weak, inviting insurrection in July 1968. After convincing key military personnel to aid their cause, the Baathists rebelled against Arif. They captured him and sent him into exile. The coup again revealed that, a half century after its invention and almost four decades after its independence, the Improbable Country remained ripe for insurrection. It would take a strongman to rule Iraq, and he had been involved in the plot against Arif—Saddam Hussein.

Up to that time, Americans had shown little interest in Iraq and Afghanistan, but that changed between the 1970s and 2000 when events in those countries and Iran—along with the emergence of al Qaeda—confronted the United States. As the United States became more dependant on foreign oil, especially after the oil embargoes of the 1970s, and as it appeared that the Soviet Union was becoming more interested in Baghdad and Kabul, Americans became more aware of problems in and around the Improbable Country and the Graveyard of Empires. East met West.

Introduction West

The United States, Saddam,
and al Qaeda, 1970s–2000

Saddam, "one who confronts" in Arabic, was born into a family of impoverished landless peasants between 1937 and 1939 in Al-Quja, a small village of mud huts on the banks of the Tigris River south of Tikrit. He never knew his father, who died or disappeared before his birth. His mother gave the baby to her brother's family, which raised him for the first years of his life. After she remarried in the clan and had three sons—Barzan, Sabawi, and Watban—Saddam returned to live with her, but his new step-father treated him harshly, publicly declaring "I don't want him, the son of a dog." Because he had no known father, other children in the village mistreated and often attacked him, so Saddam began carrying an iron bar for protection. It was a brutal existence, and by the age of ten Saddam fled to live with his uncle, Khairallah Tulfah, first in Tikrit and eventually in Baghdad. The British had imprisoned Khairallah in 1941 for his role in a revolt against their rule, and it seems likely that the uncle taught his nephew his anti-British, anti-Semitic, and pro-Arab views.

Saddam went to school, became literate, and was introduced to pan-Arabism in Baghdad. He also improved his street smarts. The young man committed his first assassination, returning to Tikrit to kill a communist politician who had forced Khairallah out of a public job. Back in Baghdad, Saddam became interested in the Baath Party, which he joined at the age of 20. The next year, in October 1959, according to legend, Saddam shot Qassim as he rode through the streets of Baghdad, only wounding him. Guards returned fire, and Saddam fled the city, some say dressed as a woman, and reached safety in Syria and eventually Egypt. Qassim recovered and sentenced Saddam to death *in absentia*, but more importantly he attempted to crush the Baath Party.

Qassim was not successful, and in 1968 the Baathists had gained the support of important military leaders. They seized the government without firing a shot in the "white," or bloodless, revolution, exiling Arif. The Baath leader, General Ahmed Hussein al-Bakr, remembered the days of 1958 when they unsuccessfully attempted to share power with the military, so shortly after the coup al-Bakr invited the director of military intelligence, who was not a Baathist, to the presidential palace. As the two men were talking, al-Bakr's relative, Saddam, walked in and pulled his gun. The official put his hand over his face, crying out "I have four children!" Saddam arrested the officer, took him to the airport, and exiled him. By the end of the year, al-Bakr appointed himself commander-in-chief, placed Baathist officers in positions of power, and granted supreme authority to his handpicked Revolutionary Command Council (RCC), effectively erasing any military opposition to the new regime. The Baathists consolidated their power by holding a series of sham trials and then executing perceived enemies and spies, many of whom hung publicly in Baghdad's Liberation Square.

During the 1970s Saddam's official position was vice president of the RCC. Many of the Baathists, including the three top government officials in the regime—al-Bakr, Saddam, and Hammad Shihab—were relatives from Tikrit who helped Saddam consolidate his power. His rural and tribal background allowed him to reach out to village leaders and solidify his clan ties, while cultivating relations with the more urban and educated Baathists in Baghdad. Publicly, Saddam traveled to Moscow to improve relations with the Soviets, who began supplying Iraq with large amounts of military hardware. Privately, Saddam took charge of the secret police, the Mukhabarat. He handpicked each member, and they patrolled all areas of the country, listening for signs of disloyalty and conducting bloody purges. He also created the Baath militia, which later would become his Republican Guard. By the end of the decade it had 50,000 loyal members.

As the Baathists consolidated power in the south, they conducted a different policy in the north. They negotiated with the Kurds, who had become increasingly important to the Iraqi economy. During the 1960s, Kurdistan produced between 40 and 50 percent of the nation's oil, and the Kurdish city of Kirkuk became the oil capital of Iraq. The Baathists, therefore, granted "autonomy" to Kurdish lands, pledged an equitable amount of oil revenues for them, and recognized both Arabic and Kurdish as official languages in their region. It was a power play. Like all previous Iraqi rulers, Saddam waited until the government in Baghdad was firmly entrenched, and then launched his attack. In 1974 he ordered 80,000 troops, now heavily armed by the Soviets, into the north. The fighting was brutal for a year. No one knows how many Kurds were slaughtered, somewhere between 50,000 and 300,000, but the bloodshed resulted in suppressing the Kurds and eventually resettling some of their areas with Arabs.[1]

The Baath government aligned itself with Egypt, Jordan, and Syria, who were eager for revenge against Israel after the Six Day War. In October 1973, on the Jewish holy day of Yom Kippur, Egypt and Syria attacked Israel. The Arabs had warned the Western nations, especially the United States, a major arms supplier to Israel, not to interfere and come to the aid of the Jewish state. In Washington, President Richard Nixon and his adviser Henry Kissinger did not heed the warning, and instead airlifted military supplies to Israel, which turned the tide against the Arabs. "I tell you gentlemen," declared the Israeli defense minister, "the tanks and ammunition our forces are firing in Egypt three weeks ago were in the United States."

The Yom Kippur War had an impact on the United States. Kissinger began "shuttle diplomacy," which eventually resulted in a ceasefire and placed America in the role of "honest broker" in the Middle East. For the next five presidential administrations, the United States would try to remain neutral and help to bring lasting peace between Israel and its Arab neighbors. While that would be a long-term policy, a more immediate result of the Yom Kippur War was the Arab punishment for American aid to Israel—by the end of 1973, OPEC declared an oil embargo on the United States. Until the 1950s, the United States had been self-sufficient concerning petroleum, but that ended as the middle class grew, as they bought record numbers of automobiles to drive on the new system of interstate freeways. By the Nixon years, the nation was importing large amounts of oil, a third of which came from the Middle East. The OPEC embargo, then, created long lines at American gas stations and soaring prices. In just the last two months of the year the price of crude quickly rose from about $3 to over $11 a barrel. Other boycotts followed, which shot prices to over $30 by the end of the decade.

The oil boycott was significant for the Nixon administration and for two old enemies in the Middle East—Iran and Iraq. The president looked for secure supplies, which opened the door for Iran's leader, Shah Muhammad Reza Pahlavi. The CIA had helped the shah take absolute power in 1953. The democratically elected prime minister at that time, Mohammed Mossadeq, nationalized the Anglo-Iranian oil company, a business dominated by the British, who had been taking more royalties each year than they paid Iran in 50 years. The British enlisted the CIA, who hired provocateurs and thugs to create chaos in Tehran. They ousted Mossadeq; the shah took firm control and remained friendly to Western oil corporations, who were given the right to distribute Iranian oil. By the early 1970s, increasing amounts of dollars were leaving the United States and flooding into the Iranian treasury, so Nixon agreed to offset the balance of trade by selling Iran a large air force, including 225 F-4s, 160 F-16s, 80 F-14s, and 900 helicopters. To train the Persians to fly the sophisticated machines, the president sent 5,000 military instructors. Another 40,000 civilians went to Iran to build airports and seaports, drill for oil, and operate refineries. The Americans lived in their own walled cities, did not learn the local language, and, like the British in Iraq earlier, created resentment in Iran. The large military build-up also created apprehension next door in Iraq, a patron of the Soviet Union. Iraq's Kurdish population traditionally had received arms from Iran to confront governments in Baghdad. Iraq also had a common southern border with Iran along the waterway Shatt al Arab, "river of the Arabs," which flowed into the Persian Gulf, the main exit point of both nations' petroleum. Sporadic gunfire had erupted on both sides of the river in the past. Eventually, Kissinger was able to get both the shah and Saddam to meet at the OPEC summit in Algiers, where both masked their hatred, embraced, and signed an agreement that ended Persian support for the Kurds and neutralized the Shatt al Arab.

During the 1970s, then, the Baathist regime was creating a relatively unified and prosperous Iraq. In 1972, it nationalized the Iraq Petroleum Company. "Arab oil for the Arabs," declared Radio Baghdad, and Saddam added, "Our wealth has returned to us." The nationalization was important, for along with rising prices because of the embargos, it contributed to petrodollars flooding the government's coffers, soaring from less than $2 billion in 1973 to almost $24 billion in 1978. Flush with funds, the regime improved roads and utilities, increased medical facilities, and opened public schools in virtually every hamlet, where it educated boys and girls in a secular state. The government built industries, housing projects, universities, airports, and communications systems. Moreover, the Baathists established free health care and subsidized consumer goods; for the first time, people living in homes, apartments, even mud huts could buy cars, air conditioners, refrigerators, and televisions. All these factors made the Baathist regime relatively popular and created a thriving capital. "Baghdad throbbed with the beat of secularism and license," recalled a journalist. The nightclubs were loud and raucous, the art scene was lively, and artists pushed the "limits of the human figure in an Islamic society. Seduction was, in fact, everywhere." Momentarily, this secularism, booming economy, and political stability overcame the deep fissures in the Iraq society.

By the end of the decade the Baath government and Iraq were almost the same. Saddam had ordered the Mukhabarat to infiltrate organizations and local governments, and they imprisoned and killed off potential enemies as President al-Bakr's stature declined. With failing health, he had almost disappeared and was president in name only. Saddam had taken over the reigns of government, highlighted by pictures of him, often in a general's uniform, on billboards throughout the country.

Then, in July 1979, Saddam announced that he had discovered a plot to take over the government. Fear ran amok in the Baath Party. A week later Saddam summoned the Revolutionary Command Council to the presidential palace. He made one RCC member confess, who named dozens of traitors. Eventually, over 20 were executed. President al-Bakr resigned for health reasons, named Saddam president, and the new leader appointed relatives and loyal friends to all the key posts in his new government, including his half-brothers Barzan, Sabawi, and Watban. The new president, in his early 40s, also named himself premier, chairman of the RCC, and leader of the Baath Party. Shortly thereafter, a foreign visitor to Saddam's office noticed many books on Stalin, the Soviet dictator, and commented, "You seem fond of Stalin." "Yes," Saddam replied, "I like the way he governed his country."[2]

Thus, after centuries of tribal warfare mixed with eras of religious strife, after Britain humiliated the people of Mesopotamia and created an improbable nation based on London's designs on petroleum and not the needs of the local inhabitants, and after five decades of palace intrigues and coups d'état, one ruthless strongman—Saddam Hussein—finally was brutal enough to have some success at nation-building. He was forging together Iraq, a prosperous nation at peace. It would not last for long.

That same year, 1979, two important events changed the course of history: one in Iran and the other in Afghanistan.

Since 1978, protesters had been demonstrating in Iran against the rule of Shah Pahlavi. Earlier, the shah had promoted his "White Revolution" to modernize his nation by installing Western ideas such as land reform, secular education, and women's rights, all of which aggravated his mostly orthodox Shiite population. Over the years, he also had become an outspoken ally of the United States and had become increasingly repressive. His secret police, SAVAK, had tossed thousands into prisons and exiled many others. One of those was Ayatollah Ruhollah Khomeini, who had become the most outspoken opponent of the shah, claiming that the shah's policies had "reduced the Iranian people to a level lower than that of an American dog." During the 1960s, the shah exiled the ayatollah, who moved to the Shiite holy city in Iraq, Najaf. In 1977 Shiite riots erupted in that city and the Baathists arrested and executed clerics and expelled some 200,000 Shiites to Iran, claiming they were "non-Iraqis." The next year, the shah asked Saddam to remove Khomeini, and the dictator was happy to expel him to Paris. Back in Iran, when some 20,000 pro-Khomeini protesters gathered in Tehran's Jaleh Square, soldiers fired into the crowd, killing 400 and wounding 4,000, which only resulted in even larger protests from angry merchants, mullahs, and students. By January 1979, protesters overwhelmed security forces, prompting the shah to leave his nation for Egypt. Two weeks later, Khomeini returned, took power, and proclaimed the Islamic Republic of Iran. American oil workers quietly left the country as the shah, ill with cancer, asked President Jimmy Carter to permit him to have medical treatment in New York. Carter agreed on humanitarian grounds, which outraged Khomeini. The ayatollah encouraged his young supporters to take to the streets, and in November hundreds stormed the fence of the American Embassy, holding almost 70 U.S. citizens hostage, and parading them blindfolded through the streets of Tehran. Khomeini praised the militants as "ten thousand martyrs" and demanded that the "Great Satan Carter" return the shah for trial, along with $40 billion that he claimed the shah had stolen from the country. If not, the ayatollah threatened to try and execute the Americans for being "spies." Eventually, Iran released some blacks and women, lowering the number of hostages to 52.

"America Held Hostage" was ABC's new nightly program on the story of the year. Every night citizens turned on their TVs to watch Iranians burning American flags and calling the U.S. the "Great Satan." Carter pledged that he would not leave the White House until he secured the release of the hostages; the next year, he broke diplomatic relations with Iran.

Carter was negotiating for their release in December 1979 when the Soviet Union shocked the world—80,000 Soviet troops invaded Afghanistan, supposedly to prop up a friendly but faltering government on their southern border in Kabul. It became their last act of the cold war.

President Carter proclaimed the Soviet invasion the "most serious threat to peace since the Second World War." He ordered a boycott of the 1980 Olympics in Moscow and cut off grain shipments to Russia; the first irritated sport fans, and the second irritated American farmers. All the while, Carter was running for reelection. With the Russians beating up on the Afghans and Iranians holding American hostages, Carter looked weak, which boosted the campaign of Republican challenger Ronald Reagan, who easily won the November contest. The new president proclaimed the end of the "era of self-doubt," and on his inauguration day in January 1981, Iran released the American hostages. Yet the crisis in Tehran meant that the new American administration remained hostile to the fundamentalist Islamic regime in Iran.

That hostility was shared by other nations and leaders in the Middle East, especially Saddam. Iraq and Iran, of course, had long-standing disputes. They had bickered for years over the status of the Shatt al Arab waterway, and the Persians had usually helped the Kurds in their revolts against Baghdad. But with a new regime in Tehran, the dispute became more personal. Khomeini called on Shiites in Iraq to revolt, create an Iraqi theocracy, and end the "infidel Baath regime." In 1980 a militant attempted to assassinate Saddam's deputy prime minister, which gave the dictator the green light for repression. His army moved south, tossed thousands of Shiites into prison, and tortured and killed many leading clerics. Saddam's army rounded up Shiites they thought were disloyal and exiled them across the border to Iran. Tempers flared, and it became a battle of Sunni secular Baathists versus Shia theocracy. Saddam declared that he and his nation would defend all Arab peoples against the ayatollahs and the "machinations of the forces of darkness." Tehran responded that the "butcher Saddam Hussein" was opposed to Islam and that "martyrs of Islam will boil in the Islamic Iraqi people . . . until Saddam Hussein's regime is completely overthrown."

Saddam planned a war against Iran. During the 1970s, his regime had used billions of petrodollars to buy military hardware. No one seemed concerned about selling weapons of mass destruction to Iraq. The regime had bought arms from West Germany, Italy, Belgium, Spain, Portugal, Yugoslavia, and Brazil. His largest suppliers, however, were France and especially the Soviet Union. From the former he acquired electronic equipment, Mirage fighters, Alouette attack helicopters, and Crotale surface-to-air missiles, and from the latter he bought SCUD missiles and hundreds of tanks. Saddam bought biological and chemical supplies from American and European corporations, usually under the guise of boosting agricultural production with fertilizers and pesticides, and by the late 1970s was manufacturing chemical weapons such as Tabun and VX nerve agents along with biological weapons such as anthrax, typhoid, and cholera. Moreover, he instructed his scientists to begin developing atomic power. Although Iraq was one of the world's largest exporters of petroleum, the French sold them the uranium and helped them build the Osirak nuclear power plant. This alarmed the Israelis. Thinking that Saddam was gaining the capacity to produce plutonium from uranium and to make atomic bombs, Israeli fighter-bombers eventually destroyed the plant.

Nevertheless, in 1980 Saddam was heavily armed and in September he ordered his army into action; 50,000 Iraqi troops moved from the southeastern provinces and crossed into Iran, winning strategic positions. Saddam thought he would win a quick victory, but in reality he had blundered into a costly war. Iran eventually counterattacked with their air force, religious fervor, and larger population, about 50 million Iranians to 18 million Iraqis. By 1981 Iran had turned the tide, become the aggressor, and the next year had reclaimed their lost territory. The war became a stalemate with massive casualties; one battle alone in 1984 cost more than 25,000 lives. Iran ordered "human wave" attacks, often using children who desired martyrdom; on one assault they almost captured Basra. The Iraqis employed chemical weapons—nerve and mustard gas—to kill the invaders. By 1987 both sides were using missiles, against Baghdad and Tehran. Saddam called for a cease-fire many times; Khomeini continually refused. Eventually, in 1987, the United Nations passed a cease-fire resolution, which the belligerents signed the next year. After eight bloody years of fighting, both sides won virtually nothing, but both leaders claimed triumph. Saddam called it a "glorious victory." The borders remained the same, but the ancient hatred had been renewed and intensified between the Iraqi Arabs and Iranian Persians, and between many Sunnis and Shiites. Both nations were deeply in debt, especially Iraq, whose oil exports had been drastically cut. Casualty figures are difficult to estimate, but most experts think that Iran suffered about 50 percent more than Iraq and that the total killed was about one million.

Toward the end of the conflict, the Kurds in northern Iraq saw their chance and rose up against the Baath regime. Saddam put his cousin, nicknamed Chemical Ali, in charge, and ordered him to "take care" of the Kurds. The regime dropped mustard and nerve gas on over 60 Kurdish towns and villages; one attack on Halabjah resulted in 5,000 dead, the most deaths at a time from chemical weapons since World War I. At the end of the Iraq-Iran War Saddam ordered his army into Kurdish lands, massacring hundreds of thousands and destroying numerous villages while forcibly relocating at least 250,000 Kurds.[3]

Meanwhile in Washington, the Reagan administration publicly watched the Iraq-Iran War from the sidelines; behind the scenes, however, it eventually supported Saddam. The administration did not sell arms to Baghdad directly, but instead allowed the Saudis to supply American arms to Saddam. In 1983, when it appeared that Iraq might lose, the president sent a special envoy—Donald Rumsfeld—to Iraq to confer with Saddam. Rumsfeld had been the secretary of defense in the Gerald Ford administration, and he returned to Baghdad and informed the dictator that the United States would consider "any major reversal of Iraq's fortunes as a strategic defeat for the West." Rumsfeld told Saddam that he could use American intelligence, and U.S. officials began supplying the dictator with satellite pictures of battlefields so he could conduct a more efficient war, which probably saved the regime. Eventually, 60 American officers were secretly providing Iraqi generals with information on the strategic troop movements of the Iranian army.

The Reagan administration also allowed American companies to continue shipping biological agents to Iraq; as a U.S. Senate report later concluded: "The United States provided the Government of Iraq with . . . materials which assisted in the development of Iraqi chemical, biological and missile-systems programs." The administration was aware of Saddam's "almost daily" use of chemical weapons during 1983 but did not complain. In fact, when Rumsfeld met Saddam, he did not even mention the use of chemical weapons. The Pentagon "wasn't so horrified by Iraqi use of gas," said an American involved. "It was just another way of killing people . . . it didn't make any difference." Eventually, the administration spoke out against using those weapons, while secretly helping Iraq develop them and supplying battlefield pictures so Saddam could gas the Iranian army.

Furthermore, the administration provided credits and loans to Saddam so he could buy food—and weapons. Initially, U.S. credits were about $300 million, which paid for U.S. military hardware from Jordan and Kuwait, but by 1987 the administration was providing billions of dollars of credit. Reagan wrote a memorandum in April 1984 directing the secretaries of state, in coordination with the secretary of defense and the CIA, to "prepare a plan of action designed to avert an Iraqi collapse." Later that year, the administration restored diplomatic relations with

Iraq, broken since the 1967 Israeli-Arab conflict, and trade between the two quickly increased over the next six years to $3.5 billion.

The Reagan administration, therefore, did not condemn Saddam for using chemical weapons. Instead, the White House was more interested in preventing Iran from defeating Iraq, a fact that became more obvious when the battlefield switched from land to sea.

In 1984 Iran had advanced into southern Iraq and that shut off Saddam's oil exports through the Persian Gulf. The U.S. administration encouraged American firms to help build new oil pipelines from Baghdad through Jordan and Saudi Arabia. By that time, both belligerents were attacking neutral tankers carrying oil out of the Gulf in an attempt to decrease each others' petroleum profits. The "tanker war" cut Iranian oil exports in half and reduced shipping in the Gulf by a quarter, prompting the UN to call for a moratorium, which both nations ignored. By 1987 Iraq attacked Iran's main petroleum terminal at Kharg Island, and Iran countered by attacking oil tankers owned by Saddam's allies, Saudi Arabia and Kuwait, which were scared of the Islamic Republic and had given large loans to Baghdad. To keep oil tankers steaming out of Kuwait, the Reagan administration sent the U.S. Navy to protect the ships from Iranian missiles, mines, and torpedoes. Then, on May 17, an Iraqi aircraft fired two missiles at the USS *Stark*, killing 37 sailors. Saddam quickly apologized, blamed "pilot error," and Washington ironically blamed Iran for escalating the tanker war in the first place. That October the president ordered a series of air and naval strikes that demolished Iranian oil platforms, and by early 1988 about ten Western navies were patrolling the Gulf, which ended the tanker war. "It wasn't that we wanted Iraq to win the war, we did not want Iraq to lose," said a Reagan staffer. "We knew [Saddam] was an S.O.B., but he was our S.O.B."[4]

Earlier during the war, the Reagan administration also had been conducting secret diplomacy with another leader whom they considered an S.O.B.—Ayatollah Khomeini—and this bizarre episode takes the reader from Lebanon to Nicaragua.

Lebanon had been torn apart by a civil war between Christians and Moslems throughout most of the 1970s and into the 1980s. Israel invaded and occupied part of the south and gave support to the mostly Christian government in the capital Beirut. Syria sent troops to support the Moslems. Shiites in Lebanon felt that the United States also supported the Christians, and in April 1983 a Shiite suicide bomber rammed his explosive-laden car into the U.S. Embassy in Beirut, killing 63 people, including 17 Americans. The French and Italians decided to intervene in an attempt to stop the fighting, and they invited Reagan to supply troops; the multinational force was supposed to provide security in the war-torn country. The president ordered the marines to Beirut, who established a barracks near the airport and attempted a peacekeeping mission. On October 23, a truck raced toward the barracks, and before the marines could stop the vehicle it detonated, unleashing a horrific blast and killing 241 U.S. troops. "It was the saddest day of my life," the president later told an aide. That same day another blast killed 58 French paratroopers. The president put on a brave face: "If others feel confident they can intimidate us and our allies in Lebanon, they will become more bold elsewhere," and in January 1984 he reiterated that the marines would remain in Beirut. But it was just tough talk. In February, Lebanon's fragile government collapsed, and as chaos returned, the president ordered a withdrawal.

The suicide bombing marked a turning point. Islamic Jihad claimed responsibility, a group believed to be made up of Shiites loyal to Khomeini, and part of Hezbollah; this was the first time that most had ever heard of the militant Islamic organization. To many in the Islamic world, the attack—and U.S. withdrawal—demonstrated that individual acts of terror could defeat a superpower, and that fueled the growth of Islamic extremism.

During the next years Hezbollah in Lebanon expanded their terrorist tactics. They hijacked a TWA airliner and held 39 hostages for 17 days, killing one who was in the U.S. Navy, and they captured some Americans and held them hostage, including the CIA station chief in Beirut, William Buckley, and USMC Lieutenant Colonel William Higgins, both of whom they executed. And they kidnapped the Associated Press journalist Terry Anderson and held him hostage for six years before they set him free.

During these hostage episodes, a Lebanese magazine with ties to the theocracy in Tehran published an article in 1986 revealing that a U.S. diplomat had visited Iran. As the story unfolded the next year, citizens learned about the unique American proposal: Iran would help to convince radical Islamists in Lebanon to release the U.S. hostages, and in return the Reagan administration would sell Khomeini arms and spare parts that he needed to continue the war against Saddam. Consequently, the Reagan administration either sold or supplied arms to both belligerents. Iran paid for the weapons, and the administration had foreign middlemen funnel millions of those dollars, along with other funds the administration had solicited from its conservative benefactors and from countries such as Saudi Arabia to Nicaragua. There, the elected leftist government of the Sandinistas was fighting a rightist rebel group known as the "Contras," whom Reagan had called "Freedom Fighters." The policy aimed to blunt the expansion of communism in Latin America, but there was a legal problem. Congress had passed the Boland Amendment, which prohibited U.S. aid to the Contras, meaning that the administration was breaking the law. The subsequent "Iran-Contra" scandal eventually resulted in numerous investigations, convictions, and damaged the last two years of the Reagan presidency.

The Reagan administration was focused on an anticommunist campaign that took it from Nicaragua to Afghanistan, a country that was demonstrating the vulnerability of another superpower, the USSR. The Soviets had become embroiled in a long guerrilla war, and the administration reacted to the conflict by supplying the *mujahedeen*, or "holy warriors," with stinger antiaircraft missiles and rocket launchers. Eventually, the Afghans shot down over 270 Soviet helicopters and aircraft while the Red Army suffered over 40,000 casualties. The war dragged on for ten years until 1989, when the Soviet leader Mikhail Gorbachev withdrew his beleaguered army from the conflict, now dubbed "Russia's Vietnam." It had been so costly for the Soviets that their nation began to fall apart as nations they had dominated since the end of World War II grew increasingly restless. Gorbachev attempted domestic reforms and began to withdraw his troops from Eastern Europe. In just two years, Germany was reunited, Eastern Europe liberated itself from communist domination, and the Soviet Union collapsed—the last empire buried in Afghanistan.

By the end of 1991, the cold war was over and the world was being transformed. The Soviet Union had been an important exporter of petroleum, but the new nation of Russia had significant infrastructure problems, temporarily decreasing its oil exports. At the same time the world's thirst for petroleum increased because of the rapidly expanding economies of the two most populous nations, India and China. All that meant more world demand for petroleum, boosting the international influence of the Middle East. Moreover, as Russia and Eastern Europe turned away from communism and toward capitalism, there was increased demand for Western goods, and that stimulated more economic globalization. At the same time, the United States became the world's only superpower. For over four decades America had been transfixed on one major enemy—the USSR. By the late 1940s, communism had replaced Nazism as the "devil we knew." Suddenly, during the 1990s, there was no devil, no hated foe. Americans, however, would not have to wait for long for a new devil—terrorism.

The end of the cold war also had an impact on Iraq. The Soviet Union had supplied Baghdad with military hardware that Saddam had employed in his long war against Iran. That war not only had destroyed a lot of that equipment but also left Iraq heavily in debt, over $130 billion, almost half of that owed to Saudi Arabia and Kuwait. By spring 1990, Iraq was low on foodstuffs, and the George H. W. Bush administration demonstrated its friendship by supplying Iraq with $400 million in agricultural credits. In May, Baghdad hosted an Arab summit meeting, and Saddam addressed the dignitaries: "Iraq is in a state of economic warfare," he claimed, because his Arab neighbors were overproducing oil and reducing its price, causing hardship in his country. Petroleum accounted for 95 percent of Iraq's revenue, and a barrel was only $12; Saddam demanded that nations cut production to increase the price to $25. We "have reached the point where we cannot sustain more pressure." He asked the Arab nations to forgive his debts, claiming that they owed Iraq billions because he had saved Arabs from the Persians. Later, the dictator continued his propaganda campaign, alleging that Kuwait had been illegally tapping oil from the joint Iraq-Kuwait Rumalyah oil field. Saddam eventually made the old claim that Kuwait was part of Iraq, that his country deserved a port free from Iranian threats, and he demanded two Kuwaiti islands in the Persian Gulf.

In mid-July, Saddam summoned the U.S. ambassador to Iraq, April Glaspie, to a meeting at the presidential palace. Fluent in Arabic, the ambassador never had met Saddam, who rarely talked with diplomats. The dictator told her that the United States should not become involved in Arab issues, and expressed anger toward the U.S. Navy patrols in the

Persian Gulf. His nation was suffering, and American support for Kuwait, he said, revealed "prejudice against Iraq." She sympathized about the dire economic situation and added, "We have no opinion on the Arab-Arab conflict, like your border disagreement with Kuwait." Glaspie stressed that the United States was eager for a peaceful solution, but she did not inform the dictator that the Bush administration would fight to save Kuwait.

As pressure mounted during the last week of July, the Bush administration contacted Iraq. A mid-level state department official gave a message to Iraq's ambassador in Washington warning against the use of force to resolve the border dispute with Kuwait. A personal message from Bush also was sent to Saddam; it contained only expressions of American-Iraqi friendship. Naturally, the dictator placed greater significance on a note from the president, and it was the message that Saddam wanted to hear.

Most likely, Saddam did not think that the United States would take military action against Iraq if he invaded Kuwait. When he had attacked Iran in 1980, President Carter did not demand that he leave that nation, and later the Reagan administration aided Saddam and was aware of his use of gas but did not complain. Instead, both the Reagan and Bush administrations provided hundreds of millions of dollars in subsidies to Saddam's regime. During the 1980s, the United States had acquiesced to the dictator's past transgressions; after receiving a friendly letter from the president, he probably thought that Bush would speak against an invasion but then accept Iraq's annexation of Kuwait and eventually return to business as usual, especially concerning oil.

Late in July, Saddam ordered 100,000 troops and 300 tanks to the Kuwait border. Western diplomats thought he was bluffing. Ambassador Glaspie flew out of Baghdad for a holiday; Secretary of Defense Dick Cheney left for his vacation in Wyoming; and Secretary of State James Baker went on a hunting trip to Mongolia. Saddam's neighbors also thought he was bluffing; they did not think the dictator would break the code that Arabs did not attack Arabs. At most, perhaps Saddam would take the Rumalyah oil field and the two islands in the Persian Gulf. King Fahd of Saudi Arabia called for a meeting and offered his services. On the last day of the month, the prime minister of Kuwait and deputy president of Iraq, both the second highest offices in their nations, met in

Jiddah. In closed session, Kuwait apparently would not accept OPEC oil quotas boosting petroleum prices, make concessions on the Rumalyah oil field, or lease to Iraq their islands in the Gulf. The next morning, August 1, the Iraqi delegation went home, boycotting another meeting with the Kuwaitis.[5]

Hours later, at 2 AM on August 2, 1990, Saddam's army invaded Kuwait. The Kuwaiti army put up no resistance; the air force scrambled to their jets and flew out of the country. A third of the population, including the emir, got in their cars and drove to Saudi Arabia. In just five hours Iraq had captured Kuwait. A week later Saddam declared "a comprehensive and eternal merger," annexing the nation as the nineteenth Iraqi province.

Whatever the occupation meant for Saddam and Iraq, it meant something different to the world and the Persian Gulf. Now, a dictator with the largest army in the Middle East was sitting on top of a gulf nation with the third-largest oil reserves in the world, stationing his troops on the border of Saudi Arabia; if he seized that country, Iraq would own half the world's known oil deposits. Secretary of Defense Cheney told the president in a cabinet meeting, Saddam "has clearly done what he has to do to dominate OPEC, the Gulf, and the Arab world. He is forty kilometers from Saudi Arabia and its oil production is only a couple hundred kilometers away. . . . The problem will get worse, not better."

"Naked aggression," President Bush labeled Saddam's occupation; "it will not stand." Later the president called the dictator "Hitler," and British Prime Minister Margaret Thatcher continued the World War II analogy by declaring that "aggressors must never be appeased." Bush froze all Kuwaiti and Iraqi assets and property in the United States. He proclaimed Operation Desert Shield for protection of other oil-rich lands from Saddam. A man with long experience in international affairs, as minister to China, CIA director, and vice president, Bush immediately pledged "to get the international community behind us." He sent Secretary of State Baker to the United Nations, and eventually the Security Council passed resolutions that placed economic sanctions on Iraq, basically ending trade and oil exports. The UN also told Saddam to evacuate Kuwait or face military action.

Saddam was not moved. "Convey to President Bush," he declared, "that he should regard the Kuwaiti Emir and Crown Prince as history. . . . We know you are a superpower who can do great damage to us, but we will never capitulate."

To prove Saddam wrong Bush began a diplomatic and military response. He ordered Joseph Wilson, the U.S. chargé d'affaires in Baghdad, to talk with Saddam. Wilson asked the dictator if he intended to attack Saudi Arabia. "We will not attack those who do not attack us," Saddam replied, a curious response since he had just attacked Kuwait, "we will not harm those who do not harm us." The president also began assembling an international armed force. By the end of the year some 700,000 military personnel from 28 countries were stationed either in Saudi Arabia or on the Persian Gulf. Bush worked the phones day and night to form a UN coalition, which included France, Germany, Britain, Turkey, and significantly, seven Arab nations, including Saudi Arabia, Egypt, and Syria.

In Washington, the Republican president asked Congress, controlled by the Democrats, for a resolution to support military action, which was required by the War Powers Act passed at the end of the Vietnam War. That created debate. Before the Senate, Secretary Cheney evoked the memories of Hitler and appeasement, saying that if not removed from Kuwait, Saddam would disrupt the world's economy and "be in the position to blackmail any nation" in the Middle East. The chairman of the Joint Chiefs of Staff, General Colin Powell, stressed that the United States had learned from the Vietnam conflict and this time would use a "combined, overwhelming, air/land/sea campaign" to bring a swift victory. Others, such as Democratic senators Sam Nunn, John Glenn, and Edward Kennedy wondered why the administration didn't wait for UN economic sanctions to work against impoverished Iraq. Was Bush claiming that "he and he alone can bring this country to war?" asked Kennedy. Cheney retorted that Bush was "within his authority" as commander-in-chief to use military force. The president did not make using military force a campaign issue for the November congressional campaigns, but after the election the administration asked for a resolution. On January 12, 1991, Congress passed a joint resolution supporting the use of the U.S. military to liberate Kuwait.

The UN passed a resolution allowing military action on January 15, and the next day President Bush declared, "The allied countries have exhausted all reasonable efforts to reach a peaceful resolution, and have no choice but to drive Saddam from Kuwait by force." This "will not be another Vietnam, our troops will have the best possible support in the entire world, and will not be asked to fight with one hand tied behind their back."

Saddam had warned that if the coalition attacked then they would be involved in the "Mother of all Battles." During the night of January 16 and 17, the U.S. Navy and Air Force launched over 150 cruise missiles; the allied air force composed of American, French, British, Saudi, and Spanish planes flew 1,000 combat sorties, bombing Iraq and their military positions inside Kuwait. Desert Shield became Desert Storm. Next morning, the residents of Baghdad awoke to find the presidential palace, Baath Party headquarters, and the ministry of defense reduced to rubble. In response, Saddam began launching SCUD missiles at Saudi Arabia and especially Israel, in an attempt to draw the Jewish state into the conflict and disrupt the coalition of his Islamic enemies. That did not work. Bush convinced Israel to remain neutral, and the missiles had little effect since Saddam did not arm them with biological or chemical warheads and since their obsolete guidance system rarely hit a target. Meanwhile, the allied air attacks pounded Iraq for six weeks, destroying most of Saddam's command structure, stunning and demoralizing his army. "Our strategy in going after this army is very simple," General Powell told reporters. "First we are going to cut it off, and then we are going to kill it." After six weeks of horrific bombardment, the coalition force commander, U.S. General Norman Schwarzkopf, ordered some 400,000 UN forces to launch the invasion, which began in the early morning hours of February 24. As Saudi and Kuwaiti troops, along with U.S. Marines, charged into Kuwait, Schwarzkopf launched the main thrust to the north and west. The American, British, French, Canadian, even some Egyptian, Syrian, and Bangladeshi, troops struck a "left hook" into Iraq, cutting communication and supply lines, which made retreating enemy vehicles and troops easy targets for the coalition air force. Pilots called it a "turkey shoot" on the "highway of death" leading north to Baghdad. Soon, more than a thousand military vehicles were burning wreckage. All the while the beleaguered and shell-shocked Iraqi troops, mostly Shiite and Kurdish conscripts, came out of their bunkers, waving white flags, and surrendered. Coalition forces liberated Kuwait and destroyed almost 400 Iraqi tanks in just 100 hours.

After the bombing campaign began, the "Mother of All Battles" was over in 34 days.

"Kuwait is liberated," President Bush announced to the world. "Iraq's army is defeated. Our military objectives are met. It was a victory for all the coalition nations, for the United Nations, for all mankind, and for the rule of law." The extent of the defeat was stated by General Schwarzkopf when he met the Iraqi generals who signed the armistice. Schwarzkopf informed them that the allies had captured about 60,000 prisoners and 15 percent of Iraq. The Iraqis made only one request—to be able to fly helicopters—since many of the nation's bridges and roads had been obliterated. The American commander agreed.

Bush's popular approval rating soared to 90 percent, as Americans again felt proud of their military. The agonizing loss in Vietnam became history, and Bush declared: "By God, we've kicked the Vietnam syndrome once and for all."[6]

Even before the formal end of the war on March 3, as Saddam's crippled army moved north, the Shiites revolted in Basra. The rebellion spread to Najaf, where angry Shiites attacked Baath Party headquarters, captured those officials, and hacked them to death. Then Karbala exploded in rage, and as some Iranians came across the border to exploit the Shiite upheaval, the Kurds joined in; some 60,000 Kurds in the Iraqi army deserted and began liberating most of the major cities in Iraqi Kurdistan. By March 20, they captured Kirkuk, meaning that almost all of the north was independent of Saddam's regime.

The American and British governments acted surprised—but they shouldn't have. They had encouraged the rebellion. In mid-February, Bush called on Iraqis, "take matters into your own hands and force Saddam Hussein the dictator to step aside," a message that was repeatedly broadcast on radio, printed on leaflets, and dropped by U.S. planes over Shia Iraq. From London, Prime Minister John Major declared that Saddam "may yet become a target of his own people."

Instead, Saddam targeted his own people. Realizing the indigenous revolt could mean the end of his regime, Saddam called on his most loyal troops, the Republican Guard. He had not used them to occupy Kuwait, fearing their destruction in the coalition invasion, so the mostly Sunni guard was relatively fresh for the attack against their own Shiite and Kurd countrymen. And attack they did, first in the south. They slaughtered Shiites in Najaf and Karbala, shelling homes, buildings, even holy shrines. All the while, the Baath press portrayed southerners as traitors to Arab Iraq and proponents of Persian Iran. Then they moved north. Helicopter gunships, allowed by the armistice, leveled Kurdish positions, and fearing a gas attack, the Kurds' resistance quickly evaporated as perhaps two million people fled in terror to the hills near Turkey and Iran.

The Kurdish leaders pleaded with the United States for help. None came. The UN armies stood by in the south while Saddam's loyal followers landed their helicopters and butchered countrymen, eventually killing over 100,000 Shiites. Years later, during the occupation of Iraq after 2003, a U.S. army intelligence officer remarked, "I don't think you can understand" the United States' problems with the occupation "without understanding the end of the '91 war, especially the distrust of the Americans."

Why did the administration stand by while Saddam slaughtered the Kurds and Shiites? There were a number of reasons, which the policymakers described later when they were criticized for their inaction. "Once you got to Iraq and took it over," Cheney declared in 1994, "what are you going to put in its place? That's a very volatile part of the world, and if you take down the central government of Iraq, you could very easily end up seeing pieces of Iraq fly off: part of it, the Syrians would like to have to the west, part of it . . . the Iranians would like to claim. . . . In the north you've got the Kurds, and if the Kurds spin loose and join with the Kurds in Turkey, then you threaten the territorial integrity of Turkey. It's a quagmire."

Moreover, the UN resolutions only mentioned liberating Kuwait, not regime change in Baghdad. That original aim was supported by Arabs in the coalition who wanted the conflict to end rapidly and Western forces to withdraw most of their military from the Middle East. "If we'd gone to Baghdad we would have been all alone," Cheney continued. "There would have been a U.S. occupation of Iraq. None of the Arab forces that were willing to fight with us in Kuwait were willing to invade Iraq." President Bush added, "Our prompt withdrawal helped cement our position with our Arab allies, who now trusted us far more than they ever had." "First and foremost," he continued, the aim was "the principle that aggression cannot pay. . . . We also believed and sought, and succeeded, to obtain the mandate of the world community to liberate Kuwait," which boosted the stature of the United Nations. Bush thought that the United States "had shouldered its peculiar responsibility for leadership in tackling international challenges, and won wide acceptance for this role around the globe. American political credibility and influence had skyrocketed."

The president added that trying "to eliminate Saddam, extending the ground war into an occupation of Iraq, would have . . . incurred incalculable human and political costs. . . . We would have been forced to occupy Baghdad and, in effect, rule Iraq . . . there was no viable 'exit strategy'. . . . Had we gone the invasion route, the United States could conceivably still be an occupying power in a bitterly hostile land."

General Schwarzkopf agreed: "I am certain that had we taken all of Iraq we would have been like the dinosaur in the tar pit—we would still be there, and we, not the United Nations, would be bearing the costs of that occupation."

Finally, there was the human cost. "Everyone was impressed with the fact we were able to do our job with as few casualties as we had," declared Cheney. "But for the 146 Americans killed in action, and for their families—it wasn't a cheap war." And then the future vice president asked an arresting rhetorical question: "how many additional dead Americans is Saddam worth? Our judgment was, not very many, and I think we got it right."

The West and their Arab allies allowed Saddam to survive. "The real problem for the Middle East is not the Gulf crisis per se," said the future UN secretary-general, Boutros Boutros-Ghali, "but the problems we will face after the crisis is 'resolved.'" All realized that Saddam was a brutal dictator with aggressive tendencies, but they had more fear of what would happen if the tribal and religious hatreds of the Sunni, Shiites, and Kurds were unleashed in Iraq, and what that invented country in the land between the rivers might do to the stability of the Middle East. Regional security and keeping the oil pipeline flowing smoothly were much more important than deposing a dictator in a region filled with many more dictators.

Saddam survived, but with the Gulf War over, the UN imposed sanctions against Iraq. The defeated nation could not sell oil, and trade was restricted on all goods except medicines. Iraq had to allow United

Nation's Special Commission on Iraq (UNSCOM) inspectors to have "unconditional and unrestricted" access to facilities that could build chemical, biological, or nuclear weapons, all of which were banned and ordered destroyed. They could not have any missiles with a range of over 90 miles. Sanctions would remain in place and be reviewed every two months until the UN confirmed that Iraq had disarmed. The idea was clear: surrender weapons of mass destruction, and the potential to build them, and the UN would lift sanctions so Iraq could rejoin the nations of the world, trade petroleum, and regain prosperity. To ensure that Saddam did not move his military around the nation and threaten his neighbors, Washington and London established the "no-fly zone" in northern and southern Iraq, and American and British planes monitored the skies.

UNSCOM inspectors attempted to search Iraq, but the regime did not cooperate. To Saddam, just the threat of having weapons of mass destruction guaranteed that he would remain a strongman in the Arab world with potential to harm his enemies and his own citizens, instead of a thug who had led his nation to a resounding defeat. The chief inspector, David Kay, arrived with his team in June 1991. At one base he discovered Iraqi soldiers removing equipment used in atomic research, electromagnetic isotope separators, from buildings and loading them into trucks. When Kay attempted to inspect, the soldiers fired shots over his head and drove their vehicles to another site, all of which the UN team captured on video cameras. A few months later UNSCOM arrived unannounced at the nuclear headquarters in Baghdad, climbed over the fence, got into the building, and discovered documents concerning a possible nuclear arms program. Soldiers rushed to the headquarters, and a standoff ensued in which Kay's team was held captive in the parking lot for days. Saddam ordered the documents and equipment dispatched to a secret compound near Tikrit. The inspection cat-and-mouse game continued for years.

Saddam frustrated the UN sanctions against exporting oil and obtained revenue for his regime by erecting a complex network of front companies and smugglers who sold Iraqi petroleum on the black market. Two years after the end of the war it was estimated that some 50,000 barrels were moving through just one border check point into Turkey, with other illegal shipments being sent through Kurdistan and Jordan.

Even most of the UN medical supplies, it was alleged, were sold on the black market, with most of the profits going to Saddam's extended family or to rebuild his military. All the while the Iraqi people starved. UNICEF claimed that in 1993 at least 80,000 children died because of the sanctions.

Back in Washington, President Bush considered how to pay for the war and rid Iraq of Saddam. On the first issue, he began Operation Tin Cup. The war cost the United States about $75 billion, but the president asked the allies to help pay for U.S. expenses since the American army had been the principal military force. The allies responded generously, and eventually the war only cost the United States a mere $7 billion— demonstrating the international significance of having a United Nations resolution supporting U.S. military action and the financial importance of having numerous allies, including wealthy nations, supporting the cause. Considering the second issue, the president authorized the CIA to begin a covert operation, hoping that the Iraqi military would turn on the dictator. But Saddam turned first, purging and executing anyone he thought might oppose him, including scores of officers and two generals in his Republican Guard. The CIA contacted the dictator's half brother, Barzan, who had been exiled to Geneva. Before his exile, Barzan had been head of Mukhabarat and had helped his brother kill off numerous Baathists, so he didn't seem a good choice to replace the butcher of Baghdad. By 1992 the CIA helped establish the Iraqi National Congress (INC). Forty groups opposed to Saddam made up the INC, and they held a meeting during June in Vienna, where they declared they would create a new government that would respect "human rights and the rule of law within a constitutional, democratic, and pluralistic Iraq." The CIA funded INC, supplying over $20 million in its first year, and one of its leaders was a man educated in the West who had not lived in Iraq since the 1950s—Ahmed Chalabi. The CIA also funded and picked a firm to manage the INC's image, the Rendon Group, owned by John Rendon, who described himself as an "information warrior, and a perception manager." The Rendon Group designed and supervised Radio Hurriah, which in 1992 began broadcasting anti-Saddam information from Kuwait.[7]

That same year President Bush ran for reelection. The Republican faced the former Arkansas Democratic governor Bill Clinton and an independent billionaire candidate from Dallas, H. Ross Perot. Bush's considerable foreign policy successes in his first two years meant little to the electorate by 1992. "The Economy, Stupid" was the sign at the headquarters of the Democratic nominee. A recession was in full swing. From June 1990 to January 1992 over four million jobs were lost, and the unemployment rate reached an eight-year high of almost 8 percent. Moreover, annual federal deficits were exploding, and that year saw the highest on record up to that time, $290 billion, which meant that the president went back on his 1988 pledge: "Read my lips. No new taxes." He signed a tax hike, to which a political cartoon responded, "Read my lips—I lied." New taxes, and the deficits, irritated his conservative base and resulted in evaporating popular support while the economy opened the door for Clinton and Perot. Both hammered the president. Clinton campaigned tirelessly, which bounced him into the lead position after the Democratic Convention. Perot bought large chunks of television time, and with a library of charts, convinced many voters that the deficit was heading the nation for ruin. In 1988 almost 60 percent thought America was moving in the right direction, but only 16 percent did by fall 1992. The result was disaster for Bush, who received only 38 percent of the vote, the lowest reelection attempt of any sitting president since William Howard Taft in 1912, another three-way race with Teddy Roosevelt and Woodrow Wilson. Perot won 19 percent of the vote, and Clinton easily won the electoral college as he picked up over a quarter of Republican votes and two-thirds of the independents, sending him to the White House.

Within hours after Clinton moved to 1600 Pennsylvania Avenue, he warned Saddam to abide by UN sanctions. Clinton's policy changed little from his predecessor—contain Saddam.

But Saddam had other plans; he attempted to kill former president Bush. The emir of Kuwait had invited the Bush family to visit his country, and many of them arrived in April 1993. Son George was not with them because he wanted to attend to his baseball business, the Texas Rangers. During the celebrations in Kuwait the local police discovered a plot: Saddam had ordered Iraqi agents to drive a Toyota Land Cruiser loaded with 200 pounds of explosives, enough to create a blast with a kill radius of four football fields, along the path of the motorcade. When detonated, it would have assassinated the former president and the emir.

The Toyota had been involved in a traffic violation when the police uncovered the plot. The CIA sent forensic experts to Kuwait, examined the bomb, and concluded it was made by Iraq's Mukhabarat. The Kuwaitis arrested, convicted, and hung the Iraqis.

Clinton responded by ordering the navy to launch 23 cruise missiles during the night, and they blew up the Mukhabarat headquarters in Baghdad. Saddam got the point—that was the last time that he attempted any aggression against the United States.

During the rest of the decade most countries lost interest in Saddam. At home, the dictator continued to obstruct UNSCOM inspections as the economy deteriorated. Because of international concern about starvation and possible epidemics, the UN modified its sanctions, developing the "food for oil" program, which began in 1996. Iraq was allowed to sell a limited amount of petroleum with the understanding that two-thirds of proceeds were to be spent on its people's humanitarian needs; three years later the nation could sell as much as it wanted, which helped the struggling economy. All the while UNSCOM officials complained that Saddam was not opening all sites to inspections, prompting tough talk from the Clinton administration. "One way or the other," declared Clinton in February 1998, "we are determined to deny Iraq the capacity to develop weapons of mass destruction and the missiles to deliver them. That is our bottom line." In an attempt to defuse the tension, U.N. Secretary-General Kofi Annan visited Baghdad. Annan and Saddam worked out an agreement; if Iraq would allow another round of inspections, then Annan would try to end all UN sanctions.

Nevertheless, Saddam's behavior had irritated the U.S. Congress, now under Republican control, and they voted for the Iraq Liberation Act. It declared that "it should be the policy of the United States to support efforts to remove the regime headed by Saddam Hussein from power," and it pledged almost $100 million to opposition groups to overthrow the dictator. Saddam responded by suspending cooperation with UNSCOM, which prompted Clinton to retaliate with Operation Desert Fox. In December, as the president was under intense pressure and an impeachment vote because of his sexual indiscretions with Monica Lewinsky, he went on television and addressed the public:

For nearly a decade, Iraq has defied its obligations to destroy its weapons of terror and the missiles to deliver them. America will continue to contain Saddam, and we will work for the day when Iraq has a government worthy of its people. . . . Saddam will strike again at his neighbors; he will make war on his own people. And mark my words, he will develop weapons of mass destruction. He will deploy them, and he will use them.

The president and Prime Minister Tony Blair ordered the attack. The Anglo-American assault lasted four days, with 650 air sorties and 415 cruise missiles, almost 100 more than were used during the entire 1991 Gulf War. They and some 600 bombs hit almost 100 sites in Iraq that UNSCOM had been prevented from inspecting. Many were damaged, some destroyed, and the attack shook Saddam. He panicked during the attack, ordering arrests and executions that backfired and destabilized his regime for months.

Desert Fox raised Republican suspicions because Congress was considering impeachment against the commander-in-chief. "I cannot support this military action in the Persian Gulf at this time," declared Senator Trent Lott, who was the Senate majority leader, and a Republican representative from California called the strike "an insult to the American people."

Clinton's strike also raised Arab concerns. They approached General Anthony Zinni, commander of U.S. Central Command (CENTCOM), which included the Middle East, and began asking questions: If you Americans overthrow Saddam, what will come next? Who is going to be the bulwark against the old threat, Iran? Who would help out during possible economic dislocations and care for the subsequent massive exodus of Iraqi refugees? "An implosion is going to cause chaos," Arabs said to Zinni. "You're going to have to go in . . . do you guys have a plan?" The general admitted, "It shocked the hell out of me."

Desert Fox was Clinton's final action toward Saddam. Although the world did not know at the time, the attack was very successful, destroying any remaining ability the Iraqis had to make weapons of mass destruction; that would be revealed in 2003 after the American invasion. But because of Desert Fox, by the end of 1998 the dictator had banned further inspections and broke off relations with UNSCOM.

Consequently, for the next few years, the international community did not have knowledge of Iraq's potential for making weapons of mass destruction. In addition, the American attack provoked international condemnation from France, China, Russia, most of the Arab world, and members of the United Nations. As conditions inside Iraq deteriorated, more nations called for an end to sanctions, especially after one UN official resigned and claimed that the sanctions caused "four thousand to five thousand children to die unnecessarily every month."

By the end of the decade, then, most nations had given up on enforcing sanctions and many were trading freely with Iraq, including France, Germany, and Russia. In December 2000 representatives of 45 countries defied the ban on commerce and attended the Baghdad International Trade Fair. By then, only Britain and the United States were still trying to enforce sanctions, which gave Saddam an opportunity. With control of the media, he blamed Israel, Saudi Arabia, Kuwait, and especially the United States for the poverty and malnutrition of the Iraqi people. That message was continually broadcast, so by the beginning of the new millennium Iraqis were hardened against the Americans. When one seasoned U.S. journalist arrived in Baghdad a woman snarled at her, "I will teach my children to hate Americans forever."[8]

The Clinton administration lost interest in Saddam as they increased their concern with what was becoming a larger threat—Islamic terrorism.

In the first month of the new Clinton administration a group of Islamic terrorists, including Ramzi Yousef, detonated an enormous truck bomb in the basement of the World Trade Center in New York City. The towers shook and swayed. The blast killed six and injured over a thousand, but the device was not powerful enough to accomplish the aim—destroy the foundation and collapse the building, killing 250,000 Americans. The number was not random, it was, Yousef explained, the number killed by the atomic bombs dropped on Japan. Yousef's bomb was the first Islamic terrorist attack on American soil, and in February 1993 he quickly fled the United States for Pakistan.

The bomb provoked the Clinton White House, especially Richard Clarke. He had been in the government since 1973 working on and researching defense and security matters. Reagan appointed him deputy assistant secretary of state for intelligence. Bush promoted him to assistant secretary of state for politico-military affairs, later appointing him to the National Security Council, and Clinton elevated him to the first national coordinator for security and counterterrorism, or "Terrorism Czar," with an office in the White House. He and his team of assistants had been tracking terrorist groups and were shocked by the events at the WTC. "They are not known members of Hezbollah or Abu Nidal or Palestinian Islamic Jihad," a CIA official told Clarke after checking the database. Clarke wondered how they got into the nation, and an FBI official astonished him: "Well, two of them just showed up at JFK [International Airport] last year without any documents or even false docs. One of the two was detained because he had 'How to Make a Bomb' manuals on him." Nevertheless, immigration let them into the United States. The FBI investigation soon revealed a network that eventually lead to Sheik Omar Abdel-Rahman, a blind Egyptian who served as a spiritual leader and who had been sentenced in absentia for terrorism in Egypt. In 1990, he had been on the State Department's visa watch list but nevertheless had received a visa from the U.S. embassy in Sudan and simply moved to New York City, where he began preaching in various mosques and soon had devoted followers. Egypt knew where he was and had requested his extradition, but to no avail, as the FBI continued their investigation. Using an Egyptian informant, the agency eventually discovered that Rahman and his followers such as Yousef had bomb-making facilities and plans to destroy landmarks, including the United Nations building, Lincoln and Holland tunnels, and the George Washington Bridge.

While Rahman was sentenced to life in prison, Clarke wondered, "Who *are* these guys?" The eventual answer was "a group that the FBI and CIA had not yet heard of: al Qaeda."

Osama bin Laden had formed al Qaeda ("the base") around 1990, and the CIA discovered that Rahman had spent time at bin Laden's guest house in Peshawar, Pakistan. But at that time it was difficult to tell which group was responsible for the World Trade Center bombing; al Qaeda did not take responsibility for the act.

There were numerous terrorist organizations with evil designs against the West, and during the 1990s the State Department listed about 40 groups worldwide. In the Middle East that included Abu Nidal or Black September in Iraq; Al-Gama'a al-Islamiyya or Islamic Group and al-Jihad in Egypt; Hamas, the Palestinian branch of the Muslim

Brotherhood; and Hezbollah or Party of God in Lebanon. These organizations had spread their message to Islamic countries in Southeast Asia, forming Jemaah Islamiyah and Abu Sayyaf, which had the aim of forming an Islamic state by combining Malaysia, Indonesia, and the southern and partly Moslem regions of Thailand and the Philippines.

All these groups hated Israel and the presence of Western troops in Saudi Arabia, and they or their associates conducted numerous assaults against Americans. In 1995 terrorists bombed the Riyadh headquarters of the U.S. military training mission in Saudi Arabia, killing five Americans. Within days the Saudis had arrested four men, obtained confessions, and beheaded them—all before Americans could interview them. The next year, also in Saudi Arabia, terrorists drove an enormous truck bomb into Khobar towers, a barrack for U.S. Air Force pilots who were enforcing the no-fly zone in Iraq. The blast killed 19 Americans and wounded nearly 400 other people. In both cases, it appeared that the culprit was Iran's Qods Force and their front, Saudi Hezbollah.

All the while, bin Laden was making plans for al Qaeda's first attack on America, and he announced it in February 1998. After conferring with other terrorists, including the Egyptian Ayman al-Zawahiri, the leader of al-Jihad, bin Laden signed the "International Islamic Front for Jihad Against Jews and Crusaders," which was published by an Islamic paper in London. Accordingly, American troops in Arabia, its embargo toward Iraq, and its support for Israel amounted to a "war on God, his messenger, and the Muslims." Therefore, bin Laden and his associates issued a fatwa, a theological order: "to kill the Americans and their allies—civilian and military—is an individual duty for every Muslim."

Six months later al Qaeda attacked—not in America—but in Africa. On August 7, on the eighth anniversary of the arrival of American troops in Saudi Arabia, the terrorist organization hit the U.S. embassies in Kenya and Tanzania. One of the reasons for this attack was that the American ambassador in Kenya was a woman, and her death would attract more publicity—although the Koran forbids killing women and children. Ambassador Prudence Bushnell was not injured, but the 2,000-pound truck bomb collapsed a seven-story building and demolished most of the embassy. Both attacks injured almost 5,000 people, mostly local inhabitants, and killed 257, including 12 Americans.

Al Qaeda faxed a claim of responsibility to London. "No matter what it takes," Clinton told the grieving relatives at the ceremony, "we must find those responsible for these evil acts and see that justice is done." The FBI placed bin Laden on its Ten Most Wanted List, and Clinton ordered the military to begin preparations to "kill bin Laden."

Americans were investigating bin Laden when one of his former business associates sought U.S. protection. The businessman had been embezzling money from the terrorist's companies and feared for his life. The informant explained the emerging terrorist network, and how al Qaeda's web had expanded to cells in 50 countries. He also noted that Ramzi Yousef and Sheik Rahman were involved in the organization. Yousef had been trained at an al Qaeda camp in Afghanistan, although it remains unclear if bin Laden sent Yousef to bomb the World Trade Center.[9]

Terrorist attacks provoked Clinton. After the World Trade Center bombing, he had proposed antiterror measures, which lingered in Congress until 1995, when two Americans—Timothy McVeigh and Terry Nichols—bombed the Murrah Federal Building in Oklahoma City. Then some laws were enacted, the most important being the Antiterrorism and Effective Death Penalty Act of 1996, which banned fund-raising for groups that supported terrorist organizations and strengthened the government's authority to bar known terrorists from entering the United States. But the new Republican Congress, along with the gun lobby and some civil libertarians, refused to allow tougher laws on black and smokeless powders, commonly used in bombs, and refused multiple wiretaps on phones used by terrorist suspects.

After the Oklahoma City bombing the federal government began to address terrorism. On June 21, 1995, Clinton signed Presidential Decision Directive 39, "U.S. Policy on Counterterrorism." It was probably the first policy document that addressed the threat of "asymmetric warfare," and it delineated the jobs of the different agencies in "consequence management," or which agencies had what responsibilities after a terrorist attack. PDD-39 also instructed the CIA to conduct an "aggressive program" of foreign intelligence gathering and covert action and to capture terrorist suspects "by force . . . without the cooperation of the host government." The next January the CIA's Counterterrorism Center established "Alec Station," a separate unit with the sole mission of collecting intelligence on bin Laden and al Qaeda, and three years later the FBI created a similar unit. In August 1996, in the heat of the presidential campaign, the president delivered a major address on terrorism, "the enemy of our generation," and during his second term he increased the counterterrorism budget over 40 percent. The next year he created a new position inside the White House, the "national coordinator" for terrorism, what the press dubbed the Terrorism Czar. The president named Richard Clarke to the post, who also became a member of the Cabinet-level Principals Committee of the National Security Council, commonly called the Principals, and composed of the national security advisor, secretaries of state and defense, CIA director, and chairman of the Joint Chiefs of Staff.

Yet it was the embassy bombings on August 7, 1998, that shifted Clinton's response to terrorism into high gear. The president called a meeting with the Principals. Clarke, the FBI, and the CIA confirmed that al Qaeda was responsible for the bombing, and Clinton signed memoranda that "authorized killing instead of capturing bin Laden," his lieutenants, and approved shooting down any private plane carrying the al Qaeda leader. National Security Adviser Sandy Berger held another meeting with the Principals; the CIA had received evidence that bin Laden was attempting to acquire or produce dangerous weapons, including chemicals, gases, and possibly a nuclear device. Cabinet members discussed a strike at one of bin Laden's factories in Sudan, possibly where gas was being produced. When there was an objection to the attack, Berger asked, "What if we do not hit it and then . . . nerve gas is released in the New York City subway? What will we say then?"

During that August, bin Laden was somewhere in Afghanistan, a guest of the Taliban regime. His exact location was a mystery, for he traveled most of the time to meetings with other terrorists, such as al Qaeda's number two man, the Egyptian doctor Ayman al-Zawahiri, and the organization's third man, Mohammad Atef. The jihadists met at bin Laden's compound in Kandahar and his camp out of town, Tarnak farm, a walled facility of about 100 acres where satellite pictures revealed women and children, and training facilities for terrorists.

"I want boots on the ground in Afghanistan," Clinton told General Hugh Shelton, Chairman of the Joint Chiefs of Staff. "I want to scare those terrorist out of their camps, and eliminate bin Laden." The president wanted Special Forces dropped into Afghanistan, but Shelton talked to Pentagon colleagues, who did not think the operation was a good idea, nor did the commander of the Central Command, General Zinni, who would have had to direct the campaign. It was almost impossible to locate bin Laden, there was no good staging area in the region, it would be hard to tell friend from foe, and it might require tens of thousands of troops. Clinton relented, and instead signed an executive order that imposed economic sanctions on bin Laden, al Qaeda, and eventually the Taliban. He also ordered the navy to fire cruise missiles at two targets: the chemical plant in Sudan and at a camp in Khost, eastern Afghanistan. The CIA had learned that bin Laden was meeting other terrorists at that camp on August 20; an attack on that camp, wrote CIA Director George Tenet, was a "no brainer."

That evening, after the missiles had been fired, Clinton informed the nation, "With compelling evidence that the bin Laden network of terrorist groups was planning to mount further attacks against Americans and other freedom-loving people, I decided America must act." The navy launched the missiles from the Red Sea, destroying the plant in Sudan, but it was a more difficult operation in Afghanistan. In order to hit bin Laden, the U.S. Navy had to fire the missiles over Pakistan and inform that government, who apparently leaked the information to the Taliban government and to bin Laden. The navy launched about 70 missiles. At 400 mph, they took two hours to reach the Khost camp, killing about 20 people, but most of the men had evacuated about an hour before the missiles arrived, including bin Laden.

"We survived the attack," Zawahiri declared. "Tell the Americans that we aren't afraid of bombardment, threats, and acts of aggression. We suffered and survived the Soviet bombings for ten years in Afghanistan, and we are ready for more sacrifices. The war has only just begun; the Americans should now await the answer."

The answer arrived at the end of the millennium. Terrorist Czar Clarke, CIA Director Tenet, and CIA Counterterrorism Center director Cofer Black all knew that al Qaeda could not miss a chance to strike the West at the end of the second Christian millennium. A year earlier, in December 1998, Tenet had sent Clinton a Presidential Daily Briefing (PDB) entitled "Bin Laden Preparing to Hijack US Aircraft and Other

Attacks," so during December 1999, Clarke sent out warnings to all U.S. embassies, military bases, and police agencies in the United States. That month Tenet and Black told the president that bin Laden was planning between five and fifteen attacks worldwide. "This set off a frenzy of activity," Tenet later wrote. The "CIA launched operations in fifty-five countries against thirty-eight separate targets." Apparently, al Qaeda had planned attacks the last day of the millennium for the Los Angeles International Airport, the Amman Radisson Hotel in Jordan, Israeli holy sites, and a Navy destroyer docked in a Yemen port. But the strike on U.S. soil was foiled by one alert customs agent who noticed a man acting nervously in the line coming into Washington State from British Columbia. She pulled him aside, and Ahmed Ressam's car held explosives, along with a map of the Los Angeles International Airport. On heightened alert, authorities apprehended conspirators in eight countries and all of the attempted attacks were thwarted, including the one in Jordan. "We have stopped two sets of attacks planned for the Millennium," National Security Adviser Berger declared at a Principals meeting, warning that bin Laden would attempt more in the future. "I spoke with the President and he wants you all to know . . . this is it, nothing more important, all assets. We have to stop this fucker."

One way to stop him was to get the Taliban to hand over bin Laden to the United States, so during 1999 the administration began sending messages to that government demanding that it turn over the Saudi. They refused, claiming it was impossible because of Pashtun traditions. In April 2000, Assistant Secretary of State Michael Sheehan delivered a message directly to the Taliban. He telephoned their foreign minister and warned: "If bin Laden or any of the organizations affiliated with him attacks the United States interests, we will hold you, the leadership of the Taliban, personally accountable. Do you understand what I am saying? This is from the highest level of my government."

That highest level had just visited India and Pakistan. On March 25, Clinton and Berger had a private meeting with Pakistan's new leader General Pervez Musharraf. The president was blunt. He "pressed Musharraf very hard and told him to use Pakistan's influence with the Taliban to get bin Laden," Berger recalled, and Musharraf responded, "I will do as much as I can," which was very little. Two months later, State Department official Thomas Pickering arrived in Islamabad and met with the Taliban deputy foreign minister. Pickering presented him with an indictment for bin Laden, charging him for the embassy bombings. "We don't think your evidence is persuasive," the Afghan replied, adding that if there were proof then the Saudi guest should be subject to judgment under sharia, or Islamic law, not American law. That was too much for Pickering, who blurted out, "People who are helping other people kill Americans are our enemies and should consider themselves as such." Eventually, the Clinton administration contacted the Taliban government 30 times concerning bin Laden. By September 2000, the administration concluded that Pakistan's aid to the Taliban reached "unprecedented" levels and that Islamabad probably had allowed the Taliban to use Pakistani territory for military operations and were "providing the Taliban with supplies, fuel, funding, technical assistance and military advisors."

The Taliban continued protecting al Qaeda, who continued attacking U.S. interests; their next strike was an unusual target—an American warship, the USS *Cole*. The guided missile destroyer had been built with the most advanced technology to fight the Soviet navy, but the enemy arrived at 11 AM on October 12 in a fiberglass fishing boat. The *Cole* was anchored in Aden's harbor in Yemen. Two sailors watched the boat come amidship; they waved to the fishermen. Then, the boat exploded, ripping an enormous hole in the ship, wounding 39 sailors and killing 17. "The destroyer represented the capital of the West," bin Laden said, "and the small boat represented Mohammed."

The *Cole* was the last terrorist strike of the Clinton years. By that time, CIA's Tenet later wrote, the "principal policy makers of the Clinton Administration understood fully the nature of the threat we were facing." As for the president himself, "I continued to push the Pentagon and the national security team for more options to get bin Laden," Clinton later wrote. "I was very frustrated, and hoped that before I left office we would locate bin Laden for a missile strike."[10]

But that was not to be. Clinton's efforts to kill bin Laden and contain Saddam became a sideshow in the United States, eclipsed by the president's sex scandal over an affair with Monica Lewinsky and his subsequent impeachment by the House of Representatives. Although the Senate did not muster the necessary votes to convict the president and force him from office on any of the three articles of impeachment, the public seemed mesmerized by the trial and then by the 2000 election campaign. Americans forgot about foreign nuisances in the Graveyard of Empires and the Improbable Country.

The Clinton presidency ended, diminished by the scandal, yet at a time of peace and prosperity in America. In the last summer of his presidency, he labored hard to get the Palestinians and Israelis to sign a treaty that would have moved the peace process further down the weary road in the Middle East, but neither side was willing to sign; at least they were talking to each other. Next door in Iraq, the economy was improving with increasing amounts of trade. Saddam had barred the UN weapon inspectors, and the U.S. and British air forces were patrolling that nation's no-fly zone. The Anglo-American policy was containing Saddam, who was not threatening his neighbors. In Afghanistan, the Taliban had consolidated its power and controlled all but the northern part of the country, while bin Laden and his men were training new members for al Qaeda. Relatively speaking, the Middle East was at peace. Few Americans realized the threat that was looming.

1

Bush, bin Laden, and the Pinnacle of World Sympathy

"Nous sommes tous Americains."
—*Le Monde*, September 13, 2001, Paris

Terrorism was not an issue during the 2000 presidential campaign, and neither were Saddam Hussein or Osama bin Laden. Opinion polls demonstrated voters were most interested in health care topics such as HMOs and prescription drug costs for the elderly, school violence, and the moral values that were revealed during the Clinton impeachment trial. The Republican candidate and governor of Texas, George W. Bush, made "values" one of his main themes. A born-again Christian, Bush roused the Republican faithful at the convention: "And so, when I put my hand on the Bible, I will swear to not only uphold the laws of our land, I will swear to uphold the honor and dignity of the office to which I have been elected, so help me God."

Throughout the campaign Bush pledged to "bring respect back to the White House." As president he would be a "compassionate conservative" who would unite Americans: "We need a uniter, not a divider." After Clinton's divisive impeachment trial, the governor declared, "I have no stake in the bitter arguments of the last few years. I want to change the tone of Washington to one of civility and respect."

Concerning foreign policy, he was asked about his "guiding principles" during the second presidential debate, and responded, "What's in the best interests of the United States? What's in the best interests of our people? . . . Peace in the Middle East is in our nation's interests. . . . Strong relations in Europe is in our nation's interest." On the next question concerning how the people of the world should perceive the United States, the Republican answered, "If we're an arrogant nation, they'll resent us. If we're a humble nation, but strong, they'll welcome us."

On another occasion he criticized Clinton's use of troops in the 1990s to stabilize the governments of Haiti and Bosnia, declaring, "I would be very careful about using our troops as nation builders." And when debating his opponent, Vice President Al Gore, the Republican added:

> I would take the use of force very seriously. . . . I think we've got to be very careful when we commit our troops. The vice president and I have a disagreement about the use of troops. He believes in nation building. I would be very careful about using our troops as nation builders. . . . If we don't stop extending our troops all around the world in nation-building missions, then we're going to have a serious problem down the road. And I'm going to prevent that.

Bush's vice presidential candidate, Dick Cheney, seconded such thoughts on *Meet the Press*, where he defended the 1991 decision not to occupy Baghdad. The United States must not act like "an imperialist power, willy-nilly moving into capitals in that part of the world, taking down governments." Concerning the armed forces, he told the Republican National Convention: "For eight years, Clinton and Gore have extended our military commitments while depleting our military power. . . . George W. Bush and I are going to change that," and he pledged to the military, "Help is on the way. Soon, our men and women in uniform will once again have a commander in chief they can respect, one who understands their mission and restores their morale."

The subsequent election was one of the strangest in American history. Gore won 540,000 more votes in the popular election but did not win the electoral college. The counting was feverishly close in Oregon, New Mexico, and Florida. Officials commenced recounts. Oregon and New Mexico fell into the Gore camp, but the work dragged on into December 2000 in Florida. There, Green Party candidate Ralph Nader had won 1.6 percent or almost 100,000 votes, which swung the state toward Bush by 537 votes. As the recount continued, the Republicans filed a lawsuit to stop it, which was quickly accepted by the Supreme Court. By a 5 to 4 vote, the majority Republican appointees stopped the recount, giving the state—and presidency—to the Republican candidate.

"Whether you voted for me or not," President-elect Bush said to the nation, "I will do my best to serve your interest, and I will work to earn your respect. I will be guided by President Jefferson's sense of purpose, to stand for principle, to be reasonable in manner, and above all, to do great good for the cause of freedom and harmony."

Given the unusual circumstances of his election, Bush began in a relatively weak political position, with most opinion polls demonstrating an approval rating only in the 55 percent range, which slowly began to decline to 50 by June. Moreover, numerous political trends demonstrated that the two main political parties had been drifting apart, more liberal and more conservative, since the 1970s, which helped to explain a divided Congress. The House was narrowly Republican, and the Senate was split 50–50; there was little mood for compromise, and there was no "honeymoon" for the new administration.

"A notion of sort of a restrained presidency because it was such a close election, that lasted maybe 30 seconds," recalled Vice President Cheney. "We had an agenda, we ran on the agenda, we won the election— full speed ahead." Yet it was slow going. Bush's campaign of compassionate conservative translated to an education reform called "No Child Left Behind," a prescription drug program for seniors, less regulation of business, opposition to abortion, and talk about privatizing Social Security. Those would have to wait, but during his first months in office he signed an executive order that established a White House Office of Faith-Based and Community Initiatives and announced that his administration aimed to develop a national missile defense shield. He signed a $1.35 trillion tax cut. In mandating his environmental policy, he rejected the Kyoto Protocol on global warming; initiated his "Healthy Forest Initiative," which opened national forest to more extensive logging; and began his "Clear Skies Initiative," which rolled back EPA pollution control requirements for power plants. While those policies received cheers from some businesses, they enraged many conservationists, including Vermont Senator James Jeffords. He quit the Republican Party and became an independent, which handed control of the Senate to the Democrats.

Meanwhile, behind closed doors the new administration discussed energy and foreign policy. On January 29, 2001, the president established his National Energy Policy Development Group, chaired by Cheney. According to a Watergate-era federal law, meetings between governmental officials and private citizens must be open to the public, but Cheney refused to release the members' names, resulting in a lawsuit against the vice president; in 2004 a federal court agreed with the administration. Nevertheless, in subsequent years it was leaked that Cheney's group was composed of cabinet secretaries, oil industry contributors to Bush's campaign, and possibly Iraqis interested in deposing Saddam Hussein. It included executives from Exxon Mobil, Enron, British Petroleum, Duke Energy, and the American Petroleum Institute. By March, Cheney and his energy task force were examining maps of Iraq's oil fields and pipelines and had a list of companies interested in doing business in a post-Saddam Iraq.

Clearly, the new administration was interested in Iraq and the Middle East. Even before the inauguration, the vice president–elect sent a message to Clinton's secretary of defense, William Cohen. "We really need to get the president-elect briefed up on some things," wrote Cheney, adding that he wanted a serious "discussion about Iraq and different options." After the inauguration, Middle East policy was immediately on the agenda. In the first meeting of the National Security Council on January 30, the president noted that his administration was going to disengage from trying to be an honest broker in the Palestinian-Israeli peace process. When Secretary of State Colin Powell said that the "consequences of that could be dire, especially for the Palestinians," Bush shrugged, "Maybe that's the best way to get things back in balance. . . . Sometimes a show of strength by one side can really clarify things."

Thus, after 30 years of engagement and an attempt by each president from Nixon in 1973 to Clinton in summer 2000 to be the "honest broker" and bring about a peace between Arabs and Israelis, the Bush administration washed its hands of the task. They would favor Israel.

In that meeting Bush had another interest, and he turned to his NSC director, Condoleezza Rice: "So, Condi, what are we going to talk about today? What's on the agenda?" "How Iraq is destabilizing the region, Mr. President." Within minutes CIA Director George Tenet had rolled out a large grainy photograph of a factory that "produces either chemical or biological materials for weapons manufacture." The photo excited the vice president, who waved to his assistants, "You have to take a look at this." One member of the NSC, Treasury Secretary Paul O'Neill, looked at the photo and commented, "I've seen a lot of factories around the world that look a lot like this one. What makes us suspect that this one is producing chemical or biological agents for weapons?" It was a good question, for Tenet admitted that there was "no confirming intelligence" about what was being produced at the factory. Nevertheless, by the end of the meeting the president had assignments for everyone. Powell would draw up new sanctions against Saddam; Tenet would improve intelligence in Iraq; O'Neill would investigate how to financially destabilize the regime; and Defense Secretary Donald Rumsfeld "should examine our military options."

During the NSC's next meeting on February 1, a State Department memo was introduced that mentioned "possible regime change." Secretary Powell discussed a new strategy of "targeted sanctions," when Rumsfeld interrupted. "Sanctions are fine," he said. "But what we really want to think about is going after Saddam."

"From the very beginning," said O'Neill, "there was a conviction, that Saddam Hussein was a bad person and that he needed to go." Going after Saddam was "topic A. . . . It was all about finding a way to do it," O'Neill continued, and he was surprised in the meeting that no one asked, "Why Saddam?" and "Why Now?"

Yet, such questions were kept secret from the public during the first months of the administration. Publicly, the new secretary of state maintained that Iraq was not a threat to the United States or to the Middle East. During a trip to Germany on February 20, Powell told a press conference that the UN and its allies "have succeeded in containing Saddam Hussein and his ambitions. His forces are about one-third their original size. They don't really possess the capability to attack their neighbors the way they did ten years ago." Four days later in Egypt, the secretary reiterated the administration's confidence: "We should constantly be . . . looking at those sanctions. . . . And frankly, they have worked." Saddam had "not developed any significant capability with respect to weapons of mass destruction. He is unable to project conventional power against his neighbors." A few months later in July, Rice made a similar statement: "We are able to keep arms from" Saddam. "His military forces have not been rebuilt."[1]

Saddam was not a threat, but he was a migraine to some in the new administration—the neoconservatives. Commonly known as neocons, these intellectuals surfaced in the late 1960s as former liberals who were horrified by violence in the streets, student rebels confronting college deans, hippies flaunting mainstream values, strident calls for "Out Now" from Vietnam, and the immediate demands for Black Power. Irving Kristol, an early adherent, described a neocon as a "liberal who'd been mugged by reality." While upset at the radical behavior of some activists in the late 1960s and the 1970s, they usually were not as interested in social issues as in foreign policy. To them, the Vietnam debacle did not demonstrate that the United States had overreached the limits of its power, as liberals believed; instead, they thought that the nation had gone soft, and when the going got tough the United States did not stay the course. They watched in dismay during the 1970s as presidents Richard Nixon and Jimmy Carter abandoned a tough containment policy toward the Soviet Union and replaced it with détente, and as they negotiated with the Russians to reduce both nations' massive stockpiles of military hardware through the SALT talks. To Norman Podhoretz, a leading neocon and editor of *Commentary* magazine, détente was the "culture of appeasement." Neocons were ashamed in 1975 as North Vietnamese tanks rolled into Saigon and forced a humiliating evacuation of the remaining Americans. These signs of weakness, they thought, were appropriately rewarded in 1979 as Iranian radicals held Americans hostage in Tehran and as Soviet tanks invaded Afghanistan.

Neocons found their hero in Ronald Reagan, a man who did not advocate negotiating with the Soviets but instead defeating the "evil empire" and spreading American democracy throughout the world. As two neocons wrote, "Reagan called for an end to complacency in the face of the Soviet threat . . . large increases in defense spending, resistance to communist advances in the Third World, and greater moral clarity and purpose in U.S. foreign policy." He "refused to accept the limits on American power."

By the early 1990s the United States was the world's only super-power, and in 1996 the neocons Robert Kagan and William Kristol, the son of Irving and editor of *The Weekly Standard*, published "Toward a Neo-Reaganite Foreign Policy," in which they posed the question: What should be America's role in the world? "Benevolent global hege-mony," they answered. "The first objective of U.S. foreign policy should be to preserve and enhance [our] predominance by strengthening America's security, supporting its friends, advancing its interests, and standing up for its principles around the world." The next year the authors helped to establish the Project for the New American Century, which included Donald Rumsfeld, Paul D. Wolfowitz, Richard Perle, James Woolsey, and Elliott Abrams. The Project advocated a tough mil-itary policy while using American power for "moral good" in the world during the next century. Concerning Iraq, the organization published an open letter to President Clinton. It claimed that the policy of con-tainment had been "steadily eroding," that diplomacy was "clearly failing," and that "removing Saddam Hussein and his regime from power . . . needs to become the aim of American foreign policy." The alternative, they claimed, would be a "course of weakness and drift." In 1998 the Republican Congress passed and the president reluctantly signed the Iraq Liberation Act, which stated that U.S. policy aimed to remove Saddam.

The Iraq Liberation Act did not mention how any administration was supposed to achieve that aim and it did not call for an American invasion to bring about regime change. Instead, it merely authorized the president to spend taxpayers' money to help exiled democratic Iraqis to find a way to end the brutal dictatorship.

Many neocons in the new Bush administration, however, began calling for more determined action against Saddam because, they believed, the dictator had been involved in aggression against the United States. One charged that Saddam was responsible for many attacks, espe-cially the 1993 World Trade Center bombing, an idea so preposterous that the Clinton administration did not investigate. Others claimed that Saddam's actions in the 1980s had doomed the Reagan administration's efforts to bring about a peace settlement between Israelis and Arabs, leading to the neocon refrain that "the road to Jerusalem runs through Baghdad." In fact, Saddam supported the peace effort.

The new president listened to the neocons and appointed more than half of the founding members of Project for the New American Century to key positions in his administration. Rumsfeld became secretary of defense, and Wolfowitz became his deputy. Abrams was placed on the National Security Council, and Perle and Woolsey were assigned to the Pentagon's Defense Policy Board Advisory Committee. Other neocons received important appointments: Kenneth Adelman was on the Defense Policy Board; David Frum became a White House speech-writer; I. Lewis "Scooter" Libby became Wolfowitz's aide at the Penta-gon and later Vice President Cheney's assistant; Stephen Hadley and Zalmay Khalilzad sat on the National Security Council; and John Bolton was appointed to the State Department.[2]

The neocons were in place, and as they began to formulate policy during 2001 other governmental officials began warning the new administration about a possible attack—not from Saddam—but from Osama bin Laden and his group, al Qaeda. "You're going to spend more time during your four years on terrorism generally and al Qaeda specifically than any issue," Sandy Berger told incoming National Se-curity Adviser Rice. In January, the terrorism czar, Richard Clarke, briefed each of his old colleagues from the first Bush administration— Condi Rice, Steve Hadley, Dick Cheney, Colin Powell—with a blunt message: "al Qaeda is at war with us, it is a highly capable organization, probably with sleeper cells in the U.S., and it is clearly planning a major series of attacks against us; we must act decisively and quickly." On January 25 Clarke sent a memorandum to Rice: "We *urgently* need . . . a Principals level review on the al Qaeda network," noting the "immi-nent al Qaeda threat."

Rice said that the Principals would not meet until their deputies had reviewed the issue. After many delays the deputies met in April. Clarke began the briefing with "we need to target bin Laden," to which Wolfow-itz responded, "I just don't understand why we are beginning by talking about this one man bin Laden." When Clarke reminded him about al Qaeda's attacks and that its terrorist network "alone poses an immediate and serious threat to the United States," the deputy defense secretary responded, "Well, there are others that do as well, at least as much. Iraqi terrorism for example." Clarke retorted: "I am unaware of any Iraqi-sponsored terrorism directed at the United States . . . since 1993 [the attempt on George H. W. Bush's life in Kuwait] and I think FBI and CIA concur in that judgment." The deputy CIA director agreed: "We have no evidence of any Iraqi terrorist threat against the U.S." Wolfowitz ignored that, commenting, "You give bin Laden too much credit. He could not do all these things . . . not without a state sponsor." Clarke again warned, that "al Qaeda plans major acts of terrorism against the U.S. It plans to overthrow Islamic governments and set up a radical multination Caliphate, and then go to war with non-Muslim states."

The new administration was not listening to its terrorism czar or to the CIA. In February, CIA Director Tenet told the Senate: "The threat from terrorism is real, it is immediate, and it is evolving. . . . Osama bin Laden and his global network of lieutenants and associates remain the most immediate and serious threat. . . . He is capable of planning multiple attacks with little or no warning." The CIA chief also met with key administration officials. On May 30, Tenet; his counterterrorism chief, Cofer Black; and Clarke met with Rice. "The mounting warning signs of a coming attack . . . were truly frightening," he reported to her, and again on June 28 Tenet and Black presented Rice with "ten specific pieces of intelligence about impending attacks." By July 10, the CIA's counterterrorism team had intercepted al Qaeda communications and other intelligence and presented it to Tenet; he was so alarmed that for the first time in seven years as CIA director he picked up the phone and requested an immediate meeting at the White House. Twenty minutes later he, Black, and an undercover agent met Rice, Clarke, and Steve Hadley. The agent began the meeting bluntly: "There will be a significant terrorist attack in the coming weeks or months!" The attack would be "spectacular" and designed to inflict mass casualties against U.S. facilities and interests. "Multiple and simultaneous attacks are possible, and they will occur with little or no warning." This was an urgent problem that had to be addressed immediately, including covert or military action to thwart bin Laden. Rice asked Clarke if he agreed, which he confirmed, but she brushed off the warning, and the men left her office frustrated. They wanted to "shake Rice," as Black later said. "The only thing we didn't do was pull the trigger to the gun we were holding to her head."

The administration also refused to heed the warnings of outgoing Clinton administration experts: Daniel Benjamin, who had been director for counterterrorism on the National Security Council staff, and Brian Sheridan, former assistant secretary of defense for special operations. Nor did they listen to the outgoing deputy national security adviser, Lieutenant General Don Kerrick. He sent a blunt memo to the NSC after Bush's inauguration: "We are going to be struck again."

"They never responded," Kerrick continued. Terrorism "was not high on their priority list. I was never invited to one meeting." Nor did they respond to warnings from the chairman of the Joint Chiefs of Staff, General Henry Shelton, who tried to warn the Defense Department. Secretary Rumsfeld did not think that counterterrorism was a military mission.

"After 9/11 some senior government officials contended that they were surprised at the size and nature of the attacks," Tenet later wrote. "Perhaps so, but they shouldn't have been. We had been warning about the threat at every opportunity." In fact, between the inaugural in January and September 11, "Bush received 44 morning intelligence reports from the CIA mentioning the al Qaeda threat, and not once did he say . . . 'let's begin a process to stop the attack.'"

The president did not show any interest in his own daily intelligence briefings. The title of his August 6 briefing was alarming: "Bin Laden Determined To Strike in US." It reminded Bush that bin Laden had proclaimed that his followers would "bring the fighting to America." It cited Egyptian sources who had informed American officials that bin Laden was planning "to mount a terrorist strike." The briefing continued, "al-Qaeda members—including some who are US citizens—have resided in or traveled to the US for years, and the group apparently maintains a support structure that could aid attacks." The briefing concluded that the FBI had information that "indicates patterns of suspicious activity in this country consistent with preparations for hijackings or other types of attacks, including recent surveillance of federal buildings in New York."[3]

The president did not respond; he was on vacation.

Instead of terrorism, the administration was focused on the old Reagan "Star Wars" policy—building a missile shield. That project had cost about $60 billion by the time Bush took office but still in numerous tests had not been able to intercept and shoot down one incoming rocket. Few military officers felt the shield was workable, or necessary, especially after the demise of the atomic-armed superpower enemy, the Soviet Union. Nevertheless, while Bush rarely mentioned administration plans to prevent a terrorist attack in his first eight months in office, he explained on at least three occasions that the nation needed the missile shield to protect against "terrorist threats that face us." Rice was scheduled to give a speech on September 11 attacking Clinton for not building a missile defense.

A week earlier, on September 4, Rice finally held the Principals meeting that Clarke had requested in January. "Tenet and I spoke passionately about the urgency and seriousness of the al Qaeda threat," recalled Clarke. But the discussion turned to the questions of funding a larger antiterrorist campaign and of attempting to use a new unmanned Predator surveillance aircraft to fire missiles at bin Laden in Afghanistan. The meeting concluded without answers. Clarke sent Rice a memorandum to complain about foot dragging: "Are we serious about dealing with the al Qaeda threat?" he asked. "Is al Qaeda a big deal?" And Clarke emphasized, *Decision makers should imagine themselves on a future day when the CSG* [Counterterrorism Security Group] *has not succeeded in stopping al Qaeda attacks and hundreds of Americans lay dead in several countries, including the US.*" Three years later, the 9/11 Commission simply concluded: "The System Was Blinking Red."

Yet to be fair, there was some significant information missing. "Throughout the summer of 2001," said deputy National Security Adviser Michael V. Hayden, "we had more than thirty warnings that something was imminent." They usually were intercepted messages, "Something spectacular is coming," but the warnings contained no specific details—no what, where, or when. Consequently, no one knows if 9/11 could have been prevented, which even Clarke admitted.

Another warning arrived on September 10 when NSA intercepted two emails that came from a suspected al Qaeda location in Afghanistan: "The match begins tomorrow" and "Tomorrow is zero hour." For the next two days, no one translated the messages.[4]

Tuesday, September 11, 2001, began as a beautiful, clear blue morning on the East Coast. Suddenly, that day—and America—was shattered.

Mohammed Atta and Abdul Aziz al Omari boarded their 6:00 AM flight in Portland, Maine, and at 6:45 arrived at Logan Airport in Boston. They and three others, Satam al Suqami, Wail al Shehri, and Waleed al Shehri, checked in and boarded American Airlines Flight 11 bound for Los Angeles and scheduled to depart at 7:45. In another Logan terminal,

Marwan al Shehhi, Fayez Banihammad, Mohand al Shehri, Ahmed al Ghamdi, and Hamza al Ghamdi checked in and boarded United Airlines Flight 175, also bound for Los Angeles at 8:00 am. None of the men were stopped by security. Nor were four other men at Newark International Airport in New Jersey. Saeed al Ghamdi, Ahmed al Nami, Ahmad al Haznawi, and Ziad Jarrah walked through security for their United Airlines Flight 93 to Los Angeles and took their seats in the first class cabin. Over 300 miles southwest, Khalid al Mihdhar, Majed Moqed, Hani Hanjour, and two brothers, Nawaf al Hazmi and Salem al Hazmi, were going through security for their flight at Dulles International Airport in the Virginia suburbs of Washington, DC. Two of them set off the alarm, but Mihdhar did not set off the alarm the second time and he passed through. Moqed did, so a screener wanded him, and he passed this inspection. The men boarded their flight for Los Angeles.

By 8:00 AM on September 11, 19 men were aboard four flights. They had defeated all the security layers that the airlines had in place to prevent hijacking. The terrorists were armed with knives, mace, box cutters, and probably some fake bombs, all stored in their carry-on baggage, yet they were not stopped by airport security. At that time, the walk-through metal detectors were calibrated to detect items with at least the metal content of a .22-caliber handgun. Moreover, security then was operated by private firms contracted by each airline, who did not want to inconvenience customers, especially those who bought the more expensive tickets. Except for two hijackers, all flew business or first class, seats closest to the cockpit.

The men also had defeated any attempts to track them as potential terrorists. They had attended flight schools, rented apartments and cars, used credit cards—all with their own names. The 19 had entered the United States a total of 33 times, through more than ten different airports, without ever being stopped or detained. Only one potential hijacker, Mohamed al Kahtani, had been refused entry in August 2001 by a suspicious immigration inspector at Florida's Orlando International Airport. The 19 had no criminal records and had not been identified by intelligence agencies for special scrutiny. As late as January 2004, a former Immigration and Naturalization Service commissioner commented, "Even under the best immigration controls, most of the September 11 terrorists would still be admitted to the United States today."

In Boston, American Airlines Flight 11 took off at 7:59 and climbed to 29,000 feet. At 8:14 air traffic control gave the pilot navigation instructions, which he acknowledged, and 16 seconds later told the aircraft to climb to 35,000 feet—which was not acknowledged. Five minutes later a flight attendant in coach, Betty Ong, was on an airphone: "The cockpit is not answering, somebody's been stabbed in business class—and I think Mace—that we can't breathe—I don't know, I think we're getting hijacked." "Nobody move," one of the hijackers said over the plane's intercom at 8:25. "Everything will be okay. If you try to make any moves, you'll endanger yourself and the airplane." The speaker did not realize that he also was broadcasting that message over the air traffic control channel, alerting Boston. Two minutes later the Boeing 767 turned south, and Ong reported that it was "flying erratically." At 8:41 air traffic controllers declared that American 11 had been hijacked and that they thought it was headed toward Kennedy International Airport in New York City. They alerted the airport to prepare and planes in the area to stay clear. At 8:43 flight attendant Madeline Amy Sweeney called the American Flight Services Office in Boston: "Something is wrong. We are in rapid descent . . . we are all over the place." An American official asked her to look out the window to see if she could determine where they were, and Sweeney responded: "We are flying low. We're flying very, very low. . . . Oh my God, we are way too low." At 8:46 American 11 crashed into the North Tower of the World Trade Center.

By that time, United Airlines 175 had lifted off from Logan Airport and had reached its cruising altitude of 31,000 feet. At 8:42 the cockpit crew reported that a few minutes earlier they had heard a "suspicious transmission" from another plane, which turned out to be American 11. That was the last communication the Boeing 767 had with air traffic control, but flight attendants and passengers were calling loved ones on cell phones: "I think they intend to go to Chicago or someplace and fly into a building," Peter Hanson said to his father. "If it happens, it'll be very fast—My God, my God," and then the phone went dead. At 9:03 United 175 slammed into the South Tower of the World Trade Center.

Earlier, at 8:20, American 77 had taken off from Dulles International Airport, and by 8:46 had reached its cruising altitude of 35,000 feet. Five minutes later the Boeing 757 made its last report to air traffic controllers. At 8:54 the aircraft deviated from its course, and 15 minutes later American

Airlines Headquarters alerted all of their flights. At 9:32 air traffic controllers at Dulles observed a "radar target tracking eastbound at a high rate of speed," which was American 77. The plane was headed in the direction of the White House but then made a 330° turn as the pilot pushed the throttles to maximum power. At 9:37 American 77 was going 530 miles per hour when it smashed into the Pentagon.

In Newark, United 93 was late. Scheduled to take off at 8:00, it sat on the ground in heavy traffic for over 40 minutes until it lifted off the runway. The crew of the Boeing 757 was unaware of the three hijackings, but by 9:00 United, American, and the Federal Aviation Administration were alert, and the two airlines began grounding all their flights in the United States. At 9:23 a United official warned their flights, "Beware any cockpit intrusion—Two a/c hit World Trade Center." At 9:26 the pilot of United 93 was puzzled by the message and asked for confirmation, but within two minutes the hijackers attacked. "May-day!" the captain yelled. There were sounds of struggle in the cockpit and seconds later, "get out of here—get out of here." Four minutes later the hijackers were in control and told the passengers: "We have a bomb on board. So sit." The new pilot then turned the plane back to the east, as two flight attendants and ten passengers made calls from cell and airphones and learned about the World Trade Center. Alarmed, the 33 passengers in coach decided to vote—and to attack the terrorists. "Everyone's running up to first class," one female passenger shouted into her phone, "I've got to go." Realizing the assault, the pilot rolled the plane violently, left, right, down, but the attack continued, as air traffic controllers listened on the ground. "Roll it!" But they kept coming. "Pull it down! Pull it down!" came from the cockpit, and as the plane flew out of control, "Allah is the greatest! Allah is the greatest!" At 10:02, United 93 plowed into an empty field in Pennsylvania at 580 miles per hour, about 20 minutes flying time from the probable targets, the White House or Capitol in Washington, DC.

Firemen and other first responders rushed to the World Trade Center and Pentagon as administration officials received news of the tragedy. The president was reading a book to children at an elementary school in Sarasota, Florida, and was slated to give a talk on education when his chief of staff, Andrew Card, whispered to him: "A second plane hit the second tower. America is under attack." The vice president was at the White House and was told to turn on the television as he wondered,

"How the hell could a plane hit the World Trade Center?" By 9:45 Bush had more information, had returned to Air Force One, and called Cheney: "Sounds like we have a minor war going on here, I heard about the Pentagon. We're at war . . . somebody's going to pay." The president wanted to return to the capital, but Card and Cheney opposed that idea, so his plane took off for an unknown destination, eventually landing at Offutt Air Force Base in Nebraska, the underground headquarters of the U.S. Strategic Command. The bunker there was built to withstand an atomic bomb. Meanwhile, the White House was warned that American 77 was approaching Washington and the secret service took the vice president to the White House bunker, where a few minutes later he learned that the Pentagon had been hit. Just after 10:00 the secret service reported an inbound aircraft, which was United 93, and at about 10:15 a military aide asked the vice president for authority to engage the aircraft. Cheney had discussed this possibility with the president, and he immediately authorized fighter aircraft to engage the inbound plane. The plane already had crashed in Pennsylvania.

The nation's air defenses had been overwhelmed, for there never had been such an attack on the United States. Confusion abounded. By 10:38 Air National Guard fighters lifted off from their base in Maryland and began patrolling the skies over Washington and a few minutes later were joined by NORAD fighters that had scrambled out of Langley, Virginia. The first group had received instructions to engage incoming planes and, if necessary, shoot them down, but the second was operating under different rules of engagement. About that same time, Cheney contacted Rumsfeld at the Pentagon, telling the secretary that he had given the order to shoot down hijacked planes, adding "it's my understanding they've already taken a couple of aircraft out."

Perhaps the most appropriate comment about what happened during the confusion of September 11 was made by an officer at NORAD's defense sector in Rome, New York: "This is a new type of war." The first major attack cost about 2,800 American lives, more than the December 7, 1941, attack on Pearl Harbor.[5]

Terrorism Czar Clarke remained at the White House, briefly went home to shower at about 1:00 AM and returned an hour later, when he was called to the West Wing, supposedly to discuss terrorism—where the next attacks might be, and what were our vulnerabilities. Clarke was shocked:

> I walked into a series of discussions about Iraq. At first I was incredulous that we were talking about something other than getting al Qaeda. Then I realized with almost sharp physical pain that Rumsfeld and Wolfowitz were going to try to take advantage of this national tragedy to promote their agenda about Iraq. Since the beginning of the administration, indeed well before, they had been pressing for a war with Iraq.

That had been confirmed hours earlier, for on the afternoon of September 11, while Rumsfeld was at the Pentagon, an aide had jotted down notes of their conversation. The secretary wanted "best info fast; judge whether good enough to hit S.H. [Saddam Hussein] at same time," not only bin Laden. "Go massive. Sweep it all up. Things related, and not."

Clarke and Tenet knew who had attacked America. At CIA headquarters, Tenet held a meeting minutes after the second plane smashed into the World Trade Center, later writing, "I don't think there was a person in the room who had the least doubt that we were in the middle of a full-scale assault orchestrated by al Qaeda." That afternoon, the president held a teleconference call from the Strategic Air Command in Nebraska and asked Tenet who attacked. "Al Qaeda," the director responded, for the passenger manifests had confirmed their suspicions. "The whole operation looked, smelled, and tasted like bin Laden."

Others agreed. "Neither of us had any doubt about who had committed the atrocity," wrote Security Council's Directorate of Transnational Threats, Steven Simon and Daniel Benjamin. From the other side of the world, CENTCOM Commander General Tommy Franks was awoken by an aide, who turned on the TV. The general was filled with rage as he watched the planes crash into the World Trade Center, clenched his fist, and barked, "Osama bin Laden. *Son of a bitch!*"

Yet the neocons had doubts. "It was too sophisticated and complicated an operation for a terrorist group to have pulled off by itself, without a state sponsor," Wolfowitz told Clarke. "Iraq must have been helping them." By the afternoon Rumsfeld was talking about "getting Iraq," when Clarke turned to Secretary Powell and declared, "Having been attacked by al Qaeda, for us now to go bombing Iraq in response would be like our invading Mexico after the Japanese attacked us at Pearl Harbor." Later in the day, Secretary Rumsfeld complained that there were no decent targets for bombing in Afghanistan and that we should consider bombing Iraq, which had better targets.

President Bush had returned to the White House the evening of September 11 and briefly spoke to the nation that evening: "I've directed the full resources of our intelligence and law enforcement communities to find those responsible and to bring them to justice," he told an audience of 80 million viewers: "We will make no distinction between the terrorists who committed these acts and those who harbor them."

The next evening he ran into Clarke and some of his staff—it was the first time that the president met with his terrorism czar. "Look," Bush ordered, "I want you, as soon as you can, to go back over everything, everything. See if Saddam did this. See if he's linked in any way." "But Mr. President," Clarke said, "al Qaeda did this." "I know, I know," Bush said, "but see if Saddam was involved. Just look." The staff did and Clarke later wrote, "All agencies and departments agreed, there was no cooperation between" Iraq and al Qaeda. The CIA concurred. Tenet later wrote that their intelligence showed "no evidence of Iraqi complicity" in the attacks and on September 16 the agency advised against attacking Iraq.[6]

Congress acted quickly after the tragedy. On September 14 the Senate voted 98–0 and the House 420–1 to give the president "all necessary and appropriate force" to respond to the terrorist attacks, and the administration did so publicly in a number of ways. The president demanded that Afghanistan's Taliban government close all terrorist camps and hand over al Qaeda leaders—or face an attack—and the State Department proclaimed that the United States had a "clear right to self defense" under Article 51 of the United Nations Charter. Bush pressured Pakistani President Pervez Musharraf to cooperate in the war against al Qaeda, and he received appropriate assurances from Pakistan. The president issued an executive order freezing the assets of groups and individuals suspected of aiding terrorists, and announced a plan to increase airport security and create a Department of Homeland Security; by the next year the new federal Transportation Security Administration was screening passengers, demanding proper identification, and mandating bulletproof, locked cockpit doors in all passenger airlines.

On September 20 the president gave one of the most significant speeches of his first term.

> Who attacked our country? The evidence we have gathered all points to a collection of loosely affiliated terrorist organizations known as al Qaeda. They are the same murderers indicted for bombing American embassies in Tanzania and Kenya, and responsible for bombing the USS *Cole*. . . . There are thousands of these terrorists in more than 60 countries.

The president then introduced Americans to the leader of the group, "a person named Osama bin Laden." America will "pursue nations that provide aid or safe haven to terrorism," he continued. "Every nation, in every region, now has a decision to make. Either you are with us, or you are with the terrorists."

It was an unrealistic choice. With the exception of al Qaeda, some radical Islamic fundamentalists, and the Taliban regime, virtually everyone was with the United States after September 11. "Nous sommes tous Americains," declared the headline of the French newspaper *Le Monde*. German Chancellor Gerhard Schroeder offered his "unlimited, I repeat, unlimited solidarity" with the United States, and 200,000 Germans supported that statement with a march in Berlin. The Irish declared a national day of mourning, and Buckingham Palace played "The Star-Spangled Banner." Many in the Islamic world sent their heartfelt condolences. Thousands of Iranians held candlelight vigils, while countless Moslem spokesmen expressed outrage over the attack. "We condemn, in the strongest terms, the incidents, which are against all human and Islamic norms," wrote the leaders of 40 different Islamic groups. The League of Arab States declared that the attacks were "deserving all condemnations," and declared a "pressing and urgent need to combat world terrorism." The NATO secretary-general announced that for the first time in its 52-year history the allies in the organization would join in appropriate action, "including the use of armed force. An attack on one is an attack on all." At the United Nations, the members passed a resolution condemning "those responsible for aiding, supporting or harbouring the perpetrators, organizers and sponsors of these acts," authorizing "all necessary steps" to respond.

In that same speech on September 20, the president used the phrase "war on terror." "Our war on terror begins with al Qaeda, but it does not end there. It will not end until every terrorist group of global reach has been found, stopped and defeated." This was not the first time a president had employed that term; Reagan had used it, but the Bush administration would make it a part of the American lexicon. Linguistically, as scholars pointed out, the term made no sense. Terror is a tactic, like the blitzkrieg. In December 1941 the United States did not go to war against the blitzkrieg but against a nation, Germany. After September 11, the president could have asked Congress for a declaration of war against the Taliban regime in Afghanistan because it was harboring bin Laden and Kabul refused to give him up. Bush was correct in maintaining that the Taliban was "harboring terrorists," and Congress probably would have supported a declaration of war; it granted a resolution allowing the commander-in-chief to use armed force in Afghanistan. Instead, the president used "war on terror," a vague term against a vague enemy, a term that eventually had profound implications. The administration felt that it had the right to deploy any type of U.S. force to pursue "every terrorist group" until they were "found, stopped and defeated." Recall that the State Department had listed about 40 groups involved in terrorism throughout the world, almost all of which never had attacked the United States or its interests. That raised the question: Who would define the terrorist enemy? The Bush administration claimed that it would, void of oversight from Congress, and any national or international agencies. And this remained the standard for the next five years until the November 2006 elections when voters swept the Democrats into control of Congress.

The administration's use of "war on terror" also had a domestic implication. At a time when level heads were needed to respond to a national tragedy, the term helped to create a "siege mentality," wrote the former national security adviser Zbigniew Brzezinski. This contributed to "a culture of fear in America" that was perpetuated for the next few years.

That culture of fear was exacerbated just one week after the 9/11 tragedy. Someone mailed letters to news organizations, including NBC and the *New York Post*, that contained traces of the bacterial disease anthrax. The anthrax letters killed one man, made others ill, and sent a wave of anxiety throughout the nation: *Is this another terrorist attack?*

Three weeks later there was a second anthrax mailing, this time to two Democratic senators, Senate Majority Leader Tom Daschle of South Dakota and the head of the Senate Judiciary Committee, Patrick Leahy of Vermont. Both mailings had messages, the letter to Daschle reading: "YOU CANNOT STOP US. WE HAVE THIS ANTHRAX. YOU DIE NOW. ARE YOU AFRAID? DEATH TO AMERICA. DEATH TO ISRAEL. ALLAH IS GREAT." The anthrax attacks killed five and sickened 17 others in the weeks after September 11.

America was afraid, angry, and perplexed. "Why do they hate us?" wondered President Bush, echoing a question asked by many of his countrymen. Why did they hate us so profoundly that they would commit suicide to attack us?—which reminded the World War II generation of Japanese kamikazes. As Americans tried to comprehend the answers, some took out their frustrations by attacking people who looked Arab or Muslim. Anti-Arab behavior was not new in America, for it was rooted in events such as the Iran hostage crisis during the Carter years, the Palestinian Liberation Organization's hijacking of the Italian cruise liner *Achile Lauro* in 1985, and the Persian Gulf War. All helped to create stereotypes of the "Islamic terrorist," negative feelings that were portrayed in the 1998 Denzel Washington film, *The Siege*. September 11 rearmed the hatred. In the week following the tragedy, Muslims made 300 reports of harassment, including assailants firing on the Islamic Center in Irving, Texas. During the next months vandals damaged a mosque in Waterbury, Connecticut, along with the Islamic Foundation in Columbus, Ohio. The president and local officials spoke out against these hate crimes, and Congress passed a resolution condemning them. Nevertheless, by the end of 2001 the FBI announced a 17-fold increase in the number of anti-Muslim crimes compared to the previous year.

The fear also appeared in October when Congress passed the USA Patriot Act. The new law was passed with little debate only 45 days after 9/11, and with only one senator opposing, Democrat Russ Feingold of Wisconsin. The act enhanced powers of immigration agents to detain and deport immigrants suspected of terrorism, and it expanded the definition of terrorism to include domestic events. It also increased the authority of law enforcement agencies to search telephone and email communications and financial, medical, and other personal records.

But it did not allow the administration to wiretap people without a court order or to pick up a citizen and detain that person without charging them with a crime, rights protected by habeas corpus and the Fourth and Sixth Amendments. That being the case, Bush signed a secret executive order authorizing the government to eavesdrop on Americans' international calls and emails without a court warrant, an act of dubious legality since 1978 when, after the Watergate scandal, Congress had passed the Foreign Intelligence Surveillance Act.[7]

Meanwhile, and quietly during the weeks after 9/11, the administration adopted secret policies. Vice President Cheney was clear about this just four days after the tragedy when he appeared on *Meet the Press*. America would not employ the military to defeat the terrorists but will "have to work . . . *the dark side*, if you will. We've got to spend time in the shadows in the intelligence world. A lot of what needs to be done here will have to be done quietly, without any discussion. . . . if you're going to deal only with sort of officially approved, certified good guys, you're not going to find out what the bad guys are doing. You need to be able to penetrate these organizations."

Cheney's words signaled the beginning of extralegal behavior, both at home and abroad, such as detention and torture during interrogations, all behavior the United States had denounced when used by other countries. In the weeks after 9/11, the government arrested at least 1,200 persons because of "possible links to terrorism." The FBI apprehended 762 Muslim aliens, mostly on immigration violations; 184 were "high interest" suspects and held in maximum security within the United States. Many were not charged or told why they were being held. The FBI took an average of 80 days before clearing or charging each with a crime. Moreover, there was little effort made to distinguish between legitimate terrorism suspects and people picked up by chance. Eventually, court papers revealed that prison guards tortured some of these suspects, violating the "cruel and unusual punishment" prohibition in the Eighth Amendment of the U.S. Constitution.

The administration took other action on foreign policy and over the weekend of September 15–16 the president held a war council at Camp David. During the first session Rumsfeld asked what the administration should do about Iraq. Wolfowitz made the case for striking that nation during "this round" of the war on terrorism, and their briefing paper specified "three priority targets for initial action: al Qaeda, the Taliban, and Iraq." Secretary of State Powell opposed, seeing no linkage between Saddam and 9/11 and saying that targeting Iraq would hurt the chances of building an international coalition against terrorism. Speaking of potential allies, Powell stated bluntly, "They'll view it as bait and switch— it's not what they signed up to do." The president returned the council's focus to al Qaeda, and the rest of the sessions concerned how to fight a war in Afghanistan.

On September 17, Bush signed a top secret presidential finding that laid out the plan for going to war in Afghanistan. The order also gave the CIA authorization to conduct a range of covert actions "to disrupt terrorist activity," including renditions, disinformation campaigns, cyber attacks, and "permission to kill, capture and detain members of al Qaeda any-where in the world." "All the rules have changed," Tenet claimed after that meeting, and his colleague Cofer Black declared "the gloves came off."

Three days later British Prime Minister Tony Blair and his ambas-sador to the United States arrived at the White House. The president advocated attacking Iraq, but Blair said, "Don't get distracted; the prior-ities" are "al Qaida, Afghanistan, the Taliban." "I agree with you, Tony," said the president. "But when we have dealt with Afghanistan, we must come back to Iraq."

The next morning, September 21, intelligence experts gave Bush the President's Daily Briefing. The PDB stated that there was "no evidence" linking the Iraqi regime to the attacks of September 11 and there was little evidence that Saddam had any ties with al Qaeda. Moreover, Saddam viewed al Qaeda as well as other theocratic radical Islamist groups as a threat to his secular regime. This information was incorpo-rated into a later CIA estimate, and like the PDB, was distributed to Cheney, Rice, and the secretaries and undersecretaries of state and defense. "What the President was told on September 21," said one former high-level official, "was consistent with everything he has been told since—that the evidence was just not there."[8]

The evidence pointed to al Qaeda, and that autumn the West became acquainted with its leader, the world's number one terrorist—Osama bin Laden.

Immediately after September 11 bin Laden denied involvement, but on October 7 he appeared on videotape and announced America's "greatest buildings were destroyed, thank God for that. There is America, full of fear. . . . Thank God for that." Then he blamed the West for Islamic "humiliation and this degradation for more than 80 years," since the occupation of the Middle East after World War I. He pledged that Americans will not have security before the Palestinians, certainly "not before all the infidel armies leave the land of Muhammad." Later, bin Laden named five Christian nations that he thought should be targeted for terror—the United States, Britain, Spain, Australia, and Canada. By 2005, all had been attacked except Canada.

Osama bin Laden had formed al Qaeda around 1990 when he was about 33 years old. Born in 1957, he was the scion of one of the wealthiest families in Saudi Arabia, one with strong ties to the royal family. His father, Mohammed bin Laden, had become rich by building highways and other projects for the royal family, including many palaces. His company was awarded the contract, and the honor, of restoring the Prophet's Mosque in Medina and the Grand Mosque in Mecca. As Mohammed bin Laden grew in fame he also grew in family. Sources differ, but it seems that he had between 22 and 24 wives officially; yet he traveled with a large entourage that included concubines and women whom he might marry in the afternoon and divorce that evening. When he died in an airplane accident in 1967 he was 59, and en route to marry another teenage bride.

The exact number of children Mohammed bin Laden fathered with his wives also is difficult to determine, but is estimated at 57; Osama was the seventeenth. His mother, Alia Ghanem, was a Syrian, the daughter of citrus farmers. Mohammed bin Laden already had taken one Syrian wife when he was introduced to Alia in 1956; he was 48 and she was 14 when she became his fourth wife. A year and a half later Alia gave birth to their only child, Osama, "the Lion." The boy spent his first years among numerous children in his father's household in Jeddah, but when Osama was about five Mohammed divorced Alia, and awarded her to one of his executives, who married her. It was a good match, creating three more brothers and sisters for Osama. The young Osama enjoyed watching television, especially American westerns, and playing soccer with other kids in his neighborhood. He was a good student at Jeddah's best public school, but when he was 14 he experienced a political and religious awakening. He became very concerned about the plight of

Palestinians, even weeping during the televised news about Palestine, and his mother later reported that he came to believe that Muslims were not "close enough to Allah." He refused to watch western shows or wear western dress and began fasting twice a week to emulate the Prophet.

As a teen, bin Laden became a deeply religious Sunni. He had been influenced by Wahhabi religious leaders, a branch of Islam with the aim of establishing a society like the one experienced by the Prophet in seventh-century Arabia, the "golden age" of Islam. These men believed that because Muslims failed to follow the teachings of the Prophet their lands were invaded by infidels, first by the Christian crusaders of the Medieval age, later by European colonialists, and after World War II by the Jews who created Israel.

The only way to bring back another golden age was to observe Muhammad's message and establish sharia, strict Islamic laws and customs. Part of those beliefs concern death. Upon death, the spirit of the deceased Muslim takes a quick journey to heaven and hell, where it sees visions of the potential bliss and torture of the afterlife. Then the spirit returns to dwell in the body, where it encounters two angels, Munkar and Nakir, who question the deceased about faith. If the dead answers appropriately and has no record of sin, then the grave is transformed into a luxurious space, making the long wait until final judgment bearable; if answers are inappropriate and sins have been committed, then the grave is transformed into an oppressive tomb, in which worms might eat the flesh and collapse the rib cage. Since the eighth century most Moslems have believed in some form of the "torture of the grave," and the idea that eventually God either condemns or resurrects the spirit. Yet, most also believed that God makes an exception to the torture—for martyrs. God rewards Islamic warriors who become martyrs and die in jihad, or "struggle," which includes armed combat against infidels to defend the Islamic world. "Do not yield to the unbelievers," declares the Koran, "but fight them vigorously." Upon death, the martyr ascends directly to paradise, where he "shall recline on jewelled couches," be served fruits, fowls, even wine, and have "dark-eyed houris, [maidens] chaste as hidden pearls . . . virgins, loving companions." Some claim this adds incentive for martyrdom.

Another custom concerns marriage; the Koran allows four wives for Moslems. Of course, wealthy Arab men, like Mohammed bin Laden, eventually have many wives, divorcing so there were no more than four at one time. Osama married his first one in 1974 when he was 17 and still in high school. His wife, Najwa Ghanem, was 14 and his cousin from his mother's village in Syria. She was tall, attractive, and meek, and according to bin Laden's sister, "constantly pregnant." Eventually they had 11 children. In 1982, Osama married a woman from Jeddah who was seven years older than him and a descendant of the Prophet. Umm Hamza had a PhD in child psychology and a teaching position at a women's college. She had his son. A few years later he married a woman from a Medina family who also held a doctorate and taught at a college; he and Umm Khaled had four children. His fourth wife, Umm Ali, was from a Mecca family, and she eventually had three children. Years later, in summer 2001, when Osama and his family were living in Afghanistan, he decided to take another wife. He sent a bodyguard to Yemen, who paid $5,000 for a 15-year-old girl for the 44 year-old international terrorist. This angered his children, mother, and wives; after 27 years of marriage his first wife, Najwa, left him and returned to Syria.

Earlier, in 1976, bin Laden had entered King Abdul Aziz University in Jeddah. He majored in economics but never completed a degree. He always was more interested in religious affairs on campus and later admitted that he and his friends "devoted a lot of time to interpreting the Quran and jihad." He went to work for his father's company and learned construction, earning and inheriting a fortune, but when the Soviet Union invaded Afghanistan he and many other Saudis eventually left their country to join the Afghan jihad. At first Osama was an important fundraiser for the jihad in the Middle East, but in 1986 he took his family to Peshawar, Pakistan, and soon was financing an all-Arab camp inside Afghanistan at Jaji. From there, bin Laden saw little combat; almost all of the war was conducted by the Afghan mujahedeen, who eventually forced the Soviets to evacuate their country in 1989.

The Soviet defeat in Afghanistan meant that when bin Laden returned to Saudi Arabia that year he was viewed by many as a hero who had helped slay a superpower. While that was more fable than reality, it was promoted in the Saudi press, and soon the 31-year-old Osama became one of the most popular men in the kingdom, which did not win him favor with the royal family. While bin Laden preached morality and piety, King Fahd practiced drinking, gambling, womanizing, and indulgence on his enormous yacht on the French Riviera or at his mansion in London. The king's son was clearly a poor role model for Islam. According to British court documents he had accepted more than $1 billion in bribes and spent it on prostitutes, pornography, racing cars, powerboats, jewelry, and palaces in Geneva and Cannes.

Bin Laden was appalled by the royal family, but he became more outraged after the 1991 Gulf War when the Saudi government decided to allow the U.S. military to station some 20,000 mostly Christian U.S. troops in the land of the Prophet. He spoke out against the soldiers and won many converts to his cause, irritating the royal family, who exiled him and revoked his Saudi citizenship. Bin Laden first went to Sudan but left in 1995 for Afghanistan, where he recruited and trained mostly Arab volunteers with the approval of the new Taliban government.

The Taliban movement had emerged in 1994 in Afghanistan. After the defeat of the Soviet Army, the country was rudderless, ruled by numerous local warlords; then, the Taliban attacked. At first these Islamic fundamentalists were popular because they brought peace and order to a country ravaged by a long civil war. Mullah Mohammed Omar, who originally had been a village cleric in Kandahar, led the new regime in 1996 when the movement seized power. Omar took on the title "Commander of the Faithful" and quickly created a theocracy with the aim of establishing a society like the one experienced in the seventh century in Arabia. By September of that year, the Taliban moved into Kabul and emptied the ministries of professionals, replacing them with mullahs who knew little about running a government. The regime burned books, except the Koran, and their minister of culture and his soldiers appeared at the Kabul Museum with axes, where they destroyed sculptures of Afghan kings and ancient Buddha statues. Later, the Taliban dynamited the enormous Buddha statues in Bamiyan, which were 1,500 years old and were the nation's greatest cultural heritage and tourist attraction. Back in Kabul, the new Taliban government established the Department for the Promotion of Virtue and Extermination of Sin, also known as the Ministry of Morality, and announced 16 decrees. "Prohibition against female exposure" declared that women must wear the burka; if they did not, their husbands would be punished. There were prohibitions banning music, dancing at weddings, playing drums, owning pictures, gambling, charging interest on loans, even "British and American hairstyles," "washing of clothes by river embankments," and "kite flying," which they claimed led to truancy and "death among children." Sharia was strictly enforced. Uncovered women were arrested and punished by the religious police, thieves had their hands cut off, and people who had sex out of wedlock were stoned to death.

Few countries granted diplomatic recognition to the Taliban regime, which was made up mostly of Pashtuns, the largest tribe in Afghanistan with about 40 percent of the population. The Tajiks in the north made up another quarter, and the Uzbeks and Hazaras in the northwest formed the remainder of the population. The Pashtuns lived mostly in the south and on both sides of the border of Afghanistan and Pakistan. The latter country established formal diplomatic relations with the Taliban, and until 9/11 so did the United Arab Emirates and Saudi Arabia.

Mullah Omar and Osama bin Laden had formed a symbiotic relationship. The Taliban regime was broke and al Qaeda provided money and some Arab fighters. Bin Laden needed a sanctuary where he could train terrorists, which Afghanistan provided. Soon, there was a closer attachment, for Omar married one of bin Laden's daughters, creating a family bond.[9]

Then, September 11, and the United States put a $25 million price on bin Laden's head. Bush demanded that the Taliban give up the terrorist, but Mullah Omar refused, and the administration responded by placing a $10 million price on Omar's head. Five days later Vice President Cheney declared that he would like to accept bin Laden's "head on a platter," and the next day the president visited the partly destroyed Pentagon. "I want justice," he declared. "And there's an old poster out West that says, 'Wanted: Dead or Alive.'"

At CIA headquarters Cofer Black gave marching orders to Gary Schroen and his team, the first unit heading for Afghanistan. "I have discussed this with the president, and he is in full agreement," declared Black. Your "mission is to exert all efforts to find Osama bin Laden and his senior lieutenants and to kill them. I don't want bin Laden and his thugs captured, I want them dead. Alive and in prison here in the United States, they'll become a symbol, a rallying point for other terrorists. . . . They must be killed. I want to see photos of their heads on pikes."

Americans were eager for revenge, which was obvious on October 7, when the president addressed the nation. "More than two weeks ago, I gave Taliban leaders a series of clear and specific demands," he said in a somber, televised address from the White House. "None of these demands were met, and now, the Taliban will pay the price." Bush announced that U.S. forces had begun "strikes on terrorist camps of al Qaeda, and the military installations of the Taliban regime in Afghanistan." The first attacks began in the evening and targeted the Taliban's air defense installations, defense ministry, electrical grids, and command centers, and hit the important cities of Kabul, Kandahar, and Mazar-i-Sharif. "The battle is now joined on many fronts," the president continued. "We will not waver, we will not tire, we will not falter, and we will not fail."

The war in Afghanistan became known as Operation Enduring Freedom. Although the Taliban told their people that they would humiliate the Americans like the mujahedeen had done to the Soviets, that was not the case, for allies and friends lined up to help the United States. Britain, Canada, Germany, Australia, and some NATO allies contributed infantry forces, deployed aircraft, or offered logistical support. France and Italy provided aircraft carrier battle groups, engineering teams, and transport aircraft. Japan sent fleet refueling ships and other aircraft. Eventually, more than 25 other nations contributed personnel, equipment, or services to the fight against the Taliban.

Operation Enduring Freedom actually had begun on September 27, when the CIA inserted Schroen and the first covert team inside Afghanistan, code-named Jawbreaker. By October 19, Special Operations troops drawn from all services, and U.S. Special Forces teams were on the ground. Meanwhile, CIA operatives were communicating and negotiating with the various warlords and their troops who made up the indigenous resistance to the Taliban, the Northern Alliance.

The American plan was to deploy massive aid and air power to support the Northern Alliance. The alliance would conduct the major ground operations against the Taliban militia and their al Qaeda allies, which included foreign Arabs, Chechens, Pakistanis, and Uighurs. To get local tribes involved, CIA teams met with tribal leaders and promised these impoverished people immediate aid for those who joined with the Northern Alliance. As fall began turning into winter, the teams called in the U.S. Air Force. Guided to exact locations by Global Positioning Systems, the planes conducted over a hundred airdrops of almost 1.7 million pounds of tents, clothes, food, medicine, horse feed and saddles, guns and munitions, even Korans. "Each drop was tailored to the specific requests of teams on the ground," wrote the CIA officer who directed the campaign from CIA headquarters in Langley, Virginia, Henry "Hank" Crumpton. "Imagine the power conferred upon the Afghan tribal leader who sided with the United States, whose clan's needs fell from the sky within seventy-two hours of his request. Their desperation was addressed, and their leader won honor and prestige among his people."

The plan worked because the CIA had done the homework. In a few weeks there were seven teams in Afghanistan, and all understood the language and culture of their hosts. One was Gary Berntsen, a 20-year veteran of the CIA's Clandestine Service, and another was Gary Schroen, age 59, fluent in Farsi and Dari; his civilian rank, SIS-3, was analogous to the U.S. army deploying a three-star general to lead an eight-man team. The average age of team members was 45, with more than 20 years on the job, and the CIA gave these professionals maximum flexibility to conduct operations, collect intelligence, and pinpoint bombing targets.

American aid and airdrops fed and armed the Afghans, saving American lives, but the strategy also meant that U.S. forces would have to rely on tribal warlords. Mohammed Fahim Khan operated in the northeast corner of Afghanistan and led a confederation of Tajiks; Rashid Dostum, an ethnic Uzbek, was based in the mountains south of Mazar-i-Sharif; Ismail Khan, a Tajik, operated in the Herat region, close to the Iranian border, as did Mohammed Mohaqqeq of the Hazara ethnic group; and Atta Mohammed, a Tajik, was at times a confederate and at other times a rival of Dostum. Eventually, the Northern Alliance was composed of Tajiks, Uzbeks, and Hazaras, all with various loyalties; some had even fought with the mostly Pashtun Taliban in the 1990s only to switch sides later. As one special forces officer remarked, "No one here is clean."

There was a long tradition of tribal rivalries, and at times it seemed that the northern warlords only seemed united in their hatred of the Taliban. At a meeting concerning the capture of the important city of Mazar-i-Sharif, the commander of CENTCOM General, Tommy Franks, told his subordinates that his priorities were to open a land bridge to another town, secure the airfield, and "Keep Dostum, Mahaqqeq, and Atta from killing each other."

The warlords also could be unreliable and more motivated by money and self-interest than by a sense of nationalism. When the first CIA team, Jawbreaker, arrived in the Panjshir Valley of northeastern Afghanistan it carried $3 million dollars in $100 bills; the team could dole it out as it pleased in an attempt to get the warlords to fight the Taliban. Within a month Jawbreaker asked for and received another $10 million. At one meeting between General Franks and the warlord Mohammed Fahim Khan, the Afghan informed the general that to attack and capture important northern towns he would need $7 million a month. "This is bullshit," Franks responded. "Translate *that.*" After negotiations, Fahim agreed to $5 million.

Nevertheless, the victory would be quick because the Taliban was not equipped to fight a modern war. Their troops rode to the front in pickup trucks with Kalashnikovs, and were easily spotted by U.S. planes and Predator drones, who launched precision air strikes. After just two weeks Taliban lines had been decimated, and the Northern Alliance was sweeping through Afghanistan. On November 9, they captured the northern city of Mazar-i-Sharif, which triggered the collapse of Taliban forces; their warlords began to change sides while others made strategic withdrawals, either back to their villages or to the tribal regions of northwestern Pakistan, often Waziristan, which was also inhabited by ethnic Pashtuns. Four days later the Northern Alliance seized control of Kabul. What remained of the Taliban militia surrendered on December 6, 2001, in the southern city of Kandahar, the spiritual capital of the Taliban movement, and two weeks later the allies celebrated the inauguration of the Afghan interim government—just 78 days after the beginning of combat operations.[10]

It was a laser-fast victory with few allied casualties, yet the world now wondered: where was Osama bin Laden? The answer was with remnants of the Taliban regime and numerous al Qaeda fighters—lodged in Tora Bora.

Tora Bora is a rugged region in Afghanistan only 20 miles from Pakistan. During the 1980s, when the Afghan mujahedeen was fighting the Soviet Union, the CIA had financed the Afghan resistance, giving them about $3 billion in weapons and funds. Part of that money was used to build miles of tunnels, bunkers, and a base camp in the steep valleys and rugged mountains of Tora Bora. The complex helped the Afghans defeat the Red Army, and after bin Laden arrived in that country, he developed the area into a cave complex that had hundreds of rooms, storage facilities, and its own generators, ventilation, and water systems—all extending some 350 yards into a granite mountain.

Under the best military conditions, Tora Bora was a difficult target. During the first half of December there was no doubt that bin Laden was there, according to the CIA field commander in the area, Gary Berntsen. His eight-man team included the CIA's finest Arabic speaker, totally fluent, who picked up a walkie-talkie, pretended to be al Qaeda hiding outside the complex, and to his surprise eventually was talking to bin Laden. They prayed together, and the operative promised supplies, while the GPS system marked the terrorist's location. Berntsen ordered in a BLU-82, a 15,000-pound bomb, which killed many but not the constantly moving bin Laden, his son Sadd, or his deputy Ayman al-Zawahiri.

Eventually, General Franks ordered about 40 Special Operations troops and a dozen Special Forces soldiers to the area to be advisers and call in air strikes. But he decided to allow Afghan troops to attack Tora Bora. As Franks later claimed, "The Afghans themselves wanted to get Tora Bora."

Berntsen disagreed, declaring that Franks was "either badly misinformed by his own people or blinded by the fog of war." The CIA field commander immediately requested 800 U.S. Army Rangers: "We need Rangers now! The opportunity to get bin Laden and his men is slipping away." Brigadier General James Mattis agreed. He was the commander of about 1,100 U.S. marines who had arrived November 25–26 and secured Camp Rhino in southern Afghanistan, 50 miles southwest of Kandahar and 300 miles east of Tora Bora. He urged the Central Command to allow him to move to Tora Bora and seal off the border of Pakistan, which was supported by the U.S. Army's Delta Force. Some of those soldiers were at Tora Bora and they asked for approval for an unconventional attack: put on oxygen, climb over the 14,000-foot ridge and attack al Qaeda troops from above. They also asked to have U.S. forces drop hundreds of land mines in the mountain passes that led to Pakistan, bin Laden's most likely escape route.

CIA officers in Afghanistan alerted Hank Crumpton at the agency's headquarters in Virginia, who drove over to the White House and met with Bush and Cheney. Crumpton briefed them with maps and satellite images. He explained the rugged terrain of Tora Bora, its tunnel complex, and the escape routes into Pakistan. The president said that Pakistani President Musharraf had been promised a billion dollars in aid to seal off the border and that he had promised he was on the U.S. side. The CIA official took out photos showing that no Pakistani troops were on the border, and he said that Afghan forces were "tired and cold and many of them are far from home," adding that "they're just not invested in getting bin Laden." Crumpton continued, "We're going to lose our prey if we're not careful." He strongly recommended that the marines at Camp Rhino or any other troops be ordered to seal the border. Bush appeared surprised, asking, "How bad off are these Afghani forces, really? Are they up to the job?" "Definitely not, Mr. President," replied Crumpton. "Definitely not."

Nevertheless, the commander-in-chief did not order the U.S. Marines to Tora Bora. General Franks had given the Afghan militia the task of capturing bin Laden. That did not change, even though U.S. Special Operations troops on the ground had informed their superiors that the militia was ill equipped, poorly trained, and had three different warlord commanders who hated each other. The troops quarreled continually and at times even exchanged gunfire. The commanders were ruthless, greedy, corrupt men, whose pockets were filled with new U.S. $100 bills. Many of their troops also were hungry for cash; when one carload of Special Operations men arrived in the area to help, they were charged a "toll" of $50 each, while at other times the Afghans charged the Special Forces teams $300 for vehicle use and $1,000 for meals.

The Afghan militia attacked, as the American teams called in U.S. war planes that unleashed a heavy bombardment, one which lasted 56 hours. In the valley below, some 2,500 militia soldiers sat freezing in the snow, while al Qaeda had the advantage of higher terrain, electricity, heat, provisions, and an abundance of commitment. The Afghans advanced, but they were repeatedly repelled by about a thousand al Qaeda fighters. Eventually, the local troops lost heart and wanted to negotiate with the enemy. They made radio contact with bin Laden's commanders and offered a cease-fire, declaring that if they surrendered they would not be handed over to the Americans but to the United

Nations, which outraged their U.S. advisers. An al Qaeda leader, most likely bin Laden's son, stalled, responding that they would think it over all night and respond the next morning.

"We'll smoke him out of his cave," Bush declared back in Washington in October, and in December he again pledged that bin Laden would be taken "dead or alive." "I don't know whether we're going to get him tomorrow or a month from now or a year from now. . . . But we're going to get him." Two weeks later, while vacationing at his ranch in Texas during the holidays, the president declared, "He is not escaping us."

Actually, bin Laden already had escaped. His son never got back in touch with the Afghan fighters the next morning. Instead, during the night of December 15, bin Laden got on his shortwave radio, praised his "most loyal fighters," said "forgive me" in case of their deaths, and announced that the battle against the "crusaders" would continue "on new fronts." He led them in a prayer, and in the cover of darkness, slipped away. As the al Qaeda fighters left Tora Bora, bin Laden and his lieutenants apparently took another route, arriving safely in the rugged Pashtun tribal lands of Pakistan. "Had bin Laden been surrounded at Tora Bora," wrote one expert, "he would have been confined to an area of several dozen square miles; now he could well be in an area that snakes across some 40,000 square miles," about the size of Kentucky. Also escaping to that area were Mullah Omar, his Taliban militia, and al Qaeda's number two man, Ayman al-Zawahiri.

To catch bin Laden at Tora Bora, therefore, General Franks sent only about 40 Special Operations troops and a dozen U.S. Special Forces. To defeat the Taliban regime that was harboring the terrorists, Secretary Rumsfeld apparently only dispatched some 130 Special Operations troops in October, growing to perhaps 350 Special Forces soldiers by early December, aided by about 110 CIA officers. By the end of that month it seems that about 4,000 marines had arrived in Afghanistan. So, by the end of 2001 the administration had sent less than 5,000 ground troops to fight and then secure Afghanistan—a country about the size of Texas with a population of about 26 million people. To put this into perspective, the commander-in-chief dispatched fewer troops to kill bin Laden, al Qaeda, and the Taliban regime harboring them, than the number of police officers assigned to any large American city, such as New York, Los Angeles, Chicago, or Houston.

The failure to commit sufficient U.S. ground forces and to allow proxy Afghan forces to bear the brunt of the ground war was hotly debated. The "strategy, accepted and expanded by CENTCOM," wrote the CIA's Hank Crumpton, "reflected much of the Afghan allies' own geographical aims." Having few Western troops on the ground avoided stirring up resentment among the Islamic population, resulted in few American casualties, and combined with massive U.S. air power, brought about a quick victory without getting tied down in a large country for years like the Soviet army did in the 1980s. The CIA also fostered cooperation between the mostly Tajik tribes in the north and Pashtuns in the south, avoiding a possible civil war. While all of that was admirable, the subsequent U.S. victory was temporary, for the strategy also allowed al Qaeda and the Taliban to escape, regroup, and attack for many years inside Afghanistan. That eventually was the first defeat for Bush's War on Terror.[11]

Operation Enduring Freedom had other unforeseen consequences. American troops captured some 600 suspected al Qaeda and Taliban soldiers, and CIA agents in other parts of the world rounded up suspected terrorists and placed them in "black sites," secret jails overseas. On November 13 the president signed an executive order proclaiming an "extraordinary emergency." Accordingly, the military could detain and try anyone who the administration deemed "enemy combatants," not in American courts but by military tribunals. The accused would have no access to the usual standards applied by federal courts and no review procedures. Detainees would have no right to remain silent, hearsay evidence and statements made during torture would be admissible, and if found guilty the detainees could receive the death penalty. "Whatever the procedures are for military tribunals," Bush said, "our system will be more fair than the system of bin Laden and the Taliban." Few disagreed, but that missed the point, countered the American Civil Liberties Union and the International Committee for the Red Cross. Congress had not declared war, stated the ACLU, so the president was "unwilling to abide by the checks and balances that are so central to our democracy."

By January 2002 the first detainees were arriving at the U.S. base, Camp X-Ray, at Guantanamo Bay, Cuba. During that month, memos written by Justice Department lawyer John Yoo and White House lawyers Alberto Gonzales and David Addington informed the president that international law, particularly the Geneva Conventions, did not apply to the Taliban or al Qaeda. That was questionable and would be debated for years, but it was what the president wanted to hear. The administration stripped enemy combatants of all the usual American legal rights, even habeas corpus—a summons to determine by a court if a prisoner has been lawfully detained—a right guaranteed by the U.S. Constitution. Later that year Secretary Rumsfeld approved "special interrogation techniques" for the detainees—a euphemism for torture.

In just months after the September 11 emergency, the administration had set aside national laws that prohibited warrantless surveillance of American citizens. It also bypassed international laws protecting foreigners from torture, secret detention, and capturing suspects and taking them to other countries for secret interrogation and torture—a tactic called extraordinary rendition.

Besides constitutional issues, there were other problems with the administration's policies toward the 770 "terrorist suspects" from over 40 countries eventually housed at Guantanamo. Some of those captured after battle obviously were enemy warriors. Camp X-Ray did house confirmed terrorists, including the alleged mastermind of the September 11 attacks, Khalid Sheikh Mohammed. But some were citizens of allies— Britain and Australia—and one, Jose Padilla, was a U.S. citizen. Moreover, later investigations revealed that most of the jailed were not terrorists. As the U.S. bombed Afghanistan the Taliban leadership quickly evacuated, leaving the battlefield filled with uneducated volunteers and conscripts, many of whom knew nothing about global terrorism and had been pressed into military service; some were teens, a few as young as 14. U.S. planes had dropped leaflets advertising bounties for the enemy, littering the country with promises of $5,000, even $10,000, or "wealth and power beyond your dreams." Afghan warlords usually were paid cash by the number of men they could hand over to the Americans. This financial incentive in an impoverished nation resulted in many locals making false reports to settle old grudges or lying about people to whom they or their family owed money. A later investigation found that dozens and perhaps hundreds of detainees were wrongfully imprisoned on the "basis of flimsy or fabricated evidence, old personal scores or bounty payments." Moreover, another investigation found that a majority of the prisoners were not caught on the battlefield, but came into U.S. custody from third parties, mostly from Pakistan, after that government targeted Arabs living in their nation after 9/11. In fact, no one really knew how many of the men imprisoned at Camp X-Ray actually were terrorists or part of al Qaeda or the Taliban. In 2002, Secretary of the Army Thomas White noted that at least a third of the prisoners did not belong at Guantanamo; later, Major General Michael Dunlavey, the commander at the base, stated that half the prisoners were a mistake. During the next six years the administration had charged only six detainees with involvement with the 9/11 attacks.

Such issues did not trouble the Bush administration. Secretary Rumsfeld labeled the prisoners "the worst of the worst . . . the most dangerous, best-trained, vicious killers on the face of the earth," and basically threw away the key as they sat in legal limbo for years at Guantanamo. That area was U.S. property but according to the administration was outside the protection granted by the U.S. Constitution, or "a legal black hole," as one attorney called Camp X-Ray. It would take two and a half years before the Supreme Court would begin ruling against the administration, beginning in 2004 with *Rasul v. Bush* and *Hamdi v. Rumsfeld.*[12]

Meanwhile, back in Afghanistan, on December 2, 2001, the United Nations picked a new leader for the interim government, Hamid Karzai. A Pashtun from Kandahar, the educated and multilingual Karzai had been a diplomat for the mujahedeen during the Soviet occupation. Although he initially supported the Taliban, he turned against them as they aligned themselves with bin Laden and enforced harsh Islamic rule. The Taliban also murdered his father, which elevated Karzai to chief of the Popolzai tribe before he fled to Pakistan. When the Americans began bombing Afghanistan in October, Karzai, "armed only with a satellite phone," went on a motorcycle campaign to Taliban strongholds in the south to try to convince Pashtuns that the Taliban would fall and to join the opposition. Many tribal leaders were impressed more by his courage than by his message, and he gradually won support. To help Karzai, the United States supplied him with weapons for his 200 fighters and a team of Special Forces advisers. When the Taliban attacked Karzai's troops near Tarin Kowt, the home of Mullah Omar, the Americans called in massive air support, decimating 30 trucks and killing 300 enemy fighters, before the remnants fled south to Kandahar. Local mullahs met with Karzai and pledged their support, and on December 7 he drove into Kandahar as thousands of Afghans cheered and threw marigolds. Seeing American Special Forces, they yelled in broken English, "Welcome!" and "Thank You!"

Karzai's capture of Kandahar effectively ended the war in the south and increased his stature in the new Afghanistan. "Hamid Karzai stood out from every other Afghan leader I'd met," wrote Gary Berntsen. "He was humble, well educated, intelligent, brave and sophisticated and also seemed to radiate a quality that I'd rarely seen in Afghanistan: hope."

There was hope for the future of a new Afghanistan, both in that country and throughout the world. The Bush administration asked its allies to send forces and supplies to avoid starvation during the winter, rebuild airfields and buildings, and to help secure the nation; 18 nations responded, and their personnel began arriving in December. French engineers and army mountain troops, German military police, British marines, even Jordanian medical personnel arrived and worked throughout the winter. The French began training a new Afghan army; the Germans, the new police force for Kabul; and the British, the national guard battalions who would provide internal security.

As the United States and its allies seemed to be securing victory in Afghanistan, Americans began feeling more hopeful. During the first Thanksgiving after September 11, citizens traveling to the homes of friends and relatives were thankful that the nation had not been attacked again, thankful that the administration was responding to the horrific attacks of September 11. Opinion polls found that 72 percent of those asked felt that the nation was moving in the right direction, and they had confidence in their commander-in-chief and his operations in Afghanistan. As allied forces routed the Taliban in November, Bush's approval rating soared to 88 percent, the highest of his presidency.

Americans that Thanksgiving also were thankful that the world had poured out so much sympathy for the United States. "We are supported by the collective will of the world," Bush said in October, and he was right. "It is sad and tragic that thousands of innocent people lost their lives," wrote a professor in Jordan. "People's reaction to it the world over, however, was truly heartening . . . protest against terror and solidarity with America."

The tragedy of September 11, and the subsequent military campaign aimed at exacting justice, marked the pinnacle of world support for the

United States. And that support was manifested in many ways, in sympathy letters to friends, candlelight parades, even on the high seas. Days after the tragedy the American navy destroyer, the USS *Winston Churchill*, the only navy warship named after a foreign national, was at sea when they were hailed by the German Navy destroyer FGS *Lutjens* requesting permission to pass close by their port side. Afterward, a young ensign on the bridge of the *Churchill* emailed home:

> Dear Dad . . . our conning officer used binoculars and announced that Lutjens was flying not the German, but the American flag. As she came alongside us, we saw the American flag flying half-mast and her entire crew topside standing at silent, rigid attention in their dress uniforms. They had made a sign that was displayed on their side that read, "We Stand By You." There was not a dry eye on the bridge as they stayed alongside us for a few minutes and saluted. It was the most powerful thing I have seen in my life.[13]

2

Rush to War

"We just have to do it now."
—President Bush to congressional leaders,
White House, September 4, 2002

World sympathy for America began declining on January 29, 2002, when President Bush gave his State of the Union address. Just four months after the 9/11 tragedy, national and international interest was unusually high, and the speech was watched and discussed throughout the world.

"Terrorists who once occupied Afghanistan now occupy cells at Guantanamo Bay," he proclaimed to applause. "And terrorist leaders who urged followers to sacrifice their lives are running for their own." He looked up into the gallery and thanked the "distinguished interim leader of a liberated Afghanistan: Chairman Hamid Karzai." He hailed the new freedom in Afghanistan, and then his tone turned more ominous, declaring that what Americans found in that country "confirmed our worst fears" about the enemy.

> We have found diagrams of American nuclear power plants and public water facilities, detailed instructions for making chemical weapons, surveillance maps of

American cities. . . . What we have found in Afghanistan
confirms that, far from ending there, our war against terror is
only beginning. . . . Thousands of dangerous killers, schooled in
the methods of murder, often supported by outlaw regimes, are
now spread throughout the world like ticking time bombs, set to
go off without warning. . . . These enemies view the entire world
as a battlefield, and we must pursue them wherever they are.

The president continued, saying that his administration would shut
down terrorist camps, bring enemies to justice, and "prevent the terrorists and regimes who seek chemical, biological or nuclear weapons from
threatening the United States and the world." Then Bush began the part
of the address for which it would be remembered:

North Korea is a regime arming with missiles and weapons of
mass destruction. . . . Iran aggressively pursues these weapons
and exports terror. . . . Iraq continues to flaunt its hostility
toward America and to support terror. The Iraqi regime has
plotted to develop anthrax, and nerve gas, and nuclear weapons
for over a decade. . . . This is a regime that agreed to international
inspections—then kicked out the inspectors. This is a regime
that has something to hide from the civilized world. States like
these, and their terrorist allies, constitute an axis of evil, aiming
to threaten the peace of the world.

Those regimes sought weapons of mass destruction, the president continued, which they could provide to terrorists and then "attack our allies
or attempt to blackmail the United States." We have to act, he declared,
for "the price of indifference would be catastrophic."

All three nations issued denials, with a blunt one coming from the
Iraqi vice president: "This statement of President Bush is stupid."

The "Axis of Evil" speech was significant on many levels, and since
the president had written in his diary that September 11 was "the Pearl
Harbor of the 21st Century," his speech should be compared with a State
of the Union one month after December 7, 1941, by Franklin D. Roosevelt. In the speech Bush declared that terrorists "confirmed our worst
fears" and talked about threats and blackmail, which were "ticking time
bombs," while Roosevelt employed a different approach: "We have not

been terrified or confused . . . for the mood of quiet, grim resolution . . . prevails," which "bodes ill for those who conspired and collaborated to murder world peace." FDR spoke of determination, unity, and of the 26 allied nations fighting Japan, Germany, and Italy. He talked of sacrifice, national mobilization, and increasing armament production to unprecedented levels, which would disrupt the "lives and occupations of millions" of Americans. And he talked about the cost, which would be paid for by "taxes and bonds and bonds and taxes," by "cutting luxuries," and sacrifice "by individual effort and family effort in a united country." In contrast, Bush said nothing about mobilization and sacrifice. Two weeks after 9/11 he had told Americans, "Get down to Disney World in Florida. Take your families and enjoy life, the way we want it to be enjoyed"; and later he told the nation to "go shopping." At his State of the Union address he declared that it "costs a lot to fight this war . . . a billion dollars a month" and then he asked Congress to make his "tax cuts permanent."

Bush's address should have sounded alarm bells. He mentioned the Taliban enemy fleeing Afghanistan and then turned to three nations that had nothing to do with the attack on September 11—North Korea, Iran, and Iraq. "If there was a serious internal debate within the administration over what to do about Iraq," wrote the conservative columnist Charles Krauthammer, "that debate is over." Democratic Representative Ike Skelton of Missouri agreed; both felt that the speech was basically a "declaration of war."

Only the most aware citizens would have realized that since the previous November the administration had been shifting its focus from al Qaeda to Iraq. "Saddam is evil," said Bush during the Thanksgiving holidays. "I think he's got weapons of mass destruction, and I think he needs to open up his country to let us inspect." In fact on November 21, 2001, Bush asked his secretary of defense: "What kind of a war plan do you have for Iraq? How do you feel about the war plan for Iraq?" Rumsfeld said that he was reviewing plans with General Franks. "Let's get started on this," ordered Bush. "And get Tommy Franks looking at what it would take to protect America by removing Saddam Hussein if we have to." "I want to know what the options are," the president continued. Six days later Franks received a call from Rumsfeld. The CENTCOM commander was engaged in obtaining air support for Afghan units pushing toward Tora Bora, when he was interrupted: "General Franks, the President wants us to look at operations for Iraq," Rumsfeld said. "What is the status of your planning?" Franks admitted that the plan was basically "Desert Storm II. It's out of date," and the secretary told him to bring it up to date and get back to him in a week.

President Bush, just 72 days after the tragedy of September 11, at a time when the outcome in Afghanistan was not clear and bin Laden and his lieutenants were evading capture, instructed the Pentagon to begin planning for a military operation against Iraq.

Two weeks later, on December 9, the administration began linking al Qaeda with Saddam. Vice President Cheney appeared on *Meet the Press* and declared that "it's been pretty well confirmed" that one of the 9/11 hijackers, Mohammed Atta, went to Prague and met with "a senior official of the Iraqi intelligence service in Czechoslovakia last April, several months before the attack."

General Franks and his staff worked on the war plan during December, and after Christmas flew to the Crawford ranch to brief the president and hold a teleconference with the national security team. "Mr. President," the general stated, "if we want to execute something like this, then what we're going to need to do is we're going to need to start posturing and building forces." The posturing came with the State of the Union address in January 2002, and as the administration slowly increased the number of troops in Afghanistan it also began to withdraw its CIA and Special Operations forces. The reason, wrote CIA operative Gary Schroen, was "in order to allow them to regroup and train in preparation for the coming war with Iraq."

More posturing appeared in the months after the State of the Union address. In early February, Secretary Powell spoke to the House International Relations Committee, "With respect to the nuclear program, there is no doubt that the Iraqis are pursuing it." A week later, one year after Powell said that Iraq was no threat, he declared to Congress, "it has long been . . . a policy of the United States government that regime change would be in the best interest of the region, in the best interest of the Iraqi people, and we are looking at a variety of options that would bring that about." In fact, Powell's State Department already was planning for regime change, for one month after the September 11 attacks the department had established The Future of Iraq Project. Diplomats contacted and organized over 200 Iraqi engineers, businessmen, lawyers, doctors, and other "free Iraqis" into working groups where they discussed topics concerning post-Saddam Iraq.

Cheney continued the message. On February 19 he insisted that Iraq harbored terrorists and that the United States would never allow "terror states" or their "terrorist allies" to threaten us with weapons of mass destruction. He repeated the message the next month, stating on CNN that Saddam is "actively pursuing nuclear weapons at this time."[1]

Was Saddam building a nuclear device? In early February the CIA sent Cheney a daily briefing that included a report from the Italian military intelligence agency, SISMI, stating that Iraq had arranged to purchase 500 tons of yellowcake uranium from the impoverished African nation of Niger. Yellowcake was the first stage toward enriched uranium that could be refined for nuclear plants or weapons, and 500 tons was an enormous amount, given that it took only 10 tons to produce enough enriched uranium for one nuclear weapon. If the report was true, it would be evidence that Iraq had revived its moribund nuclear weapons program that had been dismantled in the mid-1990s under the supervision of the International Atomic Energy Agency.

From the beginning there were problems with the yellowcake story. The Italian report first surfaced in Washington during autumn 2001. SISMI had received it from Rocco Martino, a security consultant who made a living selling intelligence. The CIA and the State Department thought that the Iraq-Niger sale was implausible because a French consortium tightly controlled Niger's two uranium mines located in the Sahara Desert. Because of more accessible mines in Canada, Niger's yellowcake was too expensive on the world market and for years had been sold and shipped only to the four countries in the consortium. In November the U.S. ambassador in Niger sent a cable to the State Department confirming that she had met with the director of the consortium who assured her that there was "no possibility" that Niger had diverted any of the 3,000 tons of yellowcake it produced at its mines. The ambassador's report was supported by the top U.S. military officer, a four-star general, in charge of relations with the armed forces of Africa. Moreover, a 500-ton deal was a large increase in production, would have had to be approved by all consortium members, and that would have left a long paper trail. As one foreign service officer who had served in Niger stated, "Twice a year 25 semi tractor trailer loads of yellowcake would have to be driven down roads where one seldom sees even a bush taxi. In other words, it would be very hard to hide such a shipment."

Cheney wanted more information, so his aide called the CIA and the request landed on the desk of one of their agents, Valerie Plame Wilson. She was married to former ambassador Joseph Wilson IV, who had been a State Department diplomat in both Niger and Iraq. The CIA sent Wilson to Africa. He spent eight days there, interviewed many, and found no proof that Niger had shipped any uranium to Iraq, which he reported back to the CIA. Wilson noted that a Niger-Iraq deal would be "absolutely impossible to hide," which confirmed the ambassador's and general's reports discrediting the yellowcake story.

The CIA debriefed Wilson. The agency informed officials in the administration, and all three reports were distributed to the State and Defense departments, readily available to Cheney. Whatever the case, between March and October the vice president declared on at least four occasions that Saddam was "actively pursuing nuclear weapons at this time."

Europeans were not so sure, and they were growing leery of Bush's foreign policy. In February, Deputy Defense Secretary Wolfowitz went to Germany for the annual conference on security. With him were Democratic Senator Joseph Lieberman and Republican Senator John McCain. Wolfowitz confronted the Europeans. "We are at war," he said, which "requires prevention and sometimes preemption." We have to "take the war to the enemy" for "the best defense is a good offense. . . . Facing the danger, countries must make a choice," he continued. They must "stand united with us in this struggle between good and evil."

McCain and Lieberman voiced their support, but the Europeans had different views. Hubert Vedrine, the French foreign minister, labeled the administration's approach "simplistic," reducing "all the problems in the world to the struggle against terror." His German counterpart, Joschka Fischer, carped that the United States was treating its European allies like "satellites," purposely using a term from the cold war. The European Union Foreign Affairs Commissioner, Chris Patten, remarked that Bush's approach was shifting into "unilateralist overdrive," and the European leaders warned the administration to obey international law and not attack Iraq.

Cheney traveled to London and the Middle East in March in an attempt to evaluate and shore up support for American policy. He had no luck in the Middle East, where he found rulers polite but not interested in a war against Iraq. The trip received little press in the United States, but it was a lead story in Britain, since a week before his arrival Prime Minister Tony Blair had warned his nation that if weapons of mass destruction fall into the hands of terrorists "then I think we have got to act on it because, if we don't act, we may find out too late the potential for destruction." Moreover, the day before Cheney arrived in London the British press reported that the Bush administration already had asked the UK to supply 25,000 troops for an American-led invasion of Iraq. The large request, wrote *The Observer*, was "unprecedented in peacetime" and it showed "the high stakes America is now playing for." The press announced that the British government was considering a joint invasion, which riled the public and divided the cabinet, and that the Bush administration quietly was drawing up a list of targets in Iraq, sending special forces to northern Kurdish areas of Iraq and Apache attack helicopters to Kuwait.

The prime minister welcomed the vice president and they held a press conference at No. 10 Downing Street. The first question was about evidence that Saddam had or will have WMDs. "Let's be under no doubt whatever," declared Blair, "Saddam Hussein has acquired weapons of mass destruction over a long period of time. . . . He is in breach of at least nine UN Security Council Resolutions about weapons of mass destruction." He continued that "no decisions have been taken on how we deal with this threat." Cheney endorsed Blair's comments, adding that "we know from the work we have been able to do in Afghanistan" that al Qaeda was "aggressively seeking to acquire the same capability, nuclear weapons, biological or chemical weapons. How far they got, we don't know, but we know they clearly . . . would use such weapons were they able to acquire them. . . . So the concern is very real, it is very great and we need to find ways as we go forward to make certain that the terrorist never acquires that capability and that it can never be used against the United States or the United Kingdom or our allies."

More Anglo-American discussions were held during the weekend of April 6–7, when Bush hosted Blair and his family at the Crawford ranch. A British reporter held an interview with the president, which aired on television in the United Kingdom but not in the United States, and asked about Iraq. "I made up my mind that Saddam needs to go," declared Bush. "That's about all I'm willing to share with you." Surprised, the reporter asked for clarification, and the president said, "The policy of my government is that he goes," later adding, "The worst thing that could happen would be to allow a nation like Iraq, run by Saddam Hussein, to develop weapons of mass destruction, and then team up with terrorist organizations so they can blackmail the world. I'm not going to let that happen."

"And how are you going to achieve this, Mr. President?" Bush replied, "Wait and see." The president continued these thoughts a couple days later when he appeared in front of a private Republican fundraiser in Greenwich, Connecticut. "History has called us into action, and this nation is responding. . . . We've got to secure the world and this civilization as we know it from these evil people. We just have to do this. And that includes making sure that some of the world's worst leaders who desire to possess the world's worst weapons don't team up with faceless, al Qaeda–type killer organizations."

In May, the secretary of defense appeared before the Senate to discuss the military budget, but his other comments were more significant. "In just facing the facts," said Rumsfeld, "we have to recognize that terrorist networks have relationships with terrorist states that have weapons of mass destruction, and that they inevitably are going to get their hands on them, and they would not hesitate one minute in using them. That's the world we live in." He talked about how terrorists were linked to Iraq, Iran, Libya, North Korea, Syria, and other nations and that they were intent on securing nuclear, chemical, and biological weapons. "We are going to be living in a period of limited or no warning," he said, adding that al Qaeda was inside America and "very well-trained."

That summer the Bush administration amplified its posturing against Iraq. On June 1 the president gave an address at West Point announcing his idea of preemptive war, which the press dubbed the "Bush Doctrine." After talking about America's previous reliance on containment, he stated that the policy was obsolete against "unbalanced dictators with weapons of mass destruction" and their "terrorist allies." "If we wait for threats to fully materialize, we will have waited too long," he warned. The

war on terror will not be won on the defensive. We must take the battle to the enemy, disrupt his plans, and confront the worst threats before they emerge. In the world we have entered, the only path to safety is the path of action. . . . And our security will require all Americans to be forward-looking and resolute, to be ready for preemptive action when necessary to defend our liberty and to defend our lives.

The speech was the clearest statement yet of the administration's intentions, and it raised eyebrows; "preemptive action" was a departure from American tradition. In the recent past, the United States had been the recipient of a preemptive strike, Pearl Harbor, or had tried to defend friends and allies against them—North Korea's strike on South Korea in 1950, Iraq's attack on Kuwait in 1990—and during the 1960s the Johnson administration argued that it was defending South Vietnam against attacks from North Vietnam. Thus, the Bush Doctrine fundamentally changed the nation's national security policy, and so it was on page one in many newspapers, including the *New York Times* and *Washington Post*. The *Times* reporter called it a "toughly worded speech that seemed aimed at preparing Americans for a potential war with Iraq."

"It was," wrote the former White House Press Secretary Scott McClellan. "Just as we'd sought to shape and manipulate sources of public opinion to our advantage in order to pass tax cuts and education reform . . . now we were setting the conditions for selling military confrontation with Iraq."[2]

In July 2002, the administration privately made the decision to go to war—eight months before their preemptive strike against Iraq. While the president and his subordinates later maintained that they had not made that decision until Secretary of State Powell presented the American case for war to the United Nations in February 2003, ample evidence suggests that they made the decision the previous summer. Richard Haas, director of policy planning at the State Department, reported that he talked with Condi Rice that month and she told him that "decisions were made." Unless Iraq gave in to the administration's demands, war was a forgone conclusion. That timing was suggested in books by journalist Bob Woodward and by at least three former insiders—the terrorism adviser Richard Clarke, NSC participant Paul O'Neill, and White House press secretary McClellan. But the most significant evidence came from a later British leak to the press on May 1, 2005—the Downing

Street memorandum. "Secret and Strictly Personal—UK Eyes Only" was the heading on the minutes of Tony Blair's meeting with his top advisers on July 23, 2002. It detailed a recent meeting between Sir Richard Dearlove, chief of Britain's secret intelligence service; Bush; and his senior advisers. Dearlove's impression of the meeting was that the president had decided to attack Saddam's regime, and the minutes continued:

> There was a perceptible shift in attitude. Military action was now seen as inevitable. Bush wanted to remove Saddam, through military action, justified by the conjunction of terrorism and WMD. But the intelligence and facts were being fixed around the policy. . . . There was little discussion in Washington of the aftermath after military action.

The administration wanted Britain to help in the invasion by deploying "up to 40,000" troops in the invasion, "perhaps with a discrete role in Northern Iraq entering from Turkey, tying down two Iraqi divisions."

The British were dubious and had been since Cheney's visit three months earlier. On March 22 the political director of the British Foreign Office, Peter Ricketts, sent a memo to his boss, Foreign Secretary Jack Straw, stating that "even the best survey of Iraq's WMD programmes will not show much advance in recent years" of nuclear, chemical, or biological weapons. He cautioned that the "programmes are extremely worrying but have not, as far as we know, been stepped up." Ricketts continued that the Bush administration was "scrambling to establish a link between Iraq and al Qaida" which was "frankly unconvincing."

The Downing Street memo also quoted others in the British government who attended the July 23 meeting. "Bush had made up his mind to take military action, even if the timing was not yet decided," said the foreign secretary, calling the case "thin" because "Saddam was not threatening his neighbors and his WMD capability was less than that of Libya, North Korea or Iran." Straw added that the Anglo-Americans should present Saddam with an ultimatum "to allow back in the UN weapons inspectors," which would "help with legal justification for the use of force." The British attorney-general agreed, stating that "regime change was not a legal basis for military action" and that an attack could be legal only if it was done in self-defense, for humanitarian reasons, or with authorization from the United Nations. That troubled Prime

Minister Blair, who hoped that Saddam would "refuse to allow in the UN inspectors. . . . If the political context were right," he continued, "people would support regime change."

Yet not all of the senior members of the Bush administration that summer were eager for war in Iraq. Some had doubts. At the Pentagon, Air Force Secretary Jim Roche, who had known Rumsfeld for 30 years, and Army Secretary Thomas White asked for a meeting with the defense secretary. "Don, you do realize that Iraq could be another Vietnam?" asked Roche. "Vietnam?" Rumsfeld roared. "You think you have to tell me about Vietnam? Of course it won't be Vietnam. We are going to go in, overthrow Saddam, get out. That's it," and he waved them out of his office.

A similar doubt concerned the only presidential adviser with combat experience—Secretary of State Powell. On August 5 the secretary dined with the president and Rice at the White House. Powell leveled with Bush, stating that Iraq "is like crystal glass," and if Bush invades "it's going to shatter. There will be no government. There will be civil disorder . . . you'll be the proud owner of the hopes and aspirations of 25 million Iraqis. *And* you become the government! You're *it*!" What about the occupation, Powell continued, the image of an American general running an Arab nation? What impact would that have on the Middle East, and how long would we be there? How would we define success? Yes, of course, Saddam was crazy, a menace, a threat, but he had been contained and deterred since the 1991 Gulf War. Once we invaded, how would we find Saddam? We had not been able to find bin Laden or Mullah Omar, and Saddam could hide in an entire nation. As for the army, the invasion would tie down perhaps 40 percent of the army for the next several years, and that's "going to remove a lot of your military flexibility. It's going to be hugely expensive. And, Mr. President, it's going to suck the political oxygen out of the environment for the rest of your presidency." Powell warned, "It's nice to say we can do it unilaterally, except you can't," for we will need allies like we had in Afghanistan. The secretary had a suggestion. "Go to the UN, and challenge the United Nations. Tell them: This is not about us and Iraq. This is a challenge to the international community."

The president did go to the UN the next month and gave a speech on Saddam, but he and his national security adviser, along with the vice president and secretary of defense, had little interest in obtaining another resolution from the United Nations. The UN already had passed many resolutions on Iraq and they had not brought about regime change in Baghdad. The president and Britain's prime minister agreed—as Blair had said, "If the political context were right, people would support regime change." But how could the administration get the right political context, especially when the vast majority of citizens were not interested in going to war in the Middle East against a nation that posed little threat to the United States and had easily been beaten in the Gulf War? In early September a CBS News opinion poll found that there was "no consensus on adopting a pre-emptive strike in general—except where a nuclear attack against the United States is contemplated."[3]

The administration began preparing for the right political context and to do that they established the White House Iraq Group (WHIG). Composed of Rice, presidential adviser Karl Rove, vice presidential adviser "Scooter" Libby, and White House Chief of Staff Andrew Card Jr., it devised "talking points," according to Scott McClellan, "to coordinate the marketing of the war to the public." When a reporter asked Card in September why the administration waited until after Labor Day to try to sell the people on military action against Iraq, Card replied, "From a marketing point of view, you don't introduce new products in August." WHIG invented most of the talking points and one the speakers constantly reiterated: Saddam's smoking gun could be a mushroom cloud. The aim was twofold, McClellan added, to introduce "intelligence" to a public uninterested in a war and to put pressure on the CIA.

That pressure arrived in the form of Dick Cheney. Although vice presidential visits to CIA headquarters had been rare in previous administrations, Cheney visited the agency's headquarters almost a dozen times, grilling agents and demanding more work on possible leads that eventually would support the administration's claims. He, and others in the administration, such as Libby and Feith, distrusted the CIA. To them, the agency had failed to predict, detect, and stop 9/11; thus, the agency was suspect. Cheney demonstrated this tension in the margin of one of Feith's reports detailing supposed evidence linking al Qaeda and Saddam: "This is very good indeed . . . Encouraging . . . Not like the crap we are all so used to getting out of CIA."

The distrust was mutual. Tenet and others at the agency called WHIG "Team Feith," and Tenet labeled their so-called intelligence "Feith-based analysis."

Not only was WHIG finding their own intelligence to support the administration's views, but the White House also had an unusual ally, a reporter for the *New York Times*. "An Iraqi defector who described himself as a civil engineer said he personally worked on renovations of secret facilities for biological, chemical and nuclear weapons," began a December 20, 2001, article by Judith Miller. She wrote that Adnan Ihsan Saeed al-Haideri "personally visited at least 20 different sites." As it was learned later, the administration had helped Miller get an interview with al-Haideri. He worked for the Iraqi National Congress, the exiled opposition group, but when telling his story to the CIA he had flunked their lie-detector test; that was three days before his interview with Miller. During 2002, Cheney's office leaked bogus information to Miller, who would report it in articles in the newspaper. Then, the conservative administration would cite the liberal *Times*. On September 8, 2002, a new Miller article appeared on the first page: "US says Saddam intensifies search for A-bomb parts." Later that morning Cheney appeared on *Face the Nation*: "According to an article in the *New York Times*," he declared, Saddam was "actively and aggressively seeking to acquire nuclear weapons."

What Press Secretary Scott McClellan later called "our campaign to sell the war" began in earnest after Labor Day. The president began his case on September 4 by inviting 18 senior members of the House and Senate to the White House. Aides handed them a letter from Bush. "America and the civilized world face a critical decision in the months ahead," it began. "The decision is how to disarm an outlaw regime that continues to possess and develop weapons of mass destruction." Since 9/11 "we have been tragically reminded that we are vulnerable to evil people. And this vulnerability increases dramatically when evil people have access to weapons of mass destruction." The president told congressional leaders that he would work with them, but that he needed a quick vote on a resolution that would grant him the authority to confront Saddam, including the use of military force. He wanted a vote on the resolution within six weeks—before members left town to campaign for reelection. The Democratic Senate majority leader Tom Daschle of

South Dakota asked if it would be better to wait until after the election in order to take politics out of such an important vote concerning war. What was the rush? What was new about Saddam, and what was the immediate threat? If there was a new threat, where was the evidence? Bush didn't answer directly but simply proclaimed, "We just have to do it now." The Republican House majority leader Dick Armey of Texas also expressed concern. He recalled what war had done to the presidency of another Texan, Lyndon B. Johnson, and warned, "Mr. President, if you go in there, you're likely to be stuck in a quagmire that will endanger your domestic agenda for the rest of your presidency." Bush asked the delegation to withhold doubts until they had seen the evidence that would be presented to the nation.

Before presenting evidence to the nation or to Congress the president went out on the campaign trail for the upcoming congressional elections. On September 7 he declared in Cincinnati that the Iraqis were "six months away from developing a weapon. I don't know what more evidence we need."

Neither did the president's subordinates, who the next day blitzed the Sunday morning talk shows, *Meet the Press*, *Face the Nation*, and *Late Edition*. "We don't want the smoking gun to be a mushroom cloud," said Condi Rice on CNN, and Cheney continued the doomsday drumbeat: "We do know, with absolute certainty, that he is using his procurement system to acquire the equipment he needs in order to enrich uranium to build a nuclear weapon." He also added a new fear: "One of the real concerns about Saddam Hussein . . . is his biological weapons ability, the fact that he may at some point try to use smallpox, anthrax, plague, some other kind of biological agent against other nations, possibly including even the United States." Rumsfeld tied it all together: "Imagine a September 11 with weapons of mass destruction," which would kill "tens of thousands of innocent men, women, and children." Later that month he told Congress, "No terrorist state poses a greater or more immediate threat to the security of our people, and the stability of the world, than the regime of Saddam Hussein."

The president gave a similar message to the American people on the first anniversary of the terrorist attacks. On September 11, 2002, he appeared in a prime-time address from Ellis Island. The speech was "a magnificent display of stagecraft," wrote one White House insider, "with the Statue of Liberty over one shoulder and a waving American flag over the other." The president declared, "We will not allow any terrorist or tyrant to threaten civilization with weapons of mass murder. Now and in the future, Americans will live as free people, not in fear, and never at the mercy of any foreign plot or power."

Next day the president took his message to the world stage at the United Nations. After recounting the numerous resolutions that the UN had passed against Iraq, and that Saddam continued to violate, Bush claimed that "Iraq employs capable nuclear scientists and technicians. It retains physical infrastructure needed to build a nuclear weapon. Iraq has made several attempts to buy high-strength aluminum tubes used to enrich uranium for a nuclear weapon. Should Iraq acquire fissile material, it would be able to build a nuclear weapon within a year." The president continued, "Iraq possesses a force of SCUD type missiles" and was working on long-range missiles that could "inflict mass death throughout the region." He also claimed, "Iraq possesses biological and chemical weapons." Bush concluded that the "purposes of the United States should not be doubted. The Security Council resolutions will be enforced . . . or action will be unavoidable. And a regime that has lost its legitimacy will also lose its power."

The UN speech was "an ultimatum," wrote Scott McClellan, "either the UN acts to disarm Saddam Hussein or the United States will." It worked—at least on Saddam. Under American and international pressure, on September 16 Iraq announced it would readmit UN inspectors without condition.[4]

That was a diplomatic coup for the Bush administration, but they did not seem interested in taking advantage of allowing UN inspectors to resolve the issue and determine if Saddam had WMDs. Instead, the administration continued to build a case for attacking Iraq. On September 20 the president hosted a private meeting with Republican governors at the White House, telling his political allies, "It is important to know that Iraq is an extension of the war on terror." He admitted, "In the international debate, we are starting to shift the burden of guilt to the guilty. The international community is risk averse. But I assure you I am going to stay plenty tough." Bush said he hated Saddam, whom he called "a brutal, ugly, repugnant man who needs to go. . . . I would like to see him gone peacefully. But if I unleash the military, I promise you it will be swift and decisive." He warned the governors not to "fall into the argument that there is no one to replace Saddam," and reassured them that "our planning will make sure there is no oil disruption; we are looking at all options to enhance oil flow." One governor asked about building the case for war, and the president answered, "There is a case to be made, and I have to make it."

The administration continued making the case during the month by attempting to establish a link between Saddam and bin Laden. Cheney had led the charge on his September 8 visit to *Meet the Press*, citing "new information" that "has come to light." He again stated that Mohammed Atta, one of the 19 9/11 highjackers, "did apparently travel to Prague on a number of occasions. And on at least one occasion, we have reporting that places him in Prague with a senior Iraqi intelligence official a few months before the attack on the World Trade Center." On September 25 Rice added, "There clearly are contacts between al Qaeda and Iraq that can be documented . . . there's a relationship here. . . . And there are some al Qaeda personnel who found refuge in Baghdad." The president continued the charge: "You can't distinguish between al Qaeda and Saddam when you talk about the war on terror." Rumsfeld added, "We have what we consider to be credible evidence that al Qaeda leaders have sought contacts with Iraq who could help them acquire . . . weapons of mass destruction capabilities." The next day Rumsfeld stated that there was "reliable reporting" of "possible chemical- and biological-agent training" and later that the evidence of Saddam–al Qaeda ties was "bullet-proof."

The president rejoined the chorus with a major address on October 7 in Cincinnati, just days before Congress was slated to vote on a war resolution. Bush began the speech by warning of the "grave threat" from Iraq: "The danger is already significant, and it only grows worse with time. . . . We know that the regime has produced thousands of tons of chemical agents, including mustard gas, sarin nerve gas, VX nerve gas" and that "Iraq possesses ballistic missiles with a likely range of hundreds of miles." The president maintained that Saddam was acquiring "manned and unmanned aerial vehicles that could be used to disperse chemical or biological weapons," including "missions targeting the United States." Moreover, "evidence indicates that Iraq is reconstituting its nuclear weapons program." Saddam "has held numerous meetings with Iraqi nuclear scientists, a group he calls his 'nuclear mujahedeen'—his nuclear holy warriors." They were attempting to build a bomb, which they could have "in less than a year." Then, Saddam would be able to dominate the Middle East, threaten America, and

> pass nuclear technology to terrorists. We know that Iraq and al Qaeda have had high-level contacts that go back a decade. Some al Qaeda leaders who fled Afghanistan went to Iraq. . . . We've learned that Iraq has trained al Qaeda members in bomb-making and poisons and deadly gases. . . . Facing clear evidence of peril, we cannot wait for the final proof, the smoking gun that could come in the form of a mushroom cloud.

The administration focused on a congressional war resolution and the November elections. At stake was control of all branches of the U.S. government. Former Republican presidents had appointed over 60 percent of sitting federal judges, including seven of nine Supreme Court justices, and the GOP narrowly controlled the House. The Senate was controlled by the Democrats—by only one vote. Bush's political strategist, Karl Rove, had written to party faithful that "we can go to the country" on terrorism and national security; Republicans should "focus on war."

Bush and Rove made the war resolution a campaign issue—unlike Bush's father in 1990. The elder Bush waited until after the November congressional elections to approach Congress for a war resolution, and members held extensive debates for two months after the elections. When a new Congress took their seats on January 3, 1991, there were additional debates before they passed the resolution nine days later. Although it passed easily in the House, it only passed by five votes in the Senate, but this debate meant two things: once America went to war the commander-in-chief had congressional support, and no congressperson complained that they had been misled by the administration. In short, in 1991 Bush senior did not want to make a potential war a campaign issue; in 2002 Bush junior did.

The administration also took its message to Congress. Rumsfeld appeared before the House Armed Services Committee and declared that Saddam "has amassed large clandestine stocks of biological weapons, including anthrax and botulism toxin and possibly smallpox.

His regime has amassed large clandestine stockpiles of chemical weapons, including VX and sarin and mustard gas." Moreover, Iraq now could attack the United States. Cheney told members of Congress that Iraq's threat consisted of a fleet of UAVs—unmanned aerial vehicles. "I was looked at straight in the face," recalled Florida Democratic Senator Bill Nelson, "and told that Saddam Hussein had the means of delivering those biological and chemical weapons of mass destruction by unmanned drones. . . . Further, I was . . . told that UAVs could be launched from ships off the Atlantic coast to attack eastern seaboard cities of the United States."

The administration's claims, and demands for a congressional resolution, resulted in a great debate that autumn in and out of the halls of Congress. Generally speaking, Democrats shied from the debate, fearful of being labeled soft on terrorism or soft on Saddam. Former vice president Al Gore spoke out against war against Iraq because "the war against terror manifestly requires broad and continuous international cooperation. Our ability to secure this kind of cooperation can be severely damaged by unilateral action against Iraq." Wisconsin senator Russ Feingold published "Why I Oppose Bush's Iraq War Resolution," and so did Representatives Nancy Pelosi and Ike Skelton, the latter saying that he had no doubts that the U.S. military would defeat Saddam's army. "But like the proverbial dog chasing the car down the road, we must consider what we would do after we caught it."

Resistance to a potential war also came from the military. The chairman of the Joint Chiefs of Staff, Army General John Shalikashvili, cautioned that it would take at least 200,000 soldiers to occupy Iraq. Quietly, Marine Lieutenant General Greg Newbold, director of operations for the JCS, resigned because of his opposition to the administration's war plans, but the retired Marine General Anthony C. Zinni spoke out. The former CENTCOM commander, and Bush's special envoy to the Middle East, urged caution in the unpredictable and violent Middle East. "We are about to do something that will ignite a fuse in this region that we will rue the day we ever started," he said, and before the congressional vote he declared in Washington:

> If we think there is a fast solution to changing the governance of
> Iraq, then we don't understand history, the nature of the country,

the divisions, or the underneath suppressed passions that could rise up. God help us if we think this transition will occur easily. The attempts I've seen to install democracy in short periods of time where there is not history and no roots have failed.

Bush and Rumsfeld held a dim view of subordinates who didn't tow the administration's line, and shortly thereafter Zinni was shunned and Shalikashvili had been retired. But that did not stop the debate, for prominent Republican foreign policy experts also spoke out that autumn. Editorializing in the *Wall Street Journal*, Brent Scowcroft declared "Don't Attack Saddam" and advocated caution, writing that the United States should finish the job against al Qaeda before beginning new adventures in the Middle East. The former secretary of state James Baker also had doubts, warning that war "cannot be done on the cheap," and Nebraska's Republican senator Chuck Hagel, a Vietnam vet, proclaimed on *Meet the Press*: "If you think you're going to drop the 82nd Airborne in Baghdad and finish the job, I think you've been watching too many John Wayne movies."

Naturally, there were numerous conservatives who supported the administration's stand against Iraq. Michael Ledeen, a contributing editor to *National Review*, wrote that "Saddam Hussein is a terrible evil, and President Bush is entirely right in vowing to end his reign of terror." He predicted that if U.S. troops entered "Baghdad, Damascus and Tehran as liberators, we can expect overwhelming popular support." Charles Krauthammer, columnist for the *Washington Post* and frequent guest on FOX News, informed his readers that "Hawks favor war on the grounds that Saddam Hussein is reckless, tyrannical and instinctively aggressive," and the neocon Bill Kristol declared that a war in Iraq "could have terrifically good effects throughout the Middle East."

In the Senate, many supported the administration's case against Iraq. The Democratic senator Hillary Clinton labeled Saddam "a tyrant who has tortured and killed his own people, even his own family members." She urged the president to return to diplomacy and get a tough UN resolution passed for unlimited weapons inspections. Nevertheless, she voted for the resolution as "a vote that says clearly to Saddam Hussein—this is your last chance—disarm or be disarmed." The Republican senator John McCain was more blunt, calling Saddam "a clear and present danger" to U.S. security, and then making the remarkable claim that the dictator "has developed stocks of germs and toxins in sufficient quantities to kill the entire population of the Earth multiple times."[5]

Stirring passions early in October was the CIA's National Intelligence Estimate. The agency sent this secret document to the chairman of the Senate Intelligence Committee, Bob Graham, summarizing the current intelligence on Iraq's relationship with al Qaeda. The CIA usually spends a number of months, about half a year, to write the NIE, checking all sources, discussing their findings, and writing it in clear prose for senior members of the administration and Congress. But under intense pressure from the administration's claims about Saddam, and from congressmembers facing a vote on a war resolution and a November election, CIA Director Tenet had to order his staff to prepare this very significant document in only three weeks.

The subsequent NIE was a mess, a report riddled with inconsistencies. The document declared that the CIA had "solid reporting" and "solid evidence" of "senior level contacts between Iraq and al Qaeda going back a decade" and of the presence of al Qaeda members in Baghdad, but another sentence cast doubts on such links after 9/11, admitting, "We have no specific intelligence that Saddam's regime had directed attacks against U.S. territory." The NIE continued that

> Iraq has largely rebuilt missile and biological weapons facilities damaged during Operation Desert Fox and has expanded its chemical and biological infrastructure under the cover of civilian production. . . . Baghdad has chemical and biological weapons as well as missiles with ranges in excess of UN restrictions. . . . If Baghdad acquires sufficient fissile material from abroad it could make a nuclear weapon within several months to a year.

That was alarming, but the NIE also expressed "low confidence" in its own findings, and it contradicted itself: "We have little specific information on Iraq's CW stockpile," and it cautioned, "We lack specific information on many aspects of Iraq's WMD programs."

Indeed, the CIA lacked a lot of information, meaning many administration claims were questionable. Three days after September 11, the CIA's Bob Walpole had a meeting with his counterparts at the NSC,

State, and Defense departments. He bluntly told those officials not to use WMDs to justify a war against Iraq; North Korea was more of a threat. Another CIA official in that meeting declared that as far as supporting international terrorism, Iran was more involved with such activities than Iraq. At that same time, the administration called a CIA Middle East expert to the White House. He was confronted by a senior NSC official who told him that they wanted to get rid of Saddam, to which the analyst responded, "If you want to go after that son of a bitch to settle old scores, be my guest. But don't tell us he is connected to 9/11 or to terrorism because there is no evidence to support that. You will have to have a better reason."

That, however, was not what the administration wanted to hear from the CIA. Thus, before the congressional vote in October Condi Rice called George Tenet and pressured him to "clarify" the agency's position with the statements from the White House. The CIA director commented that there was "no inconsistency in the views" of the CIA and "those of the president." To the public, that meant CIA intelligence supported the administration's statements about Saddam. In fact, Tenet—who submitted the NIE—later admitted that he was surprised by the administration's claims about Iraq making nuclear weapons, for those statements "went well beyond what our analysis could support. The intelligence community's belief was that, left unchecked, Iraq would probably not acquire nuclear weapons until near the end of the decade." Moreover, the CIA informed the administration about the debate over the purpose of the aluminum tubes that Iraq ordered in mid-2001. The departments of Energy and State claimed the tubes were for rocket casings, while a former worker at Oak Ridge National Laboratory claimed that they were for centrifuge rotors—which are used in isotope separation to enrich uranium, meaning Iraq was restarting a nuclear weapons program. The CIA wrote that "serious doubts existed about the intended use of the tubes," which Tenet personally told the president, but the administration decided to believe that the tubes were proof that Saddam had restarted his nuclear program. Finally, there was Cheney's claim that the 9/11 hijacker Mohammed Atta had met in Prague with a senior Iraqi intelligence agent, Ahmed Khalil Ibrahim Samir al-Ani, five months before the attack. In fact, credit card and telephone records demonstrated that Atta was in the United States at the time of the alleged meeting; moreover, al-Ani was not in Prague. The CIA and FBI briefed Cheney on Atta's location, but the vice president continued to make the false claims about an Iraq–al Qaeda link.

"Who is going to question the vice president when he keeps espousing this shit?" concerning Atta, said a U.S. counterterrorism official. "Nobody at the FBI or CIA is going to speak up and say, stop the bullshit."

"They were distorting some of the information that we provided to make it seem more alarmist and more dangerous," said the senior State Department intelligence official Gregory Thielmann. "I thought there were limits on how much one was willing to do in order to twist things." The Republican senator Hagel was as blunt: "The administration cherry-picked intelligence to fit its policy, used fear and the threat of terrorism to intensify its war sloganeering . . . and dampened the possibility of dissent by denying that it had decided to go to war even though it had already made that decision before the debate even began. It is shocking how little Congress or the media challenged the Bush administration."

It also was shocking how little U.S. intelligence agencies actually knew about Saddam's Iraq. A later report found that after Saddam expelled UN weapons inspectors in 1998 "very little new information fell into the hands of U.S. intelligence."[6]

Basically, there were four main sources on Iraq in 2002, and one was the current Iraqi foreign minister, Naji Sabri. The CIA had interviewed him and some Iraqi scientists. The agency and the French paid Sabri at least $200,000 for his inside information and offered him safe passage to exile. Sabri and the scientists told the same story—Saddam might have some "poison gas" but basically had no WMDs. On September 18 Tenet briefed Bush on Sabri's information, but Bush dismissed it as "the same old thing," worthless. The French tapped Sabri's telephone and shared the conversations with the CIA; those conversations validated Sabri's claims. When a CIA agent insisted on the significance of Sabri's information, one of Tenet's deputies responded, "You haven't figured this out yet. This isn't about intelligence. It's about regime change."

Another important informant was an al Qaeda commander, Ibn al-Sheikh al-Libi, whom the Pakistanis had captured in December 2001. He was taken to Bagram Air Base in Afghanistan and the FBI interrogated him for a few days. Asked if al Qaeda had contacts with Saddam, he was consistent, as were all other al Qaeda captives: No. Then the CIA appeared for interrogations, and al-Libi was given "extraordinary rendition." He was flown to Egypt, where he was brutally tortured. After a few weeks of coercion he changed his story and told the CIA that bin Laden wanted to develop chemical and biological weapons so he dispatched operatives to Iraq for training. That information was sent to the White House and used in speeches beginning in September 2002. When al-Libi was returned to the FBI, he recanted the entire story, affirming that his first statements were correct; there was no link. "They were killing me," he told the FBI. "I had to tell them something."

Other bits of information came from two Iraqi defectors. Ahmed Chalabi had been born in 1945 into a wealthy banking family in Baghdad that opposed the regime of Saddam. Chalabi left with his family in 1956 and lived mainly in London and the United States, eventually being granted British citizenship. He was educated at the University of Chicago where he earned a PhD in mathematics and returned to the Middle East in the late 1980s to establish the Petra Bank in Jordan. The bank collapsed in 1990, amid allegations that Chalabi had been involved in a financial scandal, and the Jordanian courts convicted him of embezzlement and sentenced him in absentia to prison. He professed his innocence, claiming it was an Iraqi plot. He returned to Iraq in the mid-1990s to organize an uprising in the Kurdish area of northern Iraq, a failed attempt that Saddam crushed, resulting in hundreds of deaths; Chalabi escaped. A Shia, like the majority of Iraq, Chalabi was secular and pro-Western, and as an English-speaker he made many Americans think that he was the perfect leader for a post-Saddam Iraq. The president invited him to sit next to the first lady at his 2002 State of the Union address. Although he did not live in Iraq, he volunteered a lot of information to U.S. officials, much of it on Iraq's WMDs, most of it inaccurate according to the agent Valerie Plame Wilson. "Despised by the CIA for his deceitfulness and lionized by the Pentagon for his ability to predict a democratic Iraq (with him as its head)," Wilson wrote, "Chalabi probably sent dozens of tantalizing but ultimately false leads into the CIA net."

Another Iraqi informant was in German custody, code-named "Curveball." The brother of one of Chalabi's top aides, Curveball fed German intelligence bogus information about Saddam's supposed mobile biological labs that he was moving all over the country to prevent detection. German's Federal Intelligence Service, BND, had informed the CIA that Curveball suffered from mental problems and that his motive for giving out untrue information was to get a German visa. "The guy's crazy," a BND official told the CIA's Tyler Drumheller, and he had a drinking problem. Iraqi officials had fired Curveball, and he was actually out of the country in 1998 when he supposedly had witnessed a biological accident that he claimed had killed 12 of his coworkers. British intelligence had doubts about his claims, but his statements found a willing audience at the NSC and the White House. Mobile bioweapons laboratories were just what the NSC officials wanted to hear, as one staffer remarked, referring to Saddam, "We got him. The bastard, we nailed his ass." Since September the White House had been using Curveball's story about mobile labs, so in October the CIA included that information in their National Intelligence Estimate.

Melvin Goodman, a retired CIA analyst, later concluded: "The U.S. rush to war against Iraq marked the worst intelligence scandal in the history of the United States."[7]

But any doubts the administration had about sources were silenced as Congress considered the resolution that October. The resolution itself was an interesting document. The title was "Joint Resolution to Authorize the Use of United States Armed Force Against Iraq," and it supposedly did just that, but it first listed 23 statements, most concerning the history of U.S.-Iraq relations since 1990, various UN resolutions, or the War on Terror. The document then shifted to Congress, declaring that the body supported the president in his efforts to get Iraq to "promptly and strictly" comply with United Nations resolutions. Finally, it declared that the president was authorized to use the military but only under two conditions: "defend the national security of the United States against the continuing threat posed by Iraq" and "enforce all relevant United Nations Security Council Resolutions regarding Iraq." What did "defend" mean? Apparently, to defend the United States against an attack. But what if there was no Iraqi threat, no attack? Nothing in the resolution gave the president power to carry out the Bush Doctrine, a preemptive attack on Iraq. The administration would have to convince the nation that Iraq was ready to launch WMDs against the United States, which meant that if the administration invaded Iraq, then it had better find what it claimed—stockpiles of weapons and a system to deliver an attack against America.

On October 11 the resolution passed the Senate, 77–23, with 29 of 50 Democrats voting with the majority, and the House, 296–133, with 81 Democrats voting in favor. The Democratic senators Joseph Biden, Hillary Clinton, John Edwards, John Kerry, and Joseph Lieberman voted for the resolution, as did all Republican senators except Lincoln Chafee from Rhode Island. Senator McCain had been advocating attacking Iraq for a year. "Very obviously Iraq is the first country," he declared on CNN in October 2001, and in January 2002 he yelled to sailors on the aircraft carrier *Theodore Roosevelt*, "Next up, Baghdad!"

Years later, as the war grinded on, the president and vice president claimed that Congress voted "for war." Perhaps "armed force against Iraq" was in the resolution's title, but actually those legislators voted to *defend* the United States. "It all comes down to the fact that we were asked to vote on a resolution based on half truths, untruths, and wishful thinking," explained the Republican senator Chuck Hagel. "I voted for this resolution that gave the president the authority to go to war in Iraq *if all diplomatic efforts were exhausted and failed.* Unfortunately, it was not his intention to exhaust all diplomatic efforts. . . . Both political parties failed to do their job in Congress. Congress abdicated its oversight responsibilities and fell silent and timid."

Others were not so silent, and many citizens began to protest. More than 60 American religious groups issued a declaration denouncing a preemptive war. On October 26, 2002, the largest antiwar march since the Vietnam War took place in Washington. Between 100,000 and 200,000 demonstrated on the National Mall, and eventually there were protests in 37 states. Cities joined the campaign, passing resolutions opposing the war; during the next months 33 city councils passed antiwar declarations. The protests were global. In August, the German chancellor Gerhard Schroeder declared that his country would not participate in or help pay for a U.S. war against Iraq, and the next month during the German election campaign his justice minister surprised many by comparing the tactics used by Bush to those of Hitler, which underscored how world sympathy had evaporated in 2002 and how much anti-Americanism now was dominating Continental politics. In November a half million Italians marched in Florence, and later hundreds of thousands demonstrated in Berlin, London, Paris, and Madrid.

But most Americans trusted the administration, and Karl Rove's prediction was proven correct during the November congressional election. The Republicans could take the war to the voters: the GOP won eight more seats in the House and delivered a majority by winning two more in the Senate. The Republicans controlled all three branches of government for the next four years. There would be no congressional oversight of the executive.

Just days after the election the United Nations acted against Iraq. On November 8 the Security Council unanimously adopted Resolution 1441, which gave Baghdad a "final opportunity to comply with its disarmament obligations." It demanded that Iraq give the UN inspectors the right to search for banned weapons. In September Iraq had announced that it would readmit UN inspectors, but this resolution gave inspector Hans Blix additional powers. The Iraqis were forced to agree to "No Notice" inspections, opening all areas of the country, even the various presidential palaces. Blix and his team, UNMOVIC, arrived in Iraq in December and had 60 days of unconditional inspections. His report was due in late January.

The Bush administration had its own views of the new UN inspections. The White House warned Saddam not to "play games." Press Secretary Scott McClellan stated that the Iraqi dictator "better not go back to his history of cheat and retreat, and deceive and deny," while Rumsfeld flatly declared that it was impossible for Iraq not to have weapons of mass destruction. If UNMOVIC did not find WMDs, he said, "it would prove that the inspections process had been successfully defeated by the Iraqis." He added, "We don't want to see a smoking gun from a weapon of mass destruction. With a weapon of mass destruction you're not talking about 300 people or 3,000 people being killed, but 30,000, or a hundred thousand." Rumsfeld also signaled that the administration was preparing to move against Saddam regardless of UN inspections. "The idea that it's going to be a long, long, long battle of some kind I think is belied by the fact of what happened in 1990," he said on a radio program. "Five days or five weeks or five months, but it certainly isn't going to last any longer than that." The U.S. military is capable "to do the job and finish it fast."

The administration also was expressing such views privately. "We've got to get in there before it gets too hot," Condi Rice told Senator Chuck

Hagel. "We've got to get this done within a window." Hagel was stunned. "Wait—you've already committed to this war?" Rice tried to calm him down, cool his apprehension, yet it was a similar story at the December 18 meeting of the National Security Council. Bush discussed the new UN inspections in Iraq and said, "It's clear that Saddam is not cooperating." "That's right," Secretary Powell responded. "That's a significant statement," the president continued. "It means it's the beginning of the end for the guy." The conversation continued, with participants debating if the United States should call Iraq in "material breach" of the UN resolution, and what that meant, until the president declared: "I think war is inevitable."

After more discussion, the president stated that the United States should not expect the world to demand action against Saddam, emphasizing "*That won't happen.*" Rumsfeld suggested giving the dictator "an ultimatum to leave to avoid war." It was clear in that meeting, wrote Douglas Feith, who took notes, that if Saddam bowed to the UN Resolution 1441, "he could avoid war. If he remained in breach, however, the President's determination was clear: to eliminate the Iraqi threat by force."[8]

Thus, five weeks before Blix's final report was due, Bush declared it was the beginning of the end for Saddam: "War is inevitable." Yet even so, the president wanted reassurance; he called his CIA director and others to a meeting at the White House. On December 21 Bush again asked Tenet if Saddam possessed WMDs, and Tenet confirmed: "It's a slam dunk." Many in the room, including Andrew Card, felt that those words were "*the* confirmation."

Perhaps, but as we have seen, the administration had been interested in going to war as early as the previous July, and they had been selling the idea throughout the autumn. As Tenet later pointed out, the president had seen a workable war plan ten months before the "slam dunk" meeting, and during the previous spring the defense department had begun shifting forces from Afghanistan to prepare for Iraq. In early October Army Chief of Staff General Eric Shinseki announced to his army commanders, "From today forward the main effort of the U.S. Army must be to prepare for war with Iraq," while at the same time the Pentagon was repositioning its assets throughout the Middle East. In Kuwait, the United States was building a helipad and runway to accommodate C-130 transports along with a pipeline from a refinery to American bases in the desert, situated less than fifty miles from Iraq. The Pentagon also was installing a deep-water pier and landing ramp in the Persian Gulf, had ordered the "stop loss" program to keep troops on active duty, and was sending troops to Kuwait. On December 6, two weeks before the slam dunk meeting, Rumsfeld issued the first major deployment order, and shortly thereafter 140,000 service personnel were moving into the region and U.S. aircraft carriers were steaming to the Gulf. The eventual theater commander, General Franks, was preparing for the war by moving into a new headquarters close to the target, in Doha, Qatar.

The CIA provided the cover. Tenet folded under pressure, his agency had been compromised, and he later admitted "marketing" the war for the administration. In January 2003 a CIA manager called a meeting at the agency and told about 50 workers, "If President Bush wants to go to war, ladies and gentlemen, your job's to give him a reason to do so." "This is awful," said an agent. "This is something that the American public, if they ever heard, if they ever knew, they would be outraged."

They didn't hear; instead, they heard from the president and his assistants who continued to claim that Saddam was trying to make nuclear weapons and had large stockpiles of WMDs.

Much of the world wanted to know if that was true. By the end of January 2003 two organizations had been scouring Iraq for 60 days, the International Atomic Energy Agency (IAEA) and UNMOVIC, and on January 27 their directors returned to give their findings to the UN. The IAEA director, Mohamed ElBaradei, reminded the audience that in 1998 his organization had verified that Iraq had no nuclear capabilities and that during the last two months they had conducted 139 inspections at 106 locations to determine if Saddam had rebuilt those capabilities. Blix had a team of about 250 inspectors inside Iraq and had conducted some 300 visits to 230 different sites. Blix reported that UNMOVIC had found a few missiles that had a range of slightly over 90 miles and some gas warheads for artillery rockets; the missiles and warheads were destroyed. He informed the world that they were continuing inspections and that his report did not "contend that weapons of mass destruction remain in Iraq, but nor do they exclude that possibility." Simply stated, there was "lack of evidence" of WMDs. ElBaradei was more direct: "No prohibited nuclear activities have been identified during these inspections." The aluminum tubes were too weak, not suitable for a nuclear centrifuge, and had been used to build small 81-mm rockets that had a range of only 20 kilometers, well within the limits imposed by the UN. ElBaradei concluded that his team "in the next few months" would be able to provide "credible assurance that Iraq has no nuclear weapons programme." These inspectors, he said, were a "valuable investment in peace" and they "could help us avoid war."

Instead of accepting the reports, or letting inspections resolve the issues, the president expressed his own views one day later in his State of the Union address:

> Our intelligence officials estimate that Saddam Hussein had the materials to produce as much as 500 tons of sarin, mustard and VX nerve agent. In such quantities, these chemical agents could kill untold thousands. . . . The British Government has learned that Saddam Hussein recently sought significant quantities of uranium from Africa. Our intelligence sources tell us that he has attempted to purchase high-strength aluminum tubes suitable for nuclear weapons production. . . . The dictator of Iraq is not disarming. To the contrary; he is deceiving. . . . Year after year, Saddam Hussein has gone to elaborate lengths, spent enormous sums, taken great risks to build and keep weapons of mass destruction. . . . Evidence from intelligence sources, secret communications, and statements by people now in custody reveal that Saddam Hussein aids and protects terrorists, including members of al Qaeda. Secretly, and without fingerprints, he could provide one of his hidden weapons to terrorists, or help them develop their own. . . . Imagine those 19 hijackers with other weapons and other plans—this time armed by Saddam Hussein.

The president said he would send Secretary Powell to the UN in a week with "information and intelligence" on Iraq. He promised to consult with other nations. "But let there be no misunderstanding: If Saddam Hussein does not fully disarm, for the safety of our people and for the peace of the world, we will lead a coalition to disarm him."

That coalition meant for the most part the British, and on January 31 the prime minister arrived at the White House. Bush told Blair that the United States was going to invade whether or not there was a second UN resolution supporting an invasion and even if weapons inspectors found no evidence that Saddam was producing WMDs. Bush already had ordered 200,000 troops to take positions in the Middle East. The prime minister responded that he was "solidly with the president" and would do whatever it took to disarm Saddam, and Bush replied, "The diplomatic strategy had to be arranged around the military planning," and the two men agreed to start the military campaign on or around March 10. Both men agreed that it was "unlikely there would be internecine warfare between the different religious and ethnic groups."

On February 5, 2003, Secretary of State Powell took the administration's case to the United Nations. The White House picked him because the general had the highest popular approval rating of anyone in the administration and had the strongest international reputation. Armed with numerous satellite photos, Powell claimed the "existence of mobile production facilities used to make biological agents," adding, "Our conservative estimate is that Iraq today has a stockpile of between 100 and 500 tons of chemical weapons agent." He continued, "We know that Iraq has at least seven of these mobile biological agent factories," and in a month they could produce enough agents to "kill thousands upon thousands of people." The secretary restated the link between Iraq and al Qaeda and declared that Baghdad had provided the terrorists "help in acquiring poisons and gases." Then, the secretary surprised the diplomats by refuting ElBaradei: "we have more than a decade of proof" that Saddam "remains determined to acquire nuclear weapons."

With few exceptions, the American media swallowed Powell's performance whole, declaring it "Impressive," "Masterful," "Overwhelming," and "Case Closed." But later, after U.S. troops were bogged down in Iraq and after Powell had retired from the Bush administration, the State Department's chief of staff, Colonel Lawrence Wilkerson, revealed that the original speech Powell was supposed to give came from Vice President Cheney's office. When Powell read it his response was "crazy. . . . This is bullshit." The secretary tossed that speech and accepted a draft from the CIA—one based on their flawed National Intelligence Estimate on Iraq. When Powell was rehearsing the talk in New York, he turned to Tenet and asked him if he stood by everything in the speech, and the director answered in the affirmative. When German's Federal Intelligence Service, BND, heard the address, they were amazed that Powell used information from Curveball about mobile factories. "We were shocked," said one German agent. "*Mein Gott!* We had always told them it . . . was not hard intelligence." As for the Niger uranium claim, the CIA by this time had warned the White House four times that it was bogus, not to use it, but they included it in Powell's address. The secretary never was informed about al-Libi, and had no idea that many intelligence officers felt his statements on al Qaeda–Saddam links were nonsense, forced by torture. Eventually, Powell blamed Tenet for giving him a flawed speech, and after he was out of office said he felt "terrible" about the address, "It's painful now."[9]

But the president had no regrets. For on the next day, Bush again upped the ante to the United Nations, repeating the claim that Iraq had "mobile factories for the production of biological agents." Then a startling claim: "Iraq has developed spray devices that could be used on unmanned aerial vehicles with ranges far beyond what is permitted by the U.N. Security Council. A UAV launched from a vessel off the American coast could reach hundreds of miles inland." Bush also charged, "Senior members of Iraqi intelligence and al-Qaeda have met at least eight times since the early 1990s. Iraq has sent bomb-making . . . experts to work with al-Qaeda," and "Iraq has also provided al-Qaeda with chemical and biological weapons training."

These statements should have raised questions. How could the administration's intelligence, based on satellite photos and exiled informants, be superior to IAEA and UNMOVIC inspectors inside Iraq who were reading documents, interviewing scientists, and conducting on-site inspections? With the most powerful air force, navy, and coast guard in the world, along with numerous satellites viewing the American coasts, how could a foreign ship launch a slow flying UAV without notice and without it being destroyed? In fact, the air force disagreed with the UAV threat, but the administration kept that quiet. Furthermore, with normal winds, how many tons of biological agents or chemicals would have to be dropped, and from what altitude, to make the agents concentrated enough to kill even one American? Even if Saddam was making such weapons, so what? He would be signing his own death certificate if he used them against a Western nation, especially the United States, or against American allies in the Middle East. Moreover, if Saddam did have WMDs—which would be his line of defense against his hated neighbor, Iran—why would he share that knowledge or weapons with the terrorist group al Qaeda, which owed its allegiance to bin Laden, a man who for years had been condemning "infidel" secular leaders like Saddam? In "the Arab world," one local expert said, "even children laugh at the thought of a relationship between Saddam Hussein and al Qaeda." The Iraq dictator was "never going to give" weapons to bin Laden, said the CIA analyst Michael Scheuer, who had directed the bin Laden unit, "because al Qaeda would have been just as likely to use them against him as they would against the United States. They hated Saddam."

But such questions did not rise to the surface during the administration's rush to war. Instead, most Americans were eager for revenge against someone, anyone for 9/11; they believed their president, were overwhelmed by events, or were not paying attention. The administration's rapid repetition of its talking points continually appeared on hyperventilating cable news networks that were competing with Internet sources for the public's attention. According to one media critic this electronic age culture scrambled news from reality, allowed "no time for fact checking," and obliterated "the demarcation between truth and fiction." Moreover, a veteran reporter later found that between September 2002 and the beginning of the war there were over 400 articles attributed to "White House sources" giving the administration's views, that 140 of them appeared on front pages, while only six raised questions about the necessity of going to war; none of those were on page one. Eventually, the administration's pronouncements had an impact on public opinion. A CBS News *New York Times* poll released two weeks after the September 11, 2001, attacks found that only 6 percent thought bin Laden had collaborated with Saddam in the strikes against America, but by the time of the Iraq invasion in March 2003, CBS News found that 53 percent believed that Saddam had been involved in September 11; other polls showed that a similar percentage had even convinced themselves that the attackers were Iraqis, when not one was from that country.

But other opinion polls were more ambiguous. The *New York Times* polls found that from January to March 2003 between 59 and 65 percent supported an attack on Iraq, but there was considerable change when Zogby International asked a much larger sample group, "Suppose U.S. military action in Iraq meant that the U.S. would be involved in a war there for months or even years," or if the war would result in thousands of American or Iraqi casualties. Then support dwindled, to about 45 percent for and against, about the same percentages as when Zogby asked the public if we should go to war "without significant UN or international support."

Others expressed doubts about a war. Behind the scenes, the CIA's Paul Pillar wrote a report on postinvasion Iraq, stating that the nation was not "fertile" for democracy and the mission would be "long, difficult and turbulent." The report was sent to the White House and Pentagon, where it was judged "too negative." The Army War College Strategic Studies Institute also did a study, citing "ethnic, tribal and religious schisms" that "could produce civil war. . . . The possibility of the United States winning the war and losing the peace in Iraq is real and serious." And General Norman Schwarzkopf told the Pentagon, "I would hope that we have in place the adequate resources to become an army of occupation, because you're going to walk into chaos."

Some Democrats wondered out loud. In the Senate, Robert Byrd of West Virginia declared, "This war is not necessary at this time" and he chastised most of his colleagues for not debating a potential conflict in Iraq. This "chamber is, for the most part, silent—ominously, dreadfully silent. . . . There is nothing." But Carl Levin of Michigan was questioning, and he asked Army Chief of Staff Shinseki his views on the war and a possible occupation. The army's top general commented that Iraq was a large country "with ethnic tensions that could lead to other problems" during an occupation. In his view, it would take "several hundred thousand soldiers" to occupy Iraq, which Levin called "very sobering," but the general's estimate drew immediate ridicule from the administration. Cheney called it "an overstatement," Wolfowitz labeled it "wildly off the mark," and the Pentagon eventually treated Shinseki as they had JCS Chairman Shalikashvili: forced retirement.

In Europe, only some eastern nations supported the conflict, those who were eager for U.S. support so they could receive American funding when they joined NATO. That prompted Rumsfeld to label France and Germany "old Europe," declaring that the "center of gravity is shifting to the east," which resulted in a stinging rebuff from the Germans and French. "Deeply irritating," said the French finance minister, and "foolish comments," wrote a German newspaper. Rumsfeld "might as well have extended the 'Axis of Evil.'" Conservative Americans responded, spurred on by their talk show hosts and media outlet FOX News, and they advocated that French toast and French fries be called Freedom toast and Freedom fries. In Munich, Rumsfeld attended the annual security conference, where in front of hundreds of diplomats he insisted that his administration had built an alliance to remove Saddam. "A large number of nations have already said they will be with us in a coalition of the willing—and more are stepping up each day. Clearly, momentum is building." Powell's speech at the United Nations, he declared, "presented not options, not conjecture, but facts." That prompted German Foreign Minister Joschka Fischer to demand: "Why now?" and at one point he switched from German to English, looked at the American delegation, and declared: "Excuse me, I am not convinced."

As the Bush administration's relations with Germany and France frayed, protests against U.S. foreign policy mounted globally. The European Parliament issued a resolution opposing a preemptive strike, and so did UN Secretary General Kofi Annan who called the war "illegal" since a preemptive attack against another nation without the consent of the Security Council violated the UN Charter. These feelings escalated on February 14, when Hans Blix returned to the UN and declared that inspections were continuing and no stockpiles of WMDs had been found in Iraq, and three weeks later ElBaradei told the organization that the documents concerning the purported sale of uranium from Niger to Iraq were not authentic; they were forgeries. Meanwhile in Australia, when Prime Minister John Howard said that he would give support with 2,000 troops, there were numerous calls for his resignation, and the country saw its largest demonstrations since the Vietnam War. Religious leaders of all faiths joined the chorus. The World Council of Churches issued a "Statement against Military Action in Iraq," and Pope John Paul II proclaimed, "No to war! It is always a defeat for humanity." Polls showed that only 2 percent of British citizens felt that the world would be a safer place after a war to remove Saddam, only 4 percent of Spaniards supported a war without UN approval, and 76 percent of French opposed the conflict.

Those feelings appeared February 15–16 as antiwar protest emerged in major cities throughout the world. Over eight million people marched on five continents against a possible war against Iraq. In the United States, millions of citizens participated in Chicago, Los Angeles, San Francisco, and New York City. Larger protests were held in Europe: a million in Madrid, more in Rome, and even more in London, the largest demonstration ever in Britain. Indeed, this was the largest global opposition to an American foreign policy in history.

The Bush administration faced a similar response in the Middle East. Although Saudi Arabia, Egypt, Syria, and Jordan had supported the Gulf War in 1991, none agreed with the Bush administration's calls for regime change in Iraq. The Saudis would not let the United States use bases to attack Iraq and neither would Turkey, which had been a staunch ally since the Truman Doctrine in 1947. There even were antiwar sentiments from Iran, no friend of Saddam. A March editorial in the *Tehran Times* had the government's view of the impending crisis: "We are where we are today because most nations and many leaders let Bush and his co-conspirators get away with their childish dreams of a 'Pax Americana' for too long; a global nightmare that begins with total control of Middle Eastern oil and total immunity for Israeli leaders' barbarism and their century-old and barely concealed plans to control 'all land from the Nile to the Euphrates.'"

Bush and Blair responded to the mountain of world criticism. The president declared that "the first to benefit from a free Iraq would be the Iraqi people, themselves. Today they live in scarcity and fear, under a dictator who has brought them nothing but war, and misery, and torture." Blair was in a much tougher position, since there was very little support for a war in Britain. Foreign Secretary Jack Straw went to the prime minister's residence and warned Blair that if he followed Bush to war without UN support then "the only regime change that will be taking place is in this room." The prime minister did not heed that advice and publicly declared that "ridding the world of Saddam would be an act of humanity. It is leaving him there that is in truth inhumane."

As the administration prepared for the invasion, conservative citizens bought t-shirts declaring "Let's Roll!," as the neocons beamed with optimism. Demolishing "Hussein's military power and liberating Iraq would be a cakewalk," wrote Rumsfeld's assistant, Ken Adelman, and his boss proclaimed that Iraqis would be "waving American flags" when U.S. troops occupied their country. Cheney declared that "we will be greeted as liberators," and Wolfowitz added, "You are going to see an explosion of joy and relief." As for the cost of the Iraq War, the administration claimed it would be cheap—since Iraq had oil. When the president's economic adviser, Lawrence Lindsey, estimated that the war might cost $200 billion, Rumsfeld mocked him; soon Lindsey was forced out of his job. Wolfowitz contended that the cost would be low because "there's been none of the record in Iraq of ethnic militias fighting one another," and Assistant Secretary of Defense Richard Perle proclaimed, "Iraq is a very wealthy country . . . they can finance, largely finance, the reconstruction of their own country." The administration's largest estimate was $50 to $60 billion, which they called "affordable."

On March 5 General Franks met with Bush and the National Security team and informed them that he had 208,000 service personnel in the region, another 50,000 were en route, and he could begin the war whenever he got the order from the White House. Two weeks later, with those forces and 45,000 British troops in Kuwait ready for the attack, Bush gave his ultimatum to Iraq. "Intelligence gathered by this and other governments leaves *no doubt* that the Iraq regime continues to possess and conceal some of the most lethal weapons ever devised. . . . And it has aided, trained and harbored terrorists, including operatives of al Qaeda. . . . The danger is clear: using chemical, biological or, one day, nuclear weapons, obtained with the help of Iraq, the terrorists could fulfill their stated ambitions and kill thousands or hundreds of thousands of innocent people in our country, or any other." Since the UN would not force the dictator out of office, he said, the responsibility rested with the United States. Bush demanded that Saddam leave Iraq in 48 hours, go into exile, or the U.S. would attack.

That ultimatum prompted a response. In Britain, three ministers quit Blair's government in protest and a third of his own party voted against his war resolution. In Paris, the French president Jacques Chirac repeated that his country would veto any UN resolution that paved the way for a war: "Iraq today does not represent an immediate threat that justifies an immediate war." The Russians, Indians, and Chinese declared their opposition, advocating a settlement through the UN, and the German chancellor Gerhard Schroeder called the ultimatum illegal, saying there was no justification for war and no reason to end inspections aimed at guiding Baghdad to disarmament. Pope John Paul II called for a peaceful resolution and his press secretary added, "Whoever decides that all peaceful means available under international law are exhausted assumes a grave responsibility before God, his own conscience and history."

Saddam naturally did not accept the ultimatum. Bush stated that the dictator had made his "final mistake."

The Bush administration rushed off to war. Only 18 months had passed since the tragedy of September 11, an event that resulted in an outpouring of world sympathy for America. Since World War II, most people in the international community had held positive views of the United States, a nation that had helped save the world from the dreaded Axis Powers, had encouraged the end of empires and the self-determination of colonial subjects, had opposed unilateralism and established the United Nations, and in times of natural disasters had been one of the greatest donors. But positive feelings dissipated as the administration called for a preemptive war against Iraq. To Bush and his team, the threat was immediate and that precluded further UN inspections and discussions of questions that would become important after the invasion: Who would rule Iraq? How would the U.S. troops deal with ethnic tensions? How long would we occupy Iraq, and what would be the responses of their neighbors, and our allies?

"Mr. President, this force is ready," General Franks informed the White House over a secure video link on the morning of March 19, 2003. "D-Day, H-Hour is 2100 hours tonight Iraqi time . . . 1300 hours East Coast time." "All right," the commander-in-chief responded, and he issued the order to attack Iraq. Bush called his war Operation Iraqi Freedom.[10]

FIGURE 1. Iraqi president Saddam Hussein waves to supporters in Baghdad, 1995. AP Photo/INA.

FIGURE 2. Osama bin Laden on Al Jazeera television at an undisclosed location, October 7, 2001. He is praising God for the September 11 terrorist attacks on the United States, and declaring that America "will never dream of security" until "the infidel's armies leave the land of Muhammad." AP Photo/Al Jazeera.

FIGURE 3. Hamid Karzai (center right, second row) with U.S. special operations troops in southern Afghanistan, October 2001. He later became president of Afghanistan. Department of Defense Photo.

FIGURE 4. Guantanamo Bay Camp X-Ray detainees in orange jumpsuits under the watchful eye of U.S. military police, January 2002. Reuters/DoD/Shane T. McCoy.

FIGURE 5. Condi Rice, Dick Cheney, George Bush, and Donald Rumsfeld at Crawford Ranch for one of many discussions about a possible war with Iraq, August 2002. Luke Frazza/AFP/Getty Images.

FIGURE 6. Smoke covers one of Saddam's presidential palaces in Baghdad during a massive U.S.-led air raid on March 21, 2003. Ramzi Haidar/AFP/Getty Images.

FIGURE 7. U.S. Marine Kirk Dalrymple watches the statue of Saddam being pulled down in Firdaus Square, central Baghdad, on April 9, 2003. Reuters/Goran Tomasevic.

FIGURE 8. The new U.S. civilian administrator to Iraq, L. Paul Bremer (L), holds a press conference after landing in Baghdad on May 12, 2003. Retired General Garner listens. Reuters/Kevin Coombs.

FIGURE 9. Aboard the USS *Abraham Lincoln*, President Bush flashes the "thumbs-up" after declaring the end of major combat operations in Iraq, May 1, 2003. AP Photo/ J. Scott Applewhite.

FIGURE 10. Iraqis chant anti-American slogans as the charred bodies of American contractors hang from a bridge over the Euphrates River in Fallujah, March 31, 2004. AP Photo/Khalid Mohammed, File.

Feb. 2, 2004   **Feb. 22, 2006**

FIGURE 11. The Askariya shrine in Samarra, one of Iraq's most revered Shiite shrines, before and after assailants detonated bombs that blew off its landmark golden dome on February 22, 2006. AP Photo/Khalid Mohammed, Hameed Rasheed.

FIGURE 12. Prime Minister Nouri al-Maliki (L) and anti-U.S. Shiite cleric Muqtada al-Sadr after a meeting in Najaf, October 2006. AP Photo/Alaa al-Marjani.

FIGURE 13. Partnering with the Afghan National Army. U.S. Marine Lt. Scott Holub of Maryland carrying a wounded Afghan soldier after a firefight with the Taliban in Marjah, February 20, 2010. AP Photo/David Guttenfelder.

FIGURE 14. The last U.S. Army combat troops withdraw from Iraq, crossing the border into Kuwait, and pose with the American flag, August 16, 2010. AP Photo/Maya Alleruzzo.

3

Operation Iraqi Freedom

"Major combat operations in Iraq have ended. In the battle of Iraq, the United States and our allies have prevailed."

—President Bush, May 1, 2003

"My fellow citizens," President Bush announced to the nation the evening of March 19, "at this hour, American and coalition forces are in the early stages of military operations to disarm Iraq, to free the people and to defend the world from grave danger. . . . Our nation enters this conflict reluctantly—yet, our purpose is sure. The people of the United States and our friends and allies will not live at the mercy of an outlaw regime that threatens the peace with weapons of mass murder. We will meet that threat now," he said, invoking the memory of 9/11, "so that we do not have to meet it later with armies of fire fighters and police and doctors on the streets of our cities."

That same evening Bush ordered the "decapitation strike." He had received intelligence that Saddam, his sons, and top regime leaders supposedly were at one of the family's residences, Doura Farms. The air strike destroyed the residence, but the intelligence proved wrong. Several hours later the dictator appeared on Iraqi television condemning the raid, and on March 21 the United States and Britain began nine hours of bombing and missile attacks.

"Shock and Awe," the media called the attack. During the first stage of Operation Iraqi Freedom, Americans dropped millions of leaflets and took control of the local airwaves telling Iraqis and their army that U.S. forces were liberating them from brutal Saddam: stay inside, away from U.S. units, or surrender.

Then combat commenced. American and British aircraft flew over 1,500 sorties a day while the U.S. Air Force and Navy launched 600 cruise missiles at Iraqi headquarters and military installations, some 3,000 targets. In western and northern Iraq, Special Operation Forces already had established forward operating bases where they harassed Iraqi forces and prevented them from returning to defend Baghdad. Then, three U.S. Army divisions, one marine division, and one British division—about 145,000 troops with about 250 Abrams tanks and the same number of Bradley fighting vehicles—left bases in Kuwait to invade southern Iraq. The marines and British commandos rushed to the Rumalyah oil fields, where over 450 active wellheads were supplying the regime with over $50 million a day. The troops quickly secured the area so the retreating Iraqi army could not sabotage the wells as they had done in 1991, which cost the nation millions in petrodollars. British troops cut off Iraq's second-largest city, Basra, from the rest of the nation and began a siege as the Americans sped up the main road to secure the bridges across the Euphrates River near the town of An Nasiriyah.

The invading army was confronted with a weak Iraqi military that was about one-third the size of their 1991 force—about 400,000 troops with 4,000 tanks and other armored vehicles. Their best equipment had been destroyed in 1991 and what remained was antiquated and in need of spare parts. Their T-55 tanks, for example, were 50-year-old death traps when fighting high-tech and fast U.S. armored vehicles. As commander-in-chief, Saddam was inept, and his political needs largely determined his military defense. He aimed to suppress local uprisings or perhaps a military coup, so even as U.S. and British troops advanced into Iraq, Saddam's forces were stationed miles from the border and were ineffective in blunting an invasion. Some of his Republican Guard troops put up a fight, but most in the Iraqi military were conscripts and they did not respond the way the U.S. administration and military officials had hoped—mass capitulation. Instead, they melted away, offering light or no resistance before they took off their uniforms and started walking home.

The most dangerous threat came from irregular forces collectively known as the fedayeen, or "martyrs," named after the Islamic fighters who defeated the Soviet army in Afghanistan. They were fanatical regime loyalists who dressed as civilians and ambushed the invading force with rocket-propelled grenades (RPGs), mortars, or AK-47 assault rifles. At the southern town of As Samawah, Sergeant Anthony Broadhead led a hunter-killer team of five Abrams and Bradleys to the bridge before the town, where a number of local people had gathered. He waved, and "total mayhem broke out!" About 200 fedayeens attacked, often at range so close that the RPGs did not have the necessary velocity to explode so they bounced off armored vehicles. The Americans returned fire, killing many before Broadhead took an AK-47 round in the chest. Fortunately, it hit his flak jacket, but a mortar round pounded a palm tree above his tank and shrapnel hit his arms, legs, and burst his eardrum. "We hauled ass out of there," Broadhead recalled, and it took a larger force and air and artillery strikes before the Americans could kill off the fedayeens, secure As Samawah, and continue north toward Baghdad. In one area along that road, fedayeens attacked U.S. units so often they labeled it "Ambush Alley."

General Franks and the military had not predicted that type of irregular war, but they were better prepared for Iraqi missiles and WMDs. During the first two weeks the Iraqis fired 17 old short-range missiles at coalition forces and facilities in Kuwait. The U.S. responded by destroying them with Patriot missiles, which had been greatly improved since they first had been deployed 12 years earlier in Desert Storm. In case the enemy employed WMDs, U.S. ground forces were supplied with the proper masks and protective gear.

Another threat came from the weather. An enormous sandstorm momentarily slowed the attack, as visibility dropped to a few meters. "It was like a tornado of mud," said Major General David Petraeus, commander of the 101st Airborne Division. A marine officer added, "That was the darkest, blackest night of my life. Night vision goggles would not even work." Wisely, theater commanders decided to use the weather to their advantage. Many enemy tanks situated south of Baghdad dug in to defend the capital. Employing infrared and thermal sensors, along with global positioning systems, Franks launched bombers that flew above the storm and delivered precision-guided bombs through the sand, decimating enemy tanks and opening the way to Baghdad. An Iraqi general later said about the bombardment, "The Iraqi will to fight was broken outside Baghdad."

After the storm the force continued at lightning speed—251 miles in six days, from As Samawah to An Najaf to Karbala—two-thirds of the way to Baghdad. "We weren't marching to Baghdad," said Franks's deputy Lieutenant General Michael DeLong, "we were sprinting there." The marines charged north from the southeast and the army rushed from the southwest toward the Karbala Gap, a narrow area with steep banks and marshy ground that led to the bridges that crossed the Euphrates, the gateway to Baghdad. For two days the Republican Guard put up a fierce defense, but by the afternoon of April 2, U.S. tanks were rolling over the bridges. "At that point," said the army commander Lieutenant General William "Scott" Wallace, "I was pretty confident that we had Saddam by the balls."

The road to Baghdad was open. On April 3, 20 Abrams and Bradleys stormed to the western outskirts of the capital, just outside Saddam International Airport. For the next 24 hours, the fighting vehicles engaged the enemy alone as waves of fedayeens attacked on any available transportation—trucks, buses, cars, motorcycles, and on foot. By daybreak, 500 Iraqi bodies littered the field when Republican Guard tanks surprised the Americans. In less than five minutes, four U.S. vehicles destroyed 12 enemy tanks; later that afternoon the Americans discovered more enemy vehicles and engaged them at short range. In 10 minutes, U.S. armor had destroyed 16 Iraqi tanks. That evening, the Abrams and Bradleys secured the tarmac and terminal and the soldiers renamed the facility Baghdad International Airport.

Just a few miles away, from the center of the capital, the Iraqi information minister announced to his listeners, "There are no American infidels in Baghdad. Never!"

Lieutenant General Dave McKiernan, the commander of all land forces for Operation Iraqi Freedom, realized that his campaign had been rewarded for audacity and thought that the Iraqis would be unable to defend Baghdad. He and his subordinates ordered the first "thunder run," charges of armored vehicles into the capital, which military planners thought would be a "hornets' nest." "Speed kills," General Franks had declared, and he was correct as about 30 Abrams and 15 Bradleys roared into the streets of the capital at first light on April 5. A U.S. officer watched the convoy pass: "It was an incredible sight! Drivers and tank commanders were firing as fast as they could, and they were *flying*! They must have been going 50 miles per hour."

The defenders were stunned that the Americans could launch an attack so fast after capturing the airport. Many were waking up, and they rushed out into the streets shooting wildly. But U.S. armor was nearly impervious to Iraqis' rifles and RPGs, and as the enemy exposed themselves they also were sighted and destroyed by A-10 Warthog antitank aircraft and helicopter gunships. "Fighting became particularly surreal as the column approached the center of Baghdad," an eyewitness reported, "women and children stood along the street or on rooftops, taking in the carnage before them with the seemingly casual interest of fans watching a soccer match on television."

About 2,000 Iraqis died. Only one Abram tank was disabled; the crew escaped unharmed, and the armor returned to the airport as the Iraqi information minister declared on radio: "The American louts fled. Indeed, concerning the fighting waged by the heroes of the Arab Socialist Baath Party yesterday, one amazing thing really is the cowardice of the American soldiers. We had not anticipated this."

Nor had the regime anticipated the second thunder run on April 7. Reinforcements had arrived, and 70 Abrams and 60 Bradleys sped out of the airport. Commanders decided that this was not to be like the first one, a "drive-by-shooting," but a bold raid to capture the palace complex, the heart of Saddam's regime in downtown Baghdad. Hundreds of fedayeen attacked, but they were mowed down all day long, and the Americans reached the palace and stayed there overnight. A few fedayeen attacked but were unaware of the capability of U.S. thermal sights and were killed by soldiers they never saw. By morning, sporadic suicide attacks were all that remained of Iraqi resistance. Most officials of the regime disappeared; many fled north, except for the Iraqi information minister, who was captured.

Two days later on April 9, embedded journalists transmitted one memorable scene back to American televisions—Iraqis pulling down the large statue of Saddam in Firdaus Square in downtown Baghdad. Once on the ground, the locals attacked the statue with sledgehammers and broke off the head, which they dragged through the streets; people spit at it and hit it with their shoes. Seeing that statue come down, said one U.S. observer, was "as good as it got, the high-water mark of the invasion." Secretary Rumsfeld put the spectacle into historical perspective, "Watching them, one cannot help but think of the fall of the Berlin Wall and the collapse of the Iron Curtain."[1]

Saddam was now a fugitive. His regime had collapsed in only three weeks, and the toll for the victors was relatively light; only 33 British troops died and 122 Americans, a majority of those caused by accidents or friendly fire. During the remainder of April, U.S. troops did mopping up operations and spread out to secure a larger portion of Iraq.

Back in America, neocons gloated. Ken Adelman, who a year earlier had called a potential war against Iraq a "cakewalk," now lambasted those "frightful forecasters" such as Brent Scowcroft who had advocated caution and opposed the Iraq war. The reason for the "crushing win," he declared, was Cheney, Wolfowitz, and his former boss Rumsfeld, who had fashioned "a most creative and detailed war plan." The administration's allies at FOX News chimed in. Bill O'Reilly had predicted that "military action will not last more than a week." "It gets easier," Fred Barnes added, "setting up a democracy is hard, but not as hard as winning a war." MSNBC's Chris Matthews summed up the jubilation: "Americans love having a guy as president, a guy who has a little swagger. . . . The women like this war. I think we like having a hero as our president. It's simple."

Victory adrenalin continued pumping on May 1 when the president flew out to the USS *Abraham Lincoln*. The aircraft carrier was outside of San Diego Bay, awaiting the commander-in-chief. Trained in the Texas Air National Guard to be a pilot, Bush and a copilot landed on the deck of the carrier and deplaned to cheering sailors. He addressed the crew, admitting that "our mission continues" and that there remained "difficult work to do in Iraq." But what was remembered from the speech was his declaration, "major combat operations in Iraq have ended. In the battle of Iraq, the United States and our allies have prevailed." Behind him waved a banner: MISSION ACCOMPLISHED.

The real mission, however, was just beginning.

"History will record that America's . . . plan for Operation Iraqi Freedom was a good plan," wrote General Franks, "and that the execution of that plan by our young men and women in uniform was unequaled in its excellence by anything in the annals of war." While it might have seemed that way when Saddam's statue was brought down in Baghdad, shortly thereafter many began questioning the plan because the general's "speed kills" also meant that the troops bypassed the fedayeen, leaving many of the enemy at large and ammunition dumps unguarded. "Why Aren't There Enough Troops in Iraq?" editorialized the retired CENTCOM commander Marine General Joseph Hoar in April. "The fact is that more ground troops are needed." A widely cited report published after the invasion concluded that occupying forces would need 20 security personnel (police and soldiers) per 1,000 people, compared to the 43 per 1,000 that sustained Saddam in power. The report noted that in order to impose order in postinvasion Baghdad, a city with over 5 million, the coalition should have had tens of thousands of military police, and to secure 25 million Iraqis living in a land mass the size of California, the coalition should have sent about three times more troops, between 400,000 and 500,000. Saddam employed at least half a million soldiers and policemen to control his population—and they spoke the language. Theater commander General McKiernan eventually agreed: "While we might not have needed" more soldiers "to remove the top part of the regime, and to get into Baghdad, we needed [them] for everything after that."

The argument over the number of troops in Operation Iraqi Freedom in many ways was a legacy from Operation Desert Storm in 1991. Then chairman of the Joint Chiefs of Staff, Colin Powell employed massive airstrikes and some 400,000 land forces to overwhelm Saddam's army and rout them out of Kuwait. This decisive intervention became known as the Powell Doctrine, and by 2001 General Zinni maintained that to control all of Iraq, the U.S. would have to deploy 380,000 troops. But when Rumsfeld became secretary of defense that same year, he advocated a leaner, faster, more mobile, high-tech, and more lethal military. In one of the first meetings on Iraq between Rumsfeld, the JCS, General Franks and his subordinates during the fall of 2001, the officers outlined a plan that called for several hundred thousand troops, as many as 500,000. Rumsfeld was irritated and told the generals that he didn't see why they would need more than 125,000, which was passed on to the war planners at Central Command. The JCS did not protest and Franks drew up a new plan. So instead of counting on the necessary troops to occupy and then police Iraq, CENTCOM hoped, even planned, that Saddam's army would capitulate, control the nation's borders, and help police their own country.

Iraqi help did not appear, and subsequent events followed preinvasion predictions made by American experts familiar with Iraq. After Saddam's "boot is lifted from the neck of the Iraqis," wrote the journalist Sandra Mackey, who had lived for years in the Middle East, "a bloodbath is likely to ensue." The Iraqis would not be able to restore order, she continued, and the "United States will be drawn into Iraq in a role it might not choose but cannot avoid." The U.S. Army's study on reconstruction had predicted an "initial honeymoon" because "of ridding the population of a brutal dictator." But it cautioned that most Iraqis and other Arabs will assume that the United States intervened for its own reasons and that a "force initially viewed as liberators can rapidly be relegated to the status of invaders."

The honeymoon never arrived in Baghdad; instead, it was a mixed response. "We drove straight through the biggest market in Baghdad," wrote one army lieutenant. "Kids bounced on the hoods of cars, waving and smiling . . . the majority of people in Baghdad really did see us as heroes, liberating them from the madness and tyranny of Saddam." At times when the troops drove by people would yell, "Bad Saddam! Good Bush!" But not always. The NPR correspondent Anne Garrels was on the scene when Saddam's statue came down, reporting that the local people had "a very mixed feeling about seeing American soldiers in their midst." An Iraqi professor standing next to her said, "You understand, you will now have to be in complete control, and we will resent you every step of the way."

Other Iraqis did resent seeing U.S. troops as they drove into their cities while attempting to secure the rest of the country during April. Northern towns such as Samarra and Mosul were tense since the area was mostly Sunni and Saddam still had a following. After a few days of bombardment, the marines attacked Saddam's home town of Tikrit, which was defended by hundreds of loyalists who melted away in a couple days. U.S. troops also drove into the western Anbar Province into Ramadi and Hit, where they were greeted with sporadic attacks. When U.S. forces arrived in Fallujah, they were met with suspicion. Days later, Iraqis demonstrated against the American presence, and someone fired shots. U.S. troops fired back, killing 17 and wounding about 70. That provoked angry demonstrations, and seven soldiers were wounded in a grenade attack. The next day, hanging on a building next to the army compound was a sign in English: "U.S. killers, we'll kick you out."[2]

The fall of Baghdad did not mean the end of Iraqi resistance. The United States never was in control of Iraq, for that would have necessitated more troops. That did not fit the administration's postwar plans and assumptions. In January 2003, President Bush had signed a national security directive that reversed tradition that went back to World War II. Instead of placing the State Department in charge of postwar planning, that task now would be under the control of Rumsfeld and the Department of Defense. The directive also established a unit within the Pentagon, the Office of Reconstruction and Humanitarian Assistance (ORHA), that would administer Iraq immediately after the fall of Saddam's regime and would report back to the Pentagon. To lead ORHA the defense secretary picked a retired lieutenant general, Jay Garner. He seemed a logical choice. At the end of the Gulf War in 1991 he had directed Operation Provide Comfort, which operated in the mountains along the Turkish border and saved thousands of Kurds.

Garner picked a group of retired military officers to be his subordinates and on February 21 and 22 he convened a meeting of various officials to discuss postwar Iraq. This was notable—just three weeks before the war began, it was the first and only time that officials in all the government agencies met to discuss postwar planning; in contrast, Americans were making postwar plans almost three years before the end of World War II. In Garner's meeting there were officials from the vice president's office and National Security Council, Pentagon and Central Command, CIA and DIA, State, Treasury, and Justice departments, and the British and Australian governments. Garner's aim was to provide postinvasion Iraq with three pillars, which he called humanitarian assistance, reconstruction, and civil administration.

The February meeting revealed major problems. Plans for running Iraq's postwar government were rudimentary, and ORHA had almost no information or ideas on the topic. As one participant said, the "humanitarian stuff was pretty well in place, but the rest of it was flying blind." Others asked about the lack of resources to do the job; one part of the plan was estimated to cost $3 billion and they only had $37,000.

Another official worried that there were not going to be enough troops on the ground "for the first step of securing all the major urban areas, let alone for providing an interim police function." A final problem was tension between Powell's and Rumsfeld's subordinates. "State and Defense were at war—don't let anyone tell you different," one Pentagon officer said. "Within policy circles, it was knee-jerk venom, on both sides."

One of the divisive points between State and Defense was the role of Ahmed Chalabi and his Iraqi National Congress (INC). Pentagon neocons eagerly embraced him, and on April 5, Wolfowitz overruled CENTCOM and ordered the military to airlift Chalabi and about 700 members of his Free Iraqi Force, armed with American weapons, into southern Iraq at Nasiriya, 230 miles south of Baghdad. The Free Iraqi Force began commandeering property and vehicles, and after those men arrived in Baghdad, CENTCOM received reports that they looted and robbed local inhabitants. "I thought Chalabi ran a political party," one Iraqi said to a CIA official. "In the United States do your political parties have their own militias?"

The State Department and the CIA distrusted and even hated Chalabi, but neocons thought that he would be an ideal leader of a new Iraq. "You know, Jay," the Pentagon's Doug Feith said to General Garner, "when you get there, we could just make Chalabi president." Garner had little trust in Chalabi, calling him "a thug, very sleazy," and he made that clear during a briefing. Afterward, Feith shouted at the general that he shouldn't be disrespectful to Chalabi, to which the general replied, "Doug, you've got two choices. You can shut the fuck up, or you can fire me."

Feith's boss, Rumsfeld, did not fire Garner, but instructed him to continue working on reconstruction issues. He did and the result was The Unified Mission Plan for Post-Hostilities Iraq. The ORHA aimed to quickly rebuild damaged utilities, get ministries running, appoint an interim government, write a constitution, hold elections, and hand over power to a new Iraqi government. The entire document was only 25 pages and it never was approved by anyone at the Pentagon; nor was it distributed to the ORHA team. The document was dated a week after the fall of Baghdad.

"That wasn't a plan," said an ORHA member, Barbara Bodine. "It was an outline that never saw the light of day. The 'plan' was to be out of Iraq by the end of August." Garner told some ORHA team members that he expected to be out of Iraq in 90 days, and when Rumsfeld's spokesman Larry Di Rita met with ORHA's senior officials, he declared, "We're going to stand up an interim Iraqi government, hand over power to them, and get out of there in three to four months." He continued, "All but twenty-five thousand soldiers will be out by the beginning of September."

Thus, the administration behaved the same way rushing to war as preparing for postwar Iraq. In both cases it constructed its own reality and expected everyone else, now including all Iraqis, to behave accordingly. The Pentagon and White House convinced themselves of the most optimistic assumptions. "Our plan called for . . . victory in as quick as sixty days," wrote Lieutenant General DeLong, "and we believed that once Baghdad fell, the war would be won." The White House concurred. The president convened a meeting on April 15 and told his top aides to develop a plan to withdraw from Iraq and the Pentagon issued orders that month—later reversed—that U.S. troops would be withdrawn and reduced to a force of only about 30,000 by August 1. That would be possible because a large number of Iraqi troops, security forces, and police supposedly would be willing to switch sides and support the occupation. "The concept was that we would defeat the army," recalled Condi Rice, "but the institutions would hold, everything from ministries to police forces." The Pentagon leadership assumed the same thing. Those officials thought U.S. troops would arrive to find "a fully functioning Iraqi bureaucracy," recalled the OHRA member, Bodine. "They would all be in their offices, at their desk, pen and paper at the ready. And we would come in and essentially . . . take them off the pause button." As soon as civilian Iraqis were freed from dictatorship there would be "a *Wizard of Oz* moment," recalled another OHRA member, Major General Carl Strock. Cheering Iraqis would hail their liberators, support American troops, help in their own reconstruction, and quickly establish a democratic Iraq. Moreover, the administration assumed that Iraqi oil exports would pay for much of the rebuilding and that the economy would rebound. In fact, Saddam's economy was in a state of near collapse and had been throughout the 1990s because of sanctions imposed after the 1991 Gulf War. "By the time Iraq was occupied in 2003," wrote one expert, "the country had one of the most dysfunctional and distorted economies of the world." The administration even had convinced itself that the international community—including nations who had opposed the war, along with nongovernmental organizations (NGOs)— would come to the aid of the new country. In that April 15 meeting the president discussed soliciting international troops. The Pentagon thought that the administration could convince four nations, even Arab countries and NATO, to send divisions. Supposedly, those foreign troops would arrive during the summer and take over peacekeeping duties in Iraq.

Believing in those assumptions meant that there was little reason to draw up a detailed and sophisticated postwar reconstruction plan, so-called Phase IV. "There was no real plan," said the Pentagon officer Lieutenant General Joseph Kellogg Jr. "The thought was, you didn't need it. The assumption was that everything would be fine after the war, that they'd be happy they got rid of Saddam."

Such assumptions led to surreal situations after the invasion. On the second day of the war a U.S. Agency for International Development (USAID) official met with civil-affairs officers just inside Iraq. "What's the plan for policing?" one official asked another. "I thought you knew the plan," the other responded. "No, we thought you knew." "Haven't you talked to ORHA?" the first one asked. "No, no one talked to us."[3]

Soon, the victorious U.S. Army became caught in the swift currents of geography, history, ethnic identity, religion, sectarianism, tribalism, and a large number of resentful former members of the defeated Baathist government. In an astonishingly short period of time, Iraq began to disintegrate.

Just days after Saddam's statue was pulled down, thousands of looters appeared and began to pillage government buildings in Baghdad. U.S. bombs had disabled telephone switching centers and had damaged much of the city's electrical capacity. Now, looters destroyed even more of the city while American troops stood by, for the Pentagon had issued no rules of engagement for the army occupying the city. Within days, 17 of 23 ministries were ransacked. The Iraqi police force abandoned their posts and looters picked clean their stations; they did the same to the city's computerized control center. Hoards then turned on schools, hospitals, wealthy neighborhoods, and even the sewage treatment plants. They stole computers, air conditioners, tables, chairs, telephones, televisions, virtually anything that they could carry away. In the ministries, they often carried away file cabinets that contained important documents, personnel rosters, and necessary blueprints to restart a new government. Looters walked into power plants and stripped copper wire from the electrical and communication systems, took down transmission lines, destroying electricity and telephone service. "They just started at one end of the transmission line and worked their way up, taking down the towers, taking away valuable metals, smelting it down, selling it in Iran and Kuwait," said a USAID official. "The price of metal in the Middle East dropped dramatically during this period of time." In May, a survey of Iraq's electrical system showed 13 downed transmission towers; four months later the total was 623.

Looters also attacked the Iraq Central Bank and Baghdad's National Museum. Bank security guards vanished, or helped in the theft, and men drilled or blew holes in safes and ran out with bags of money, much of it in euros or U.S. dollars. Between April 10–12, looters broke into one of the greatest museums of the ancient world and stole 15,000 ancient objects, including Abbasid wooden doors; Sumerian, Akkadian, and Hatraean statues; gold and silver necklaces, pendants, and pottery. What they could not carry away they smashed and destroyed, including the 4,000-year-old head of a terra-cotta lion from Tell Harmal and 2,000-year-old Roman statues. A reporter was on the scene, seeing rooms stripped bare, and "people with crowbars running in to pry open cases . . . floors covered in shattered, broken pottery." For the first time he began to think, "We've come here without a plan. It would have taken one tank in front of this building to have protected it."

The lawlessness was televised around the world and back to Washington, where Secretary Rumsfeld was holding a press conference. When asked about looting in Baghdad, he replied, "Stuff happens. Freedom's untidy, and free people are free to make mistakes and commit crimes and do bad things. . . . And while no one condones looting, on the other hand one can understand the pent-up feelings that may result from decades of repression." He asserted that the repeated television images of Iraqis ransacking buildings represented "a fundamental misunderstanding" of what really was happening in Iraq. One image played over and over again was of a man stealing a vase from the museum. Playing for laughs, he asked, "Is it possible that there were that many vases in the whole country?"

Iraqis weren't laughing in Baghdad, where the looting continued for two months. "This was going on in view of American soldiers, sometimes literally across the street," recalled the NPR reporter Ann Garrels. Another journalist on the scene added, "People were shocked that the U.S. did nothing, and they will forever remember that virtually the only building . . . that was protected was the Oil Ministry; that just summed up to so many Iraqis why the U.S. was there, and confirmed their worst fears." Moreover, the Iraqi Army had stored ammunition and arms throughout the country; with the collapse of that force most of that cache was not guarded, and soon looters were walking away with about one million tons of weapons and ammunition, everything from handguns to rocket-propelled grenades. The looting wasn't just Iraqis letting off steam, reveling in their new freedom, Garrels continued, "It was Baathists destroying documents—making Iraq ungovernable." Without personnel rosters, OHRA officials did not know who had run or who could now run the ministries. The lawlessness also had another impact on the populace—a growing distrust of their liberators. "We're incompetent, as far as they're concerned," said an American legal adviser. "The key to it all was the looting. That was when it was clear that there was no order. There's an Arab proverb: Better forty years of dictatorship than one day of anarchy."

The lawlessness meant that Iraqis' first taste of freedom was chaos. Saddam had been brutal, but at least the Baathists had maintained order, prevented violence in the streets, and kept on the water and electricity that ran the lights, computers, water pumps, and air conditioners in Baghdad. Now, in the wretched summer heat, often over 110 in the day, Saddam's certainty and stability had been replaced by American instability and uncertainty. "Anarchy ruled" in Baghdad, recalled an Army officer trying to impose security. "Banks were robbed, assassinations were common, and young attractive women were snatched from their homes. It was as though we'd popped the cork on Iraqi society after decades of repression, and it was ugly. . . . I felt like Wyatt Earp in Tombstone."

Eventually, American officials did a rough calculation of the looting—$12 billion. Thieves made the greatest single heist in history by stealing $900 million in U.S. bills and as much as $100 million worth of euros from the Iraq Central Bank. Some 15,000 items were stolen out of the National Museum; fortunately, archivists had confiscated many of the finest exhibits and hidden them in vaults. Still, 40 of the most famous pieces were stolen. Fifteen were eventually recovered, along with over 5,000 items of lesser importance. The gutted buildings, missing office files and computers, and damaged infrastructure would haunt every aspect of the massive task ahead—reconstruction.

The violence kept the U.S. reconstruction team stuck in Kuwait City, where they had been headquartered at the Hilton Hotel since mid-March. General Garner and about 400 members of ORHA did not arrive in the capital until April 21–23, moved into their headquarters at the Republican Palace on the Tigris River, and realized that the city had virtually no electrical power or telephone systems. Food and drinking water were scarce and so was gasoline; petroleum delivery trucks were attacked and soon lines at filling stations stretched over a mile. Moreover, Saddam had emptied prisons of thousands of criminals as he fled the city. Crime soared. "Carjackings are endemic," reported one official in Baghdad. "The evening air is full of gunfire." Garbage was piling up in the streets, and without television, there was no way for ORHA to get their messages, advice, and information to the people of Baghdad. Nor were there enough translators or military escorts to provide security for American personnel who were supposed to make contact with Iraqis who could help reestablish some political and social security in the capital. In postconflict reconstruction, said an American official, "you need to have the ability to deliver the resources right away. People in a desperate situation need help. Boy, that's a blindingly obvious insight."

In the confusion, Garner and his staff tried to find out which Iraqis could help them in reconstruction. By April 28, ORHA had contacted many local leaders and Garner held a meeting with 350 Iraqis at the Baghdad Convention Center. He told his audience that his eventual aim was to begin planning to turn political power back to the Iraqis, and he and his subordinates talked of protecting individual rights and the need for a new constitution. After a while a tribal sheikh stood up and said, "I have no running water, no electricity, no security—and you are talking about a constitution?" Another sheikh asked Garner, "Who's in charge of our politics?" and the ORHA director replied, "You're in charge."

There was a loud gasp in the room, said one witness. One American adviser realized that the Iraqis "were losing faith in us by the second."

The meeting revealed that, after 35 years of authoritarian government, no one was in charge of Iraq.[4]

While Garner tried to help the Iraqis form a provisional government, the U.S. military was conducting a massive search of the country. Saddam's regime had fallen, but there appeared a conspicuous problem: the dictator had not used Bush's casus belli—weapons of mass destruction—against U.S. or British troops.

"We know where they are," Rumsfeld claimed on March 30. "They're in the area around Tikrit and Baghdad and east, west, south, and north somewhat." Almost two weeks later, as the administration was beginning to feel heat from reporters, the White House press secretary Ari Fleischer declared, "We have high confidence that they have weapons of mass destruction. . . . This is what this war was about and is about. And we have high confidence they will be found."

Actually, WMDs never would be found since they did not exist, which surprised many Americans and Iraqis. Only Saddam, his sons, and his closest aides were aware of the nation's weapons supplies, and since Iraq had used chemical weapons against Kurds and Shiites and against Iran, the generals naturally thought that the dictator had hidden WMDs somewhere in the country. No Iraqi general knew where, or who possessed those weapons, and the military had made no preparations for the use of them before the U.S. invasion. In December 2002 Saddam had held meetings with his Revolutionary Command Council, Baath Party bosses, and top military commanders and shocked them—Iraq did not possess WMDs. Aware of that, the official who oversaw Iraq's military industry, a man in the position to know, wondered why the Bush administration continued to make WMD charges; in fact, he admitted after the invasion that the constant charges made him actually think that perhaps Saddam did have some hidden away someplace in Iraq.

The president ordered the army to find WMDs and eventually some 1,400 military and civilian personnel were searching for weapons, people the military desperately needed for security. To help in that task, U.S. inspection teams began chasing tips from Iraqis who were paid reward money for evidence, bogus or not, so scamming became big business in Iraq.

Back in Washington, administration officials waited nervously for news of WMDs. It was a "roller coaster," said one press aide. One day the army reported they found what they thought were containers of ricin, but it turned out to be curdled milk. Another day it was drums with an unknown powder, which proved to be pesticide. Then soldiers found "suspicious glass globes" which was cleaning fluid, and a trailer "mobile unit" had equipment but it was for separating water into hydrogen to be used in weather balloons. On and on. "We were getting lots of Elvis sightings," said a CIA spokesman. "As each day passed," recalled Assistant Secretary of State Carl Ford Jr., "it became more and more difficult to hold to the line that we're going to find them." Ford was reading classified reports coming from Iraq concerning interrogations of senior Iraqi officials and scientists. They all said the same thing, that they had no idea where Saddam had hidden WMDs. The U.S. Army gave them lie detector tests; they all passed. Some administration officials simply thought that the Iraqis were good liars, but others were beginning to realize that Saddam might not have WMDs. "Our common reaction" at the State Department, Ford recalled, was "holy shit, we're in trouble."

Trouble was brewing for the administration and that became obvious on May 3 when the president began to *reinterpret* his previous statements about WMDs. Speaking with reporters at his Crawford ranch, Bush first offered the standard line: "We'll find them. And it's just going to be a matter of time." Then he continued, "but what we're going— the world will find is, the man had a *program to develop* weapons of mass destruction." That sentence was significant. The president was beginning to change the talking points. Instead of there being "no doubt" that Iraq possessed and concealed "some of the most lethal weapons ever devised" and that we are going to find "stockpiles of chemical and biological weapons," as he and his subordinates had declared for over nine months, Bush now was talking about "a program to develop" WMDs. On May 29, the president gave an interview to a Polish journalist, one of the few nations who joined his coalition. The reporter prodded Bush, "But still, those countries that did not support the Iraqi freedom operation still use the same argument—weapons of mass destruction have not been found." "We found the weapons of mass destruction," the president now claimed, stating that two mobile laboratories "to build biological weapons" had been located, promising more to come. "We found them." The talking points had shifted again; Bush saw no distinction between facilities and weapons. A month later, the White House spokesman Ari

Fleischer put a new twist on Saddam and the weapons issue. "I think the burden falls on those who think he *didn't have them* to explain when he destroyed them and why, after he destroyed them, he didn't tell anybody or show anybody." So, the fact that Saddam did not have WMDs was the fault of people who doubted that he possessed them in the first place, not the administration who took the nation to war to prevent Iraq from attacking the U.S. with "some of the most lethal weapons ever devised." Since they never could locate any WMDs, the administration continued to talk about mobile biological laboratories for months. By the end of the year, the new interpretation was stated by the president during an interview: "we got rid of him and there's no doubt the world is a safer, freer place as a result of Saddam being gone."

During the next months and years Bush, Rice, Tenet, and many other administration officials stated that every government in the world thought Saddam had WMDs. True, the dictator did nothing to dissuade his neighbors from that belief—especially his hated enemy Iran, who he feared would launch an attack against his country—but it is untrue to say the world thought Saddam had WMDs. Frankly, most nations did not know, and there even was doubt within U.S. intelligence agencies. The CIA's Paul Pillar admitted that in the agency there was a lot of disagreement about Saddam's WMD threat, if he had a nuclear weapons program, and if there was a connection between Iraq and al Qaeda. Secretary Powell later admitted that he had doubts, as did his chief of staff, Colonel Lawrence Wilkerson, who, like many, labeled the administration's use of evidence "cherry picking." As for other nations, most of them wanted the UN to conclude its inspections inside Iraq to determine if Saddam possessed WMDs, and they certainly didn't think that the possession of those weapons was casus belli. Nevertheless, almost everyone in the Bush administration had convinced themselves that Iraq had WMDs.

"The truth is that, for reasons that have a lot to do with the U.S. government bureaucracy," Paul Wolfowitz admitted in May, "we settled on the one issue that everyone could agree on, which was weapons of mass destruction as the core reason" to go to war.

There also was another type of WMD missing from Iraq. No one could locate the "smoking gun in the form of a mushroom cloud," an Iraqi atomic bomb or at least the appropriate equipment and African uranium to build such a device. "We do know, with absolute certainty," Cheney had declared, that Saddam was "using his procurement system to acquire the equipment he needs in order to enrich uranium to build a nuclear weapon." That talking point also began to unravel on May 6 when the *New York Times* columnist Nicholas Kristof wrote in his opinion piece that there were "indications that the U.S. government souped up intelligence, leaned on spooks to change their conclusions and concealed contrary information to deceive people at home and around the world." He was writing about the "Niger caper," Iraq's alleged attempts to buy uranium from Niger so it could build nuclear weapons. His source was a former U.S. ambassador who had been dispatched more than a year before to Niger, debunked the uranium sales story, and reported that back to the administration. Two months later, the former ambassador Joseph Wilson confirmed Kristof's article in his own op-ed piece, entitled "What I Didn't Find in Africa."[5]

Thus, less than two months after Bush started the war, the administration's rationale for the conflict was being questioned, and so was Jay Garner's mission in Baghdad. Bad news reached the White House from many sources, including the British. London had put their ambassador to Egypt, John Sawers, in charge of their occupation in Iraq, and he sent a message to 10 Downing Street entitled "Iraq: What's Going Wrong?" "Garner's outfit, ORHA, is an unbelievable mess," Sawers reported. "No leadership, no strategy, no coordination, no structure, and inaccessible to ordinary Iraqis. . . . Garner and his team of 60-year-old retired generals are well-meaning, but out of their depth." Americans in the country were reporting similar concerns through other channels, while at home, citizens were watching the violence and looting on their televisions, which prompted reporters to continually question Rumsfeld. The secretary concluded it was time for a change in Baghdad.

Rumsfeld dismissed Garner, dissolved the ORHA, and on May 6 introduced his new man to head the Coalition Provisional Authority (CPA), L. Paul "Jerry" Bremer, with a mandate to provide security, get the economy moving, and eventually work to create an interim or provisional government. Jerry Bremer had attended Yale University and in 1962 joined the State Department. He had been an assistant to former secretaries of state Henry Kissinger and Alexander Haig, ambassador to the Netherlands, and head of the department's office on counterterrorism.

After retiring from the department in the late 1980s he worked for Kissinger and Associates, the former secretary of state's business consulting firm. Bremer, a bedrock Republican and devout Catholic, was not an expert on the Middle East, but that did not concern Rumsfeld. He wanted someone who did not hold preconceived notions about the area; many of the government's Arab experts did not feel that Iraq would be a good proving ground for democracy, an idea which ran counter to the neocons' view. The new appointee only had about a week to prepare for one of the most difficult jobs in the world, and on May 12 he landed in the Iraqi capital and moved into his headquarters, a secure area that became known as the Green Zone. He quickly concluded, "Baghdad was burning."

As Bremer settled in his new job, the U.S. military command was rapidly changing in Iraq and the United States. Most of the top American commanders began leaving the Iraq theater. On July 1, General Franks retired. He had decided not to accept the position of army chief of staff. "I'm a warfighter," Franks said to Rumsfeld, "not a manager." He recommended General John Abizaid, who became the new commander of CENTCOM, while the theater commander in Iraq, Lieutenant General McKiernan, was replaced by a smaller force and staff under the command of Major General Ricardo Sanchez. "Allowing McKiernan to leave was the worst decision of the war," one general recalled. On McKiernan's staff were several hundred intelligence officers who were trying to comprehend the immediate situation inside Iraq; they were replaced by fewer than 30 such officers. "We were starting from scratch," stated an officer in Iraq, "with practically no resources."

At the time when experience and knowledge were desperately needed to secure the occupied country, to bring about stability and put local people back to work, the White House and Pentagon brought in new commanders and administrators inexperienced in Iraq, including Jerry Bremer, who had no experience in nation-building, had never been to Iraq, and did not speak Arabic.

Bremer's tenure as head of CPA got off to a rocky start. He was not interested in accepting advice from Garner, who remained in the country for a couple of weeks, and he was brash with the remaining American military commanders in Iraq, Lieutenant General Scott Wallace and Major General Ricardo Sanchez. "I'm the CPA Administrator and I'm in charge," Bremer declared in his first meeting with Wallace. No one questioned that Bremer was the senior U.S. representative in Iraq, the president's envoy, but the Pentagon never clarified the command relationship between Bremer and the U.S. military in Iraq. Bremer was not a proconsul; he was not the commander of the military and the CPA. In fact, both worked for Rumsfeld. Bremer demanded that Wallace move his headquarters into the Green Zone. The general moved the command. Shortly thereafter Wallace made a comment to the press expressing his concerns about a potential insurgency, noting that his forces did not have plans for that type of enemy. Bremer was angered, the Pentagon relieved Wallace of duty—the last general with combat experience in Iraq. Sanchez, who had been in the country for only three weeks, was promoted to lieutenant general and on June 10 became the commanding general of U.S. forces in Iraq.

From his office in the Green Zone, Bremer began making decisions that would have an impact on millions of Iraqis. Before the invasion, President Bush had decided on de-Baathification, to purge the ministries and country of the leading members of the Baath Party. The power structure had to be eliminated, and Bremer felt that it was essential to make clear to the local public that the Baathist ideology, which had been part of Saddam's dictatorship, would be extirpated from the society, as the United States did in post–World War II Germany, with de-Nazification of the former Third Reich. The comparison did not make much sense, since Germany was a homogeneous society, which was not the case with Iraq. Nevertheless, the question was, how deep to purge? Under Saddam, party membership had been a requirement for almost all government jobs. Virtually all civil servants, including teachers and professors, professionals and managers, military personnel, had no choice—they had to join the party. U.S. intelligence estimated that the Baath Party had about 600,000 to 700,000 members; others thought that there might be as many as two million with between 15,000 and 40,000 senior members, depending on how one distinguished that tier. The top echelon held the important positions running everything from the secret police to the universities and hospitals to waterworks. Even the exiled Iraqis disagreed on this issue. Ahmed Chalabi advocated a deep de-Baathification process, even disbanding the Iraqi military, while another influential exile, Ayad Allawi, favored a limited program that left many top civil servants on the job. Bremer wrote his opinion in a memo to the Pentagon. He wanted to ensure that "my arrival in Iraq be marked by clear, public and decisive steps to reassure Iraqis that we are determined to eradicate Saddamism."

Eradication, of course, was not easy. "There was a sea of bitching and moaning," Bremer emailed to his wife. Indeed. "*Holy Christ*," Garner said to himself when he heard the plan. "*We can't do this*." Garner went to Bremer's office, "Jerry, this is too harsh," and urged him to soften the order. "Absolutely not," Bremer responded. Another official who was overseeing five ministries said that the Baathists were "the brains of the government," the "ones with a lot of information and knowledge," and if they were sent home the CPA would have "a major problem" running the ministries. Bremer responded that the order was not open for discussion. The CIA station chief urged Bremer to reconsider; he refused. Do this, warned the CIA official, and "by nightfall you'll have driven 30,000 to 50,000 Baathists underground. And in six months, you'll really regret this." Other CPA officials agreed, urging caution and delay, but on May 16, Bremer issued Coalition Provisional Authority Order Number One, "De-Baathification of Iraq Society." The commission was co-chaired by Chalabi, who obtained party membership records and began the purge. No one knows how many were fired. Bremer later maintained only 15,000 to 30,000 but critics maintain as many as 100,000 civilians were forced from their positions, which closed some of the factories, ministries, and public facilities that had remained open after the invasion. In some Sunni areas, only one or two teachers now were able to work at a school. Whatever the number tossed out of work, it meant that CPA officials were spending the next months doing background checks on thousands of Iraqis who wanted to return to their previous jobs. "It was a terrible waste of time," recalled one official. "There were so many more important things we could have been doing, like starting factories and paying salaries."

That same day, May 16, Bremer and General Abizaid met with exiled Iraqi leaders who had returned to their native country to begin the process of establishing a provisional Iraqi government. Invited to the meeting were Chalabi of the Iraqi National Congress, Ayad Allawi of the Iraqi National Accord, Jalal Talabani and Massoud Barzani of Kurdish parties, Ibrahim al-Jaafari of the Shiite Islamic Dawa Party, and others who represented the Supreme Council for the Islamic Revolution in Iraq (SCIRI). Bremer informed the exiles that the Bush administration wanted a broader coalition and that the CPA was "not about to turn over the keys to the kingdom," which is what many of the exiles wanted. They all thanked the American generals for ridding the nation of Saddam but complained about the violence in the streets. "There is a security vacuum," said Allawi. "Lawlessness, street crime that we have never experienced before." General Abizaid asked the Iraqis to come up with "practical solutions" to help solve the problem, and Bremer changed the topic and announced that the "path to representative government will be incremental," which dismayed the former exiles. Talibani warned against "squandering a military victory by not conducting a rapid, coordinated effort to form a new government." Another urged, "Ambassador, you must hasten the political progress. The 'street' is waiting for the freedom you promised." Bremer again said that the process would be incremental, adding, "this body is not representative. There is only one Arab Sunni leader among you. There are no Turkmen here, no Christians, no women."

Bremer concluded the meeting by asking them to meet again in two weeks and told them that he hoped the next time he would see a broader group that included indigenous Iraqis. The former exiles left, unhappy with Bremer. The United States and Britain compounded the problem by sponsoring a UN resolution that would basically give them the status of occupying powers in Iraq, which again frustrated many Iraqis. Many began to wonder if the U.S. and U.K. were trying to establish a colony and if Bremer was the new proconsul.

Bremer worked for two months to form an indigenous government, which seemed a long time to many Iraqis. To them, liberation was turning into occupation. In mid-July he finally picked 25 Iraqis, whom the UN presented to the country. Some were former exiles but most were indigenous and they formed the Iraqi Governing Council (IGC). The CPA director worked with the IGC to accomplish three responsibilities: appoint ministers to the Iraqi cabinet, approve a budget for 2004, and begin the process of writing an Iraqi constitution. The first president was a physician and Shiite leader, al-Jaafari, but that office rotated to a new person every month, resulting in many months of an ineffective Iraqi leadership. All the while Bremer remained in control; an American made the final decisions.

On the local level, de-Baathification meant that mayors were dismissed and the occupying forces had to find new leaders. The result was an ad hoc affair in which military commanders tried to find "figures of local influence." Since the coalition military leaders did not know Arabic and had too few translators, their initial picks often displayed their ignorance of Iraqi society. In Basra, for example, the British first announced that they had "a tribal leader," but when they announced his name there was almost a riot since he had been a former high ranking officer in the army and Baath Party. Embarrassed, the British dropped him and after a few days announced a new leader who they described as "the wealthiest businessman" in the city. Again, locals were outraged since it was well known that this candidate, like most wealthy Iraqis, was a business partner of Saddam's son, Uday Hussein.[6]

A week after Bremer announced de-Baathification, on May 23, he issued Order Number Two, "Dissolution of Entities," abolishing the Iraqi military. The Pentagon leadership ordered this, but it was opposed by the State Department, Jay Garner, and the top three U.S. generals in the theater. Garner had publicly stated in Baghdad that he wanted to employ the former Iraqi Army in reconstruction and security. As one intelligence officer said, Saddam's army "is solid, it has structure and discipline, and credibility inside Iraq." In mid-April General Abizaid had "strongly recommended" that a large Iraqi army be reestablished immediately to "take over internal security functions as quickly as possible," and in another memo the general declared an "urgent need to maintain order, suppress various militias, put an Iraqi face on security and relieve burden on Coalition military." At that same time, one of Garner's top planners, Colonel Paul Hughes, was meeting with former Iraqi officers. They told Hughes that they had the names of between 50,000 and 70,000 former soldiers who would come forward and form a security and police force if the CPA only would pay their salaries. By mid-May some 30,000 former members of the Iraqi army had registered for emergency payments and desired to return to active duty.

Bremer refused. Order Number Two meant that, in effect, the United States double-crossed the Iraqi army. The U.S. Air Force had dropped millions of leaflets telling Saddam's soldiers not to fight, or as General Zinni said, "We had spent a decade psyopsing the Iraqi army, telling them we would take care of those who didn't fight." America invaded, the Iraqi army didn't put up much resistance, and instead of taking care of those veterans, Bremer fired them, tossing 400,000 men out of work. Soon, many former soldiers were picketing outside the gates of the CPA. One banner read that disbanding the army was a "humiliation to the dignity of the nation."

In one week, therefore, the CPA issued two orders that fired over a half million people—without pay for them and their families. Many had no pension. That had a profound impact on Iraq. When Bremer disbanded the Iraqi army, said an American colonel, "the insurgency went crazy. May was the turning point . . . that was it. Every moderate, every person that had leaned towards us, was furious. One Iraqi who had saved my life in an ambush said to me, 'I can't be your friend anymore.'" In late May and early June, dismissed workers and soldiers held demonstrations. The protest continued, and on June 18 some 2,000 former soldiers gathered outside the Green Zone, some carrying placards: PLEASE KEEP YOUR PROMISES. "We will take up arms," one declared. "We are all very well-trained soldiers and we are armed. We will start ambushes, bombings and even suicide bombings. We will not let the Americans rule us in such a humiliating way." U.S. soldiers panicked and fired into the crowd, killing two.

Bremer then announced an order of lesser importance but also with the potential of affecting many Iraqis. He initiated a program long advocated by many neocons, shifting Iraq from a more socialist economy with many state-run industries—including petroleum and electricity—to a free market system. The CPA aimed to "corporatize and privatize" almost 190 publicly owned companies, cutting subsidies to them, firing employees or forcing retirements. That alienated many workers and managers who were part of the middle class, a sector of society that already had been negatively affected by de-Baathification. Privatizing those industries was a long and difficult process, which by the end of the year was abandoned because of high Iraqi resistance and unemployment.

During his first month on the job, Bremer made significant decisions that reversed Garner's stated aims and alienated hundreds of thousands—perhaps millions—of Iraqis. Garner planned to turn power over to Iraqis while Bremer made sure they knew that the CPA was the ruler; Garner's team had been working with top civil servants to get the ministries functioning while Bremer's de-Baathification program fired most of them;

Garner had advocated recalling the Iraqi army while Bremer dissolved the armed forces. "We made hundreds of thousands of people very angry at us," said a Western diplomat in Iraq, "and they happened to be the people in the country best acquainted with the use of arms." CIA official John Maguire, who was on the scene, agreed that the orders "disenfranchised people with guns," while they "got rid of the technocrats—the people who ran the society—because it was a militarized society. It was a cataclysmic mistake." A State Department official added that the administration had "committed one of the greatest errors in the history of U.S. warfare: It unnecessarily increased the ranks of its enemies."

"We've made three tragic decisions," Garner told Rumsfeld on June 18 after he returned to Washington, DC, "terrible mistakes," and described them. "Well," said Rumsfeld, "I don't think there is anything we can do, because we are where we are." "They're all reversible," Garner countered, but Rumsfeld ended the conversation: "We're not going to go back."[7]

That same month Bremer unveiled plans for a New Iraqi Army that was aimed at helping coalition forces police the society, patrol borders, and provide security. CENTCOM had advocated immediately recalling about 100,000 former soldiers during the next nine months, but the Pentagon gave the orders. Bremer proposed a force one-third that size, which would be established slowly during the next two years.

By the first summer of the occupation, what little goodwill left toward the Americans began to evaporate in the hot Iraqi sun. Some of the problems were with the CPA. Like the administration in Washington, Bremer made rosy predictions about the situation in Iraq. Reporters described CPA briefings as "bizarre" and "cognitive dissonance." In one press conference, Bremer assured his audience that Baghdad was receiving 20 hours of electricity daily. "It simply isn't true," said an Iraqi journalist. "Everybody in Baghdad knows it," since the real number of electricity outside of the Green Zone was eight. Reconstruction would take years, and the Bush administration had underestimated the task. The CPA team had veteran professionals at senior positions but they rotated in and out of Iraq and lost continuity; only seven of Bremer's staff remained with him for the 14-month existence of the CPA. At lower levels the administration staffed the CPA with inexperienced Republican loyalists and campaign workers. Pentagon neocons often screened potential staff to make sure that they had the proper outlook and loyalty, not expertise in what they would be doing—nation-building. "The criterion for sending people over there," admitted the deputy director of the CPA's Washington office, "was that they had to have the right political credentials." The hiring process included interviews that asked questions that most employment lawyers would consider illegal: Who did you vote for? What are your views on *Roe v. Wade?* Are you a Muslim or Christian? Many of the employees were right out of college; perhaps half of them never had left the United States and they got their first passport to work in Iraq. One 24-year-old who never had worked in finance was given the job of opening a stock market in Baghdad, while the young daughter of a prominent neocon commentator with no background in accounting was chosen to manage Iraq's budget. Many of these 20-something conservatives aimed to complete Bush's "mission" of remaking Iraq in America's image and then get back to the United States so they could join the president's reelection campaign in 2004. Politics and contacts also were important for older job applicants. To privatize Iraq's industry, the administration sent a top Bush fundraiser with no experience in economic transactions or international law, which prohibits an occupying power from selling off the assets of a conquered country. To rebuild Iraq's health care system, Wolfowitz replaced one of the foremost experts in postconflict public health, an MD who served in Kosovo, Somalia, and Haiti, with a man without a medical degree, a Republican political appointee in Michigan who had worked at an adoption agency encouraging women not to have abortions. To run Iraq's higher education system, the Pentagon picked a person who was the former president of a small college with 500 students and a friend of the wives of Dick Cheney and Don Rumsfeld; and to rebuild the nation's public schools, they picked a man from the conservative Hoover Institution who had written on the need for school vouchers. None of these people had worked in postconflict reconstruction, spoke Arabic, or had any expertise in, or had been to, the Middle East. Nor did the Bush administration send enough people. The CPA was composed of only 1,147 Americans in July, of which just 34 were career Foreign Service Officers, with a charge of reconstructing an entire nation. The CPA staff was overwhelmed, working very long days. During the summer Bremer begged for more people, but the administration never could fill half of the mid-level and junior positions in the CPA.

Another problem was tension between the CPA and the U.S. military. On the lower level, many of the 20-something conservatives in the Green Zone treated soldiers like their errand boys, which resulted in ample resentment from troops. If these combat vets who dealt with the locals every day and got shot at didn't agree with the young officials' optimistic predictions about the future of Iraq, then the youngsters labeled them "defeatists." On a higher level, there was friction between CPA director Bremer and the top military commander Lieutenant General Sanchez; neither liked each other and the commander had openly opposed disbanding the military and de-Baathification. "We ordered military commanders to continue the recall of Iraqi former policemen," recalled Sanchez, and "every single policeman was a former member of the Baath Party."

By the summer, life in the Green Zone also began to irritate Iraqis. A seven-square-mile area on the west side of the Tigris River that had been home to Saddam's Republican Palace in central Baghdad, the Green Zone represented the West, not Iraq. Iraqis usually had to go to the zone to secure a reconstruction contract and eventually hundreds of locals worked as secretaries or translators where they witnessed the living situation of many young CPA officials. "Life in the Green Zone is thoroughly disconnected from the reality around," reported a journalist, it was "a little like Disneyland." While there was "anarchy" outside in the "Red Zone," inside Americans ate at cafeterias and restaurants that served bacon and pork in a Muslim land. They had laundry and bus services, and worked in air-conditioned comfort since they had their own diesel generators to produce electricity; fuel tankers arrived daily from Kuwait to keep the generators humming 24/7. Americans also had ways to relax, including listening to rock on Freedom Radio; attending the regular Bible study classes; taking a swim at the pool; pumping iron in one of the gyms; drinking beer, wine, or spirits at the half dozen bars; even going to the disco "at the al-Rashid Hotel where girls," the journalist continued, "would pack hot pants and four-inch heels" and dance "atop an illuminated Baath Party star." Being in the Green Zone "was sort of like taking a happy pill. And then you'd go out, and the real Iraq would confront you."

The real Iraq was difficult to comprehend, for during the first months of the occupation the nation was awash with rumors. With the end of Saddam's regime, the CPA advocated a free press and to transmit their interpretation of news it established the Iraq Media Network. Soon Iraqis became involved, and by June there were at least 85 new newspapers in the country, some aligned with new political parties, others with tribes or important clerics. The CPA did not censor. "President Bush said he had come as a liberator, not as an occupier," editorialized one Iraqi journalist. "However, Operation Iraqi Freedom cost the Iraqis thousands of martyrs, wounded, missing, and handicapped, who were all innocent." New local radio and television stations appeared, and so did regional ones, especially satellite channels such as Al Jazeera and Al Arabiyya, channels that had taken an antiwar stance before the invasion and ran stories about chaos and insecurity in Iraq. The Iranian station, Al Alam, beamed slanted messages to the Shiite majority. Internet service also became available during the summer, another venue to spread malicious stories about the occupation or rumors, especially about Israel and the Jews. By June, people were claiming that Jews were swarming into Baghdad to "buy homes, control the media, control trade," that Israeli brothels were built to look like mosques, and that the allegedly Jewish Coca-Cola logo really meant "No Mecca, No Muhammad."

Yet rumor and innuendo did not diminish reality on the street, for the real Iraq was unemployed and hungry, in need of massive reconstruction projects to restore public facilities. During the first four months after the fall of Saddam, the CPA only spent $23 million on reconstruction projects such as sewers, schools, bridges—less than a dollar for each Iraqi; billions more would be needed. "Infrastructure is the key now," a U.S. Army captain told a journalist in a slum south of Baghdad. "If these people have electricity, water, food, the basics of life, they're less likely to attack."[8]

Insurgents conducted scattered attacks during the hot, dusty summer. On June 13 the enemy struck in a town 20 miles north of Baghdad and the U.S. Army responded with massive force, killing at least 20. It was the bloodiest attack since the fall of the capital. "The undeniable fact," recalled General Sanchez, "was that we were still at war." While Rumsfeld dismissed the attacks and labeled the enemy as "just a bunch of dead-enders," Sanchez was not so sure. "We really had no idea what was in these uncleared areas and were very leery that there may have been organized elements of the enemy present." Saddam and most of his staff were alive and possibly in communication with his loyal followers; many wondered, had Saddam planned an insurgence? That month, as U.S. troops moved into cities, snipers often ambushed them, and there were close-range shootings on crowded streets. For grunts trying to win Iraqi hearts and minds, walking streets was "scary as hell," said one soldier. "Any man shaking your right hand could shoot you in the face with the gun in his left. . . . We were all on edge." Insurgents also began using roadside improvised explosive devices (IEDs) that blew up American trucks and Humvees. Soon grunts were making searches of anything on the sides of roads that might be hiding an IED—abandoned vehicles, piles of garbage, rotting dead dogs and horses.

There was another military problem—Iraq's porous borders. During the invasion thousands of Iraqis had fled to bordering nations and some of these people were beginning to supply the insurgency with money and men. Iraq had over 2,200 miles of borders, including 900 with Iran, 150 with Kuwait, almost 500 with Saudi Arabia, about 110 with Jordan, over 370 with Syria, and more than 200 with Turkey. In all of these nations there were potential insurgents who did not want American and British Christians occupying an Islamic country in the Middle East. "We did not seal the borders because we did not have enough troops to do that," recalled Jay Garner, "and that brought in terrorists."

Attacks on U.S. troops escalated throughout June. The press noted at the end of the month that more than 65 U.S. troops had died since Bush declared that major combat had ended on May 1. Moreover, WMDs had not been found, provoking additional criticism. To quell some of it, Rumsfeld held a news briefing at the Pentagon, where a reporter asked him to comment about two terms that commentators now were using about the conflict: "guerrilla war" and "quagmire." Privately, the CIA already had informed the president and his top aides that he faced a "classic insurgency," but the administration could not face reality, and the secretary responded that he didn't use "guerrilla war" "because there isn't one." The enemy were unorganized groups of "looters, criminals, remnants of the Baathist regime, foreign terrorists who came in to assist and try to harm the coalition forces, and those influenced by Iran." As for "quagmire," Rumsfeld said, "we're in a war. We're in a global war on terrorism."

The administration fought back the next day, July 1, when the president held a news conference. Naturally, he was asked about increasing attacks on U.S. troops in Iraq. "Anybody who wants to harm American troops will be found and brought to justice," Bush promised, and after saying that the United States was not going to leave prematurely, he switched to a combative tone: "There are some who feel like . . . the conditions are such that they can attack us there. My answer is bring them on. We got the force necessary to deal with the security situation."

"Bring them on" provoked outrage from Democrats. "I am shaking my head in disbelief," declared Senator Frank Lautenberg of New Jersey. "When I served in the Army in Europe during World War II, I never heard any military commander—let alone the commander-in-chief—invite enemies to attack U.S. troops." Representative Dick Gephardt lamented "the phony, macho rhetoric. . . . We need a serious attempt to develop a postwar plan for Iraq, and not more shoot-from-the-hip one-liners." There even was outrage in Baghdad, where one army officer saw the statement on CNN News and later wrote, "My soldiers and I were searching for car bombs . . . and scanning rooftops for snipers, and our president was in Washington taunting our enemies and encouraging them to attack us." Moreover, the officer continued, "The enemy was already 'bringing it on' all over Baghdad."

Privately, General Sanchez agreed. Struggling to stabilize Iraq, realizing that he was undermanned, Sanchez asked the new commander of CENTCOM, General Abizaid, to reverse General Franks's order to draw down American troops in Iraq. On July 11, Abizaid issued the reversal, writing that the "operational environment in Iraq is fluid and continuously being evaluated." Military forces that were scheduled to deploy back to the United States would remain in Iraq for one year. Rumsfeld reluctantly agreed, "but the Secretary really had no choice by then," wrote Sanchez. "It was either that or total chaos . . . we were facing an insurgency." When Abizaid returned to the Pentagon that month, he was asked about the situation in Iraq, and he responded that opponents of the occupation were "conducting what I would describe as a classical guerrilla-type campaign against us. . . . It's war, however you describe it."

To avoid an insurgency, the administration had planned on the help of foreign troops, but as soon as the international community saw the U.S. stumbling, few nations were eager to join what Bush had called the "coalition of the willing." The Saudis placed so many conditions on sending troops that it amounted to a refusal, and the United Arab

Emirates were not interested in sending troops to protect southern Iraqi oil fields. The Pentagon sent a general to India to ask that nation if they would deploy an entire division, about 30,000 troops, to help secure northern Iraq, but they refused because the invasion was not endorsed by the UN. The Australian, Italian, Spanish, and South Korean governments each sent a couple thousand troops, and, of course, the United Kingdom invaded with about 46,000. Although the British division was successful in combat and security in Basra, it was not very helpful in the rest of Iraq.

By August, a few thousand troops arrived from other nations, eventually reaching a 36-nation coalition, including forces from the Ukraine, Hungary, Slovakia, Georgia, Thailand, Poland, Nicaragua, Honduras, El Salvador, the Dominican Republic, and even Mongolia. They volunteered because the U.S. administration offered them financial and military aid. The Pentagon wanted to prove that there was international support for the Anglo-American policy in Iraq, when in fact, the coalition was plagued with problems; it was, recalled General Sanchez, "an extraordinary challenge." Language was a headache. The Pentagon did not require English-speaking troops, so for the Mongolian unit English policies and commands had to be translated into Polish, then into Russian, and finally into Mongolian. Moreover, the governments had placed so many restrictions on their service that Sanchez had to carry "a five-page spreadsheet listing all the countries [and] their rules of engagement." Sometimes the foreign contingents would follow an order, other times not, and they always were checking back with their own governments. Most of the international troops rarely saw any combat. The Lithuanian contingent was four doctors and a platoon, about 35 people, and a Ukrainian brigade was barely able to defend itself and retreated during their first serious attack. "So every time the use of offensive force was necessary to maintain security," wrote Sanchez, "we had to send American troops."[9]

All the while the situation deteriorated in Iraq. The insurgency didn't begin with an announcement from a religious leader or a former Baathist or with one significant event, but during August attacks increased against U.S. and British troops, against allies such as new Iraqi police and politicians, and against unguarded international agencies arriving during the summer such as the United Nations, International

Monetary Fund, and World Bank. On August 7, a car bomb detonated outside the Jordanian embassy in Baghdad, killing 11 and wounding more than 50. Many Iraqis felt that Jordan had helped U.S. troops during the invasion. As cars burned outside the embassy, General Sanchez arrived and proclaimed, "We're still in a conflict zone."

Chaos continued. On August 14, a U.S. helicopter accidentally knocked over a religious banner in Sadr City, Baghdad's Shiite slum named for the martyred father of Muqtada al-Sadr. Only 30, Sadr was a radical Shiite cleric who had a fanatical gang of several hundred armed followers, the Mahdi Army, and he was using his men to gain control of mosques; they were linked to recent killings and attacks on coalition forces. Sadr jockeyed with other clerics for influence that summer, such as the Grand Ayatollah Ali al-Sistani, the nation's highest Shiite cleric, and Ayatollah Mohammad Baqir al-Hakim, another important cleric in the holy city of Najaf and the leader of the Supreme Council for the Islamic Revolution in Iraq (SCIRI). When an American reporter met with leading clerics in Najaf, he was warned, "if the political system is against Islam, then we will fight it. No Muslim can be ruled by a non-Muslim."

The incident in Sadr City unleashed protests, riots, and more violence. Protestors called Sadr and asked him if they should now shoot at Americans. "Yes," he told them. "It is your duty." Thousands took to the streets and were met by U.S. troops, resulting in at least one Iraqi killed and many wounded. That same day insurgents killed a British soldier and wounded two others outside of Basra. The next day the enemy blew up an oil pipeline in Northern Iraq, which resulted in a large fire and disrupted petroleum exports to Turkey. On August 17, someone destroyed water mains in Baghdad, and five days later the enemy again attacked in Basra and killed three British soldiers. The next day insurgents attacked and killed three new Iraqi security guards in Najaf. In all of these attacks the U.S. military noticed that the insurgents were employing more sophisticated weapons with more precision and accuracy, synchronizing IED and assault weapon fire, and employing remote devices or suicide personnel to set off vehicles loaded with explosives.

A more deadly demonstration of the rising insurgency occurred on August 19. A suicide bomber crashed a cement truck filled with explosives into the headquarters of the UN mission in Baghdad. The blast was the most powerful since the invasion; it blew out windows a half mile away, shook homes within five miles, killed 23 people and wounded another 70. One of the dead was the chief of the mission, Sergio Vieira de Mello.

The death of de Mello and attack on the UN mission rattled international resolve to help in Iraq. UN Secretary-General Kofi Annan decided that the country was not safe enough for their diplomats and the mission staff was decreased from almost 800 to about 20. That meant that there remained no neutral force to shepherd the political process. Some important Iraqis, such as the Grand Ayatollah Ali al-Sistani, who would not meet directly with foreign occupiers, now had fewer options to get Shiite opinions to the Americans and British. That made it easier for insurgents to frame the emerging conflict as Iraqis vs. Occupiers. The bombing also convinced other international organizations that could help with reconstruction to leave, and shortly thereafter they were pulling out, including the World Bank, the International Monetary Fund, Oxfam, and Save the Children.

The spike in attacks was directed not only at coalition forces and agencies but also against domestic targets. On August 29, two huge car bombs exploded as the Shiite leader Ayatollah Mohammad Baqir al-Hakim was leaving the Imam Ali Mosque in Najaf. The SCIRI leader and the brother of Abdul Aziz Hakim, a member of Iraq's Governing Council, the ayatollah had been a voice of moderation compared to Muqtada al-Sadr. Hakim had been leading Friday prayers at the holy shrine when he and many followers walked out into the blast. The massive explosion was the deadliest attack since the end of Saddam's regime, killing 124 and wounding over 140. Relatives dug through rubble throughout the night and next morning searching for survivors; many of the bodies they found were burned beyond recognition.

The death of Hakim provoked tens of thousands of Shiites to take to the streets and stage demonstrations and riots. Rumors spread. Many Iraqis thought that coalition forces might be responsible for the ayatollah's death since the popular cleric had been calling for an end to the occupation and the establishment of an Iraqi government. Others blamed Sadr's Mahdi Army, while others thought the assassination probably was the work of radical Sunnis. No one took responsibility. General Sanchez reported that "we were not only seeing an escalation of the insurgency, but for the first time we were witnessing signs of a civil war in Iraq."

The escalation of violence had a significant impact on America's war effort in Iraq. Foremost, there were not enough troops or equipment to confront the emerging enemy, one that was illusive and difficult to identify. By the end of August, Sanchez noted that the "battlefield had clearly expanded all across the country—to Mosul in northern Iraq, to Baghdad and Najaf in central Iraq, and to Basra in southern Iraq." The rising insurgency and increasing U.S. casualties convinced the general that "our ground forces were wholly lacking in sufficient armored protection, and we simply didn't have enough armored Humvees for our troops." The violence also had an impact on the CPA. "Reality on the ground made a fantasy of the prewar scenario under which Iraq would be paying for its own reconstruction through oil exports within weeks or months of liberation," wrote Jerry Bremer, who later admitted, "We were clearly involved in a long-term project of nation-building here, like it or not." He figured that reconstruction alone would cost between $55 and $75 billion, more than the administration had planned for the entire war and reconstruction, and that security needed to be improved. Bremer could not open the Baghdad International Airport because of potential strikes from heat-seeking missiles, and he had to beef up his own protection. The CPA director moved out of his first office, a trailer that could be targeted by mortars and rockets, and into a concrete and armored-glass command post. He also had a new team of bodyguards, tough former Navy SEALs, armed with short black submachine guns, from the contractor Blackwater USA. Bremer no longer traveled freely, and his convoy now consisted of "two armored Humvees, a lead armored Suburban with Blackwater 'shooters,' my armored car, another armored Suburban with more shooters, and two following Humvees."

The attacks of August also had an impact on the Pentagon. "I need information," Rumsfeld told Sanchez, and the general began ordering his troops to bring in suspects to interrogate. "Actionable intelligence is the key to countering the insurgency," General Abizaid said later, and troops on the ground picked up suspects to answer questions: Who was the enemy? How were they organized and trained? Who were the leaders, and what did they want besides expelling U.S. and British forces?

Shortly thereafter, experts in Iraq were beginning to answer those questions, unlike neocons in the Bush administration who refused to acknowledge or even use the word "insurgency" and who increasingly referred to the enemy as "terrorists." In fact, at that time the enemy was composed of former Baathists, security agents, military officers and fedayeen, loyal to the former dictator. In addition, the enemy had smaller contingents of tribal leaders, criminals, disaffected unemployed men, and possibly militia aligned with clerics, such as the Mahdi Army, who felt that fighting the mostly Christian occupiers was an Islamic imperative. There also were a few foreigners moving into Iraq, young men aligned with terrorist organizations from places like Saudi Arabia, Jordan, Yemen, and Syria.

Identifying the enemy by picking up scores of suspects presented an immediate problem—it alienated large numbers of the population who at one time might have supported coalition troops. After all, many had done nothing wrong so it reminded locals of Saddam. Once captured, there was the question of where to house thousands of Iraqi men. There was only one complex in the country that could hold 4,000 prisoners at one time. It was 20 miles west of Baghdad—Abu Ghraib.

By August 2003 coalition forces faced an insurgency in Iraq, and during the next years many asked if this had been inevitable. Naturally, there would have been some level of resistance, especially from Saddam loyalists but probably not the subsequent full-scale insurgency and civil war. The commander-in-chief never ordered and his top officials never developed an effective postwar plan; instead, the neocons created their own reality based on hopes and ignorance of the nation they were about to invade. They had an aversion to learning from the past—Vietnam— and to "nation-building" but did not realize that after Shock and Awe they would be involved in rebuilding Iraq. The Pentagon—Rumsfeld and Wolfowitz—did not provide an adequate military force. "We had momentum going in and had Saddam's forces on the run," said one army officer. "But we did not have enough troops" for security or intelligence gathering in each city in Iraq. General Franks was a battle commander who aimed to capture Baghdad, the "center of gravity," but he was not concerned about planning for either an occupation or a possible guerrilla war. The subsequent U.S. force did not have enough translators, military police, civil affairs units, or intelligence and special forces. The quick rotation of American commanders back to the United States left relatively inexperienced officers in charge of a situation on the ground that was becoming more dangerous every day, and except for the British, the multinational "coalition" was ineffective, more for political show in Washington and London than to provide security for Iraq. Moreover, the change in leadership from Garner to Bremer meant that the occupation basically floundered during the first crucial month and the initial contacts with Iraqis had to be remade. When Bremer postponed local elections, Anglo-Americans came to be seen as occupiers. It also became clear that the United States would be running Iraq for years while the nation wrote a constitution, held elections, and formed a stable national government. However, the CPA itself, securely and comfortably housed in the Green Zone, did not have much presence outside of the capital. U.S. commanders joked that CPA stood for "Can't Provide Anything." Bremer and the Iraqi Governing Council were remote from the population and to many citizens they appeared arrogant; by the end of autumn a survey demonstrated that 75 percent of Iraqis had little or no confidence in the IGC. The Bush administration thought the cost for reconstructing Iraq would be only $3 billion so they did not provide the necessary funds immediately after the invasion to adequately staff the CPA and put locals to work on a robust reconstruction program. When CPA officials announced that they would not have electricity at prewar levels until October, Iraqis wondered how the United States could put a man on the moon but could not restore electricity, water, and other necessary facilities? American prestige plummeted. Then, de-Baathification and disbanding the Iraqi army outraged civil servants and former military. "In retrospect," wrote experts later, "it would have been better to put all Iraqi army personnel on inactive status, continue to pay them, and recall individuals incrementally and selectively." Those orders tossed hundreds of thousands—many with guns—out of work and into poverty, and so by the end of summer it was common knowledge that enemies of the occupation could hire local men for $50 to $100 to shoot at Americans.[10]

Thus, only six months after the invasion, by the end of summer 2003, the "cakewalk" in Iraq that had begun as Operation Iraqi Freedom had become an insurgency. Next it would become Bush's War.

4

Bush's War

"I have seen this movie, it was called Vietnam."

—General Tony Zinni

In 1951, after the United States military became mired in a conflict against communist expansion in Korea, the Republican senator Kenneth Wherry proclaimed, "This is Truman's war." During America's next conflict in Southeast Asia, activists demonstrating against the escalation in Vietnam in the 1960s called it "Johnson's War." In 2004, the Democratic senator Edward Kennedy labeled the war in Iraq "George Bush's Vietnam," and four years later PBS *Frontline* aired a program simply called "Bush's War."

Between September 2003 and the end of his administration in January 2009, U.S. troops fought Bush's war in Iraq, which on September 7, 2003, he blended with his war on terrorism. In a speech to the nation, he recounted September 11 and declared, "We acted in Iraq, where the former regime sponsored terror, possessed and used weapons of mass destruction. . . . We have carried the fight to the enemy. . . . Iraq is now the central front" of the war on terror. During the first half of his speech on Iraq, about 20 minutes, he mentioned "terror," "terrorists," or "terrorism" 24 times.

Another reason for the speech was less rhetorical and more significant—money. "I will soon submit to Congress a request for $87 billion" to restore basic services and raise an Iraqi army. That was an admission that the war was not going to cost between $50 and $60 billion, which six months earlier administration officials had called "affordable." Contrary to the neocon Richard Perle's prediction, Iraq would not be able to "finance, largely finance, the reconstruction of their own country." In fact, by September the war was costing more than $1 billion a week. Funding for reconstruction stalled, was not approved until November, and was not headed to Iraq until the next February.

By the first autumn of the occupation, as one journalist wrote, "The reassuring forecasts of Cheney, Rumsfeld, and Wolfowitz went into the dustbin of history." Instead, the insurgency intensified. "Resistance to the occupying troops was strengthening," Lieutenant General Sanchez warned in October. Americans should "brace themselves for more casualties."

Those casualties appeared three weeks later when the enemy began its Ramadan Offensive. On October 26, the first night and early morning of the holy month, insurgents began mortar and rocket attacks west of and inside Baghdad. Wolfowitz was visiting, staying in the Green Zone, and that morning his hotel was hit by six rockets, killing one colonel, and wounding 17 others, but not the deputy secretary of defense. The attack was politically significant, threatening the life of an American war manager, but the insurgents also attacked Iraqis. They assassinated one of the capital's deputy mayors and the next day bombed four police stations—the first major attack on their own security forces—killing ten. That day, October 27, a truck disguised as an ambulance exploded at the office of the International Committee of the Red Cross, killing 35 and wounding over 240, marking the bloodiest day since the fall of Saddam. The ICRC had been providing humanitarian aid to Iraq since 1980; their staff was in total shock. So were the Italians two weeks later, when a car bomb rammed into their military headquarters in southern Iraq, killing 18 Italians and eight Iraqis, the deadliest attack on a coalition member.

Attacks intensified and became more sophisticated during Ramadan. The previous summer the enemy had attacked U.S. troops about 10–15 times a day, but that soared to 45 a day during Ramadan. Moreover, for the first time the insurgents attacked aircraft. They shot down Black Hawk and Chinook helicopters, killing almost 40 soldiers, and they launched rockets at planes attempting to land or take off from the

Baghdad International Airport. By the end of that holy month, more U.S. troops had died in combat since May 1 than during the initial invasion.

"We're going to get pretty tough," declared General Sanchez, "that's what's necessary to defeat this enemy." Even Rumsfeld had changed his tune. He privately told his staff that winning in Iraq would be "a long, hard slog," and finally admitted publicly, "We're in a low-intensity war that needs to be won, and we intend to win it."

Ramadan violence provoked the Bush administration to formulate a three-pronged policy: return sovereignty to the Iraqi people, get more intelligence about the emerging enemy, and rebuild Iraqi security forces.

In November, the White House sent three senior officials to Baghdad to assess the insurgency and they returned, urging political action. Earlier, the CPA director Bremer had surprised his superiors by announcing a two-year, seven-step plan to return sovereignty to the Iraqis. The Pentagon advocated a shorter turnover, but Bremer told Wolfowitz that the Iraqi Governing Counsel was "ineffective. . . . Those people couldn't organize a parade, let alone run the country." Then Ramadan and the violence provoked Bush to recall Bremer for more discussions. Shortly thereafter, the White House announced the November 15 Agreement. Iraq would become a sovereign nation in less than eight months—by July 1, 2004.

Meanwhile, the United States continued searching for actionable intelligence to understand the enemy and its leaders. The CIA expanded the number of case officers so that by spring 2004 its office in Iraq became its largest in the world with some 500 personnel. To discover intelligence, U.S. troops conducted cordon and sweep operations, entering Iraqi homes at night, "breaking down doors, waking up residents roughly, yelling orders . . . pushing people around . . . punching and kicking and striking with rifles," reported the International Red Cross. "Individuals were often led away in whatever they happen to be wearing at the time of arrest . . . underwear."

There was a "complete lack of cultural understanding by the troops," reported NPR's Anne Garrels. Soldiers had received no training in Iraq culture and customs and had few interpreters; they often were left to communicate their instructions with gestures and sign language. "The result was that American troops were blind and deaf to much of what was going on around them," wrote a journalist, "and the Iraqis were often terrified."

One of them looked especially terrified and confused when he was captured—Saddam. During the first six months of the occupation, the Bush administration thought that capturing Saddam was an important step toward ending the resistance for it would finish off the remnants of the Baathists. Consequently, about one thousand CIA paramilitaries and Special Operations forces were devoted to finding Saddam and his top allies, even though the death of his two sons in July had no effect on the insurgency.

"We got him!" Bremer exclaimed to the press on December 14. After 38 weeks of searching and announcing a $25 million reward, U.S. forces received a tip that an important person was hiding in a hole on a farm 10 miles south of his hometown, Tikrit. Soldiers removed a prayer rug, then a lid, revealing a hole. Before the troops dropped a grenade or fired into the shaft, two hands surrendered. "I am Saddam Hussein. I am the president of Iraq and I am ready to negotiate."

"President Bush sends his regards," replied the American soldier. Bremer told Iraqis the arrest was a "turning point," a "great day in your history," but it had no impact on the insurgency, for opinion polls demonstrated massive Iraqi suspicion of American intentions. Only 5 percent of Iraqis surveyed thought that the United States invaded "to assist the Iraqi people," only 1 percent believed it was to establish democracy, while about half thought it was "to rob Iraq's oil." As one CPA adviser recalled, "I realized that Bremer and his most trusted CPA advisers simply did not grasp the depth of Iraqi disaffection, suspicion, and frustration." A November 2003 survey demonstrated that 47 percent of Iraqis expressed confidence in the CPA; by March 2004 it was 14 percent.[1]

That spring there was no confidence in Americans in Fallujah, a mostly Sunni city of 300,000 west of Baghdad in Anbar Province. On March 31, 2004, two vehicles with four private security employees of Blackwater USA drove into the city. With a shortage of U.S. troops, the Bush administration had resorted to contracting security guards, eventually some 20,000. As the British drew down their troop strength, this private army became the second-largest armed force in Iraq, larger than the rest of the coalition combined. While these guards were of international origins, many were former U.S. Special Forces, who were expensive, usually costing between $1,000 to $1,500 a day while a corporal or sergeant earned only about twice that for an entire month in Iraq.

Fallujah was tense. There had been recent firefights, one leaving a dozen Iraqis dead, and when the Blackwater vehicles drove into the city, they ran into an ambush. Insurgents threw grenades, opened fire, and pulled the wounded Americans from their cars. They captured one alive, beat him with bricks, and while cheering and dancing, they cut off his arm, leg, and head. They doused the dead with gasoline, lit them, chanting "Allahu Akbar!" (God is Great). Cameramen arrived as two torsos were dragged to a bridge, where they were hung, their bodies dangling like "slaughtered sheep" for ten hours; they were taken down and thrown on a pile of burning tires as the crowd cheered. CNN beamed images of the charred bodies back to the United States as one man warned, "This is the fate of all Americans who come to Fallujah."

"We've got to pound these guys," Rumsfeld declared to General Sanchez. The defense secretary wanted the Sunnis on the Iraq Governing Council "to step forward and condemn this attack. . . . It's time for them to choose. They are either with us or against us." Attack, Rumsfeld ordered. "We need to make sure that Iraqis in other cities receive our message."

Instead, Generals Sanchez and Abizaid urged caution. The marines had been trying to peacefully engage the Sunnis, which had worked in some parts of the country with the Shiites. Moreover, attacking Fallujah would result in massive collateral damage—many civilian deaths and refugees along with a huge rebuilding cost—Sanchez told President Bush on video teleconference. What impact would destroying the town have on Iraq, the general asked, and on the Arab world? Al Jazeera already had journalists in the city and their pictures would be sent out to the world. "Yes, we understand," the president replied. "We know it's going to be ugly, but we are committed." Attack.

On April 5, USMC Major General James Mattis, the commander in Fallujah, launched Operation Vigilant Resolve. It was almost a year since U.S. troops had commenced the thunder runs that captured Baghdad, over 11 months since President Bush had declared that "major combat operations in Iraq have ended," and only three months until the CPA planned to hand over sovereignty to the Iraqis. After blocking all roads in and out of the city, about 2,500 marines stormed and were confronted by 1,200 insurgents who were prepared for battle. The fighting was close quarters, street to street, door to door; sometimes combat occurred in alleys so narrow that tank commanders could not fully rotate their turrets. The marines called in air power, and AC-130 gunships and Cobra attack helicopters pounded the low-rise cinder block buildings that dominated the poor, industrial city.

For some months, U.S. forces had been training Iraqi police and army and there was pressure to use Iraqi forces that seemed ready for combat. Yet during the battle, local policemen either abandoned their posts or joined the other side, as did the town's police commissioner. Almost half of the first battalion of the New Iraqi Army deserted on their way to Fallujah and the battalion recruited from Sadr City had 80 percent absenteeism. "So much for the Iraqis taking over their own security," complained Bremer, and Sanchez griped, "Their participation was a flat-out failure."

As the battle raged, the president was commencing his reelection campaign and he told supporters, "We still face thugs and terrorists in Iraq. . . . We will defeat them there so we do not have to face them in our own country." From the combat zone, General Sanchez had a different view of the rising insurgency. "To say that the Fallujah offensive angered the Sunni Muslims of Iraq would be a gross understatement." Up to then, many had still been on the sidelines and were working with the occupation to create a more stable government, but when citizens saw the bloody images on Al Jazeera, Sanchez continued, "most Sunnis felt Fallujah was an attack on their very existence."

Tribal leaders called for men with arms, and soon most of Anbar Province erupted—and so did the Shiites in Sadr City and in southern Iraq. By that time, Muqtada al-Sadr had at least 5,000 and perhaps 10,000 armed followers in his Madhi Army, and there were increasing attacks on U.S. forces in Sadr City and Najaf. When Sadr's newspaper *Al Hawza* ran an editorial stating that the 9/11 attacks on America were a "blessing from God," Bremer shut down the paper, which sparked massive protests and boosted the cleric's prestige among Shiites. On April 3, Bremer issued an arrest warrant for Sadr and U.S. Special Forces executed a raid in Najaf that led to the capture of one of the cleric's lieutenants. That night the Mahdi Army attacked and took over five police stations in Sadr City and the next morning opened fire on an American patrol, killing eight. The Mahdi Army then extended their operations and seized control of four southern provincial capitals—Najaf, Al Kut,

Nasiriyah, and Basra—taking over government buildings. Sadr appeared at the Great Mosque in the holy city of Kufa, where hundreds of his army had driven out Iraqi security forces, and declared during Friday prayers, "Every person has to take a stand, either with us or against us. Neutrality doesn't exist between us and the Americans." The CPA labeled Sadr a "hostile force" and planned a campaign to defeat the Mahdi Army in order to restore the CPA and stability in the southern provinces. A few days later, Sanchez and Bremer had a video teleconference with the White House. Bush declared that the United States couldn't allow Sadr "to change the course of the country. It is absolutely vital that we have a robust offensive operation everywhere down south." Concerning Sadr and the concurrent battle in Fallujah, Bush got excited. "Kick ass! If somebody tries to stop the march to democracy, we will seek them out and kill them!" The president suddenly gave Sanchez a pep talk: "Stay the course! Kill them! Be confident! Prevail! We are going to wipe them out! We are not blinking!"

Nor were Shiite insurgents blinking. Southern Iraq was particularly vulnerable since the area was occupied mostly by coalition forces. British forces in Basra allowed the Madhi Army to take over government buildings, and other members of the coalition often deserted their posts. To be fair, the Bush administration had not supplied the military equipment they promised to coalition forces and had told them that their troops would be needed only for peacekeeping and security, not combat; by summer many of those forces were heading home. Consequently, when the Mahdi Army moved into cities, Polish, Spanish, and Italian troops refused to confront them, and instead of guarding the bridges of Kufa, the Ukrainians withdrew to their safe compound and allowed Sadr's forces to take over the city.

"The crises are converging," Bremer declared, while international pressure mounted. Al Jazeera, CNN, and other international networks beamed images of destruction in Fallujah and chaos in southern Iraq. Americans and especially British citizens demanded that their governments end the combat, and Prime Minister Tony Blair conveyed that to the White House. The United Nations called for peace, and about a half dozen members of the Iraqi Governing Council, including the ministers of interior and human rights, declared that if the United States did not end the offensive they would quit the government—which would destroy American plans for sovereignty of Iraq. "We were at the most critical crisis of the occupation," wrote Bremer. "The stakes couldn't be higher."

The military urged continuing the battle for Fallujah. In a video teleconference call, General Abizaid asked the commander-in-chief to allow the marines just three or four more days to kill a pocket of 500–800 insurgents and secure the city. But Bremer opposed the request, and Bush refused. The president then turned to General Sanchez asking, "Do these people even want us here? . . . Can you find anybody to thank us for giving them democracy and freedom?"

The administration wanted to keep the Iraqi Governing Council together, on track for the transfer of sovereignty, and did not want pictures of destruction in Iraq on television while the president was running for reelection. Just three days after the offensive began, the White House gave the order, and on April 9 Bremer announced that the marines would cease offensive operations in Fallujah. Just two days after the president had ordered "Stay the course," he reversed course.

The commander-in-chief's order outraged American commanders in Iraq. "Thirty-nine Marines and U.S. soldiers had died," griped General Mattis in Fallujah, "for what?" A standstill at best; encouraging insurgents at worst. "Fallujah was like a siren," said a marine officer, "calling to the insurgents." The offensive, televised throughout the Middle East, stimulated the flow of foreign terrorists into Iraq, and that included the Jordanian-born terrorist Abu Musab al-Zarqawi, a man who had ties with Osama bin Laden. There was "no link between al-Qaeda and Iraq," wrote Sanchez, "or a major presence of al-Qaeda in Iraq, until after the aborted battle of Fallujah."[2]

Fallujah remained a dangerous insurgent stronghold, and violence spiraled out of control in Iraq late in April, when CBS aired a program on 60 Minutes II. It contained shocking pictures from Abu Ghraib.

Earlier, in February 2002, the administration had issued a memorandum stating that the Geneva Conventions of 1949 did not apply to members of al Qaeda or the Taliban. Bush's legal counsel Alberto Gonzales and Secretary Rumsfeld declared that the conventions were "obsolete," that those captured in the war on terror were "unlawful combatants" who did not qualify for the usual treatment for prisoners of war. That opened the door for torture at Guantanamo Bay's Camp X-Ray.

It also had an impact on suspects the army picked up in Afghanistan and Iraq, setting aside the military's usual legal constraints, training guidelines, and rules of interrogation.

As the insurgency emerged in autumn 2003, the Pentagon demanded that U.S. forces get actionable intelligence, but that raised a question: Where to hold thousands of suspects? In Saddam's prison, Abu Ghraib, which was built to hold about 4,000 prisoners and was located 20 miles west of Baghdad. By late autumn 2003, Abu Ghraib contained about 6,000 to 7,000 prisoners, while Camp Bucca in southern Iraq had over 5,000. These suspects were held for as long as 90 days before they were interrogated. Eventually, U.S. officials estimated that most were innocent and that about 90 percent had no useful intelligence for the occupation forces.

By October, it was obvious that more guards were needed at Abu Ghraib. Some prisoners were camped in tents on the grounds, while the ones that the army thought had information were kept in the permanent part of the prison. To guard that secure area, the military sent the 372nd Military Police Company, an Army Reserve unit from the foothills of the Appalachians in Maryland. During subsequent investigations, these MPs admitted that they took prisoner abuse and torture, already common, "to another level." Moreover, they took digital pictures "just for fun," said one. Those photos sickened another MP, who collected many of them, placed them in an envelope, and slid it under the door of the U.S. Army's criminal investigator, who began the probe.

Eventually, the pictures were leaked to the media and shown on cable news in Iraq, where some marines saw them on the mess hall television. General Mattis walked in and asked, "What's going on?" and a corporal looked up and responded, "Some assholes have just lost the war for us."

The photos were shocking. One showed a man naked and hand-cuffed to his cell door; another handcuffed to a bed with women's underwear over his head; a third had PFC Lynndie England holding a dog's leash with the end attached to a naked man on all fours; and then a picture of a group of men with hands and legs cuffed all stacked into a nude pile. One Iraqi translator saw the pile and later stated that the guards "stacked them on top of each other by ensuring that the bottom guy's penis will touch the guy on top's butt." The subsequent investigation revealed more sordid behavior. Some detainees were forced to masturbate in front of female guards while another was sodomized with a stick. One was hooded and put on a box, had wires attached, and was told that he would be electrocuted if he fell off the box, while another told investigators that he was made to "bark like a dog . . . crawl on his stomach while MPs spit and urinated" on him before he was beaten unconscious. The Pentagon eventually released the morbid facts: 20 Iraqi prisoners had died while in U.S. custody at Abu Ghraib.

"When you lose the moral high ground," said General Mattis, "you lose it all." Previously, the world saw Arab insurgents shooting at U.S. soldiers, exploding IEDs, and dead civilians laying in the streets; now, they saw the pictures of American torture at Abu Ghraib. "Unquestionably, the abuses constituted criminal behavior by soldiers in my chain of command," wrote General Sanchez, who had authorized some of the interrogation tactics, "and clearly violated the Geneva Conventions."

Al Jazeera and other satellite networks condemned Abu Ghraib. One sheikh from Fallujah asked, "Where is the freedom? Where is the democracy? The jails are now fuller than they were in Saddam Hussein's time."

Iraq spiraled out of control. Militias formed rapidly, or, as one CPA adviser noted, "metastasized like a malignant cancer in the body politic of Iraq." Militiamen attacked U.S. troops in many towns—Mosul, Tikrit, Baqubah, Baghdad's Sadr City, Najaf—all the way to Syria. Insurgents attacked Western trucks delivering supplies and even the highway from Baghdad to its airport was informally renamed the "Road of Death." In many towns Iraqis painted anti-American graffiti on walls; one in Abu Ghraib proclaimed, "We shall knock on the gates of heaven with American skulls."

The chaos again elevated the status of Abu Mussab al-Zarqawi. This extremist Sunni terrorist had formed the group al Qaeda in Iraq with the aim of establishing a caliphate, an Islamic fundamentalist state. While he and Osama bin Laden agreed on that goal, they differed concerning Shiites. Zarqawi labeled Shiites "the lurking snake, the crafty and malicious scorpion, the spying enemy," even "the most evil of mankind," but bin Laden had reached out to form alliances with some Shiites. After the invasion, Zarqawi saw an American-Jewish-Shiite alliance aimed at destroying Sunnis, and since Shiites were a majority in the country, he was horrified by the thought of a democratic Iraq. To him, Shiites who worked with or for the American occupiers were no better than the infidels and deserved to die. In February 2004, U.S. forces had intercepted a letter from Zarqawi to bin Laden in which the Jordanian revealed his terrorist plan—a sectarian war between Shiites and Sunnis. His aim was to "awaken the inattentive Sunnis as they feel imminent danger" from the Shia majority. "We were on top of the system. We had dreams," a Sunni Baathist told a reporter. "Now we are the losers. We lost our positions, our status, the security of our families, stability. Curse the Americans. Curse them." "To the paranoid Sunni mind," wrote a freelance journalist, "American devils and Shia traitors worked together."

Shortly thereafter, some Iraqis began to draw a distinction between insurgents and terrorists. One newspaper wrote that the "Iraqi resistance believes in ending the occupation using armed resistance, while the goal of terrorism is the failure of the entire political process in Iraq."

By April 2004, then, Bush's War had become a much more complicated conflict than he or his war planners had predicted, or as one expert wrote, "unintended consequences broke out in Iraq with a vengeance." The early insurgency of 2003 was a mélange of former Baathists, military officers, and other loyalists to Saddam. The first enemy had smaller portions of tribal leaders, criminals, disaffected unemployed men, and some militia aligned to clerics such as Muqtada al-Sadr, with a few Arab foreigners. During and after the battles in Fallujah and Najaf, along with the televised torture at Abu Ghraib, the enemy expanded. The siege of Fallujah outraged the Sunnis; the confrontation with Sadr estranged many Shiites; and the pictures from Abu Ghraib angered the rest of Iraqis and enraged the Islamic world. Shiites, after centuries of being marginalized in Iraq, now aligned themselves with the ayatollahs and the Iranians and attempted to take control. Sadr's Shiite Mahdi Army attacked Sunnis, Western forces, and the emerging Iraqi security forces. That stimulated a wave of revulsion and fear throughout the Sunni minority, who responded by attacking Western forces and Shiites. With the arrival of Zarqawi and his Sunni terrorists, U.S. troops were facing sporadic attacks from all three—terrorists, Sunni insurgents, and the Mahdi Army.[3]

Zarqawi exacerbated the violence. His organization began kidnapping foreigners, one of them an American contractor named Nick Berg. An international businessman, Berg had been in Iraq trying to win contracts to help rebuild the nation's infrastructure. Instead, the insurgents released a shocking video over the Internet. The footage showed men wrestling Berg to the ground, a terrorist pulling a long knife from his shirt, decapitating the American, and holding his head up at the camera. The killer was Zarqawi.

Zarqawi's terrorists continued kidnapping and videoing public beheadings of American and British contractors that summer, prompting international corporations to stop many reconstruction projects. General Electric and Siemens pulled their staff from project sites. Security costs soared for reconstruction, while over the next year insurgents killed over 400 contractors and construction workers, a number that almost doubled by the end of 2006.

Violence spiraled out of control. In mid-May, a car bomb exploded outside the Green Zone, killing seven Iraqis, including Ezzedine Salim, that month's president of the Iraqi Governing Council. Next door, the Sadr City slum again erupted. Ten times the size of Fallujah, with unemployment over 70 percent, maintaining security there was impossible. Soon, rumors ran wild that insurgents would overrun Baghdad. They conducted assassination attempts on government ministers who needed small armies of guards, including one who had 30 bodyguards. Iraqi politicians and ministers suffered, and so did common people. Assassins were easy to hire; in one market killers put up a poster advertising their service at between $300 to $400 a murder. "Baghdad sounded like a free-fire zone," noted a journalist; the city's morgue averaged 25 new bodies a day. Another journalist reported, "The Baghdad morgue became a charnel house filled with bodies, heads, limbs, and buckets of flesh."

During that instability, the Americans changed its team in Baghdad. Earlier, in October 2003, the president had shifted most of the responsibility for Iraq from Rumsfeld to Rice and her Iraq Stabilization Group; she had a better relationship with Bremer. In 2004, Rice informed Bremer that he would be replaced that summer by the career diplomat John Negroponte, former U.S. Ambassador to the UN. The administration replaced Lieutenant General Sanchez with General George Casey Jr., formerly army vice chief of staff, who was knowledgeable in political-military affairs. Unlike the Bremer-Sanchez strained relations, Negroponte and Casey worked smoothly together. At the same time, Lieutenant General David Petraeus became commander of Security Transition Command Iraq and concentrated on accelerating the training of new Iraqi security forces.

Leadership also changed in Iraq. The Bush administration was in a quandary over whom to hand over the government to, so they asked the UN for a special envoy. Lakhdar Brahimi arrived in April and met with hundreds of Iraqis and helped the CPA form a caretaker government before the elections scheduled for January 2005. On June 28, outgoing Ambassador Bremer dissolved the Iraqi Governing Council and handed over control of the country to the new interim government composed of a Sunni president, Ghazi al-Yawar; Shia and Kurd deputy presidents, Ibrahim Jaafari and Rowsch Shaways; and a Shia prime minister, Ayad Allawi. Fearing attacks, and behind the security of the Green Zone, the Americans secretly transferred power two days before it was scheduled. After a brief private ceremony, Bremer was quietly taken to the airport, where he and his bodyguard boarded a C-130. After waiting on board a few minutes, they ran to a helicopter that flew them to a different runway, where they boarded a jet that hustled them to Jordan. "What had started with neoconservative fantasies of cheering Iraqis greeting American liberators with flowers and candy," wrote a former American diplomat, "ended with a secret ceremony and a decoy plane."

That same day Bremer sent the news of the transfer of power to Rice who delivered a note to the president, "Iraq is sovereign." Bush wrote on the margin "Let freedom reign!"

Something else was reigning in Iraq. A "civil war," recalled General Sanchez. "And what's more, we had created these conditions ourselves." Bremer also was despondent, admitting to Rice, "We've become the worst of all things—an ineffective occupier."

Back home, many Americans agreed, as former prowar columnists turned up the heat on the administration during spring 2004. "This administration needs to undertake a total overhaul of its Iraq policy," editorialized Thomas Friedman of the *New York Times*. "Otherwise, it is courting a total disaster for us all." His conservative colleague at that paper, David Brooks, labeled the administration's prewar perceptions and claims about Iraq "childish fantasy," and the neocon Robert Kagan wrote that "Bush Administration officials have no clue about what to do in Iraq tomorrow, much less a month from now."

Furthermore, that summer the administration's justifications for the war continued to fall apart because of the publication of reports by independent groups: the British Butler Review; the U.S. Senate Report of Pre-war Intelligence on Iraq; and most importantly the 9/11 Commission, which after 15 months of pressure finally forced the administration to hand over important documents, including the president's daily intelligence briefings. The findings from these investigations were confirmed by the administration's own Iraq Survey Group headed by the U.S. weapons inspector Charles Duelfer. The administration's prewar claims in their rush to war were bogus. Saddam had no WMD program, no stashes of chemical or biological weapons, no UVAs, and no links with al Qaeda.

To many Americans, those findings meant that the war was unnecessary, but that had little impact on General Casey, who was developing tactics to fight the insurgency in Iraq. He increased the number of U.S. advisers partnering with Iraqi troops and aimed to eliminate safe havens for insurgents—particularly Fallujah—and Shiite rebel strongholds in the south. Then in August, Muqtada al-Sadr's Mahdi Army stormed into Najaf and made their stand around the Imam Ali Shrine. Casey ordered retaliation, fighting intensified, and the battle destroyed large parts of the holy city, killing 400 enemy and wounding 2,500 insurgents and civilians. Eventually, the Grand Ayatollah Ali al-Sistani, the nation's highest Shiite cleric, used his influence to bring about an agreement, which increased his stature as the leader of Iraq's Shia. He brokered a ceasefire, the CPA dropped attempts to arrest Sadr, and Western forces withdrew from the holy cities of Najaf and Kufa. Sadr's bruised Mahdi Army disarmed and left the city, many going to Basra.

Sadr, however, needed a new strategy. The battle in Najaf outraged the local inhabitants; their livelihoods depended on thousands of Shia pilgrims who visited the Imam Ali Shrine. They demonstrated against the Mahdi Army and behind the scenes Shia tribes boosted their own loose force, the Badr Organization, which had ties to Iran. Sadr's army was not strong enough to defeat the U.S. Army or to eliminate his rivals, so by October he began working within the political system. He held discussions with Prime Minister Allawi, who offered amnesty to fighters who surrendered their weapons. Sadr called on his followers to put down their arms and eventually he made an alliance with Ahmed

Chalabi, who was under increasing criticism for feeding U.S. intelligence officials untrue information. In response—and since the United States had not made him the leader of a new Iraq—Chalabi began attacking his former benefactor. "What did fourteen months of occupation achieve?" he asked in July 2004. "The electricity still doesn't work, thousands are dead, the United States has lost the moral high ground in the Middle East."[4]

It seemed that the United States also was losing a war, one that was becoming increasingly complex. "In other wars, the front line was exactly that, a line to advance toward and cross," wrote a journalist embedded with the troops, "but in this war, where the enemy was everywhere, it was anywhere out of the wire, in any direction: that building, that town, that province, the entire country, in 360°. . . . Suspicion in 360°."

Suspicion was heightened by the roadside bomb—what the military called Improvised Explosive Devices (IEDs)—which became the enemy's weapon of choice against the occupation in Iraq and eventually in Afghanistan. At first these weapons were rather primitive: an artillery shell, TNT, or plastic explosive attached by a line to a person who would detonate them as troops walked or drove by. Occupation forces soon learned to spot the lines and attack the assassin. By 2004, however, most of the bombs were remotely controlled, set off using cellular phones, car alarm transmitters, or other electronic devices.

Ground troops were unprepared for this type of warfare. Rumsfeld's rapid force meant that many vehicles had speed but lacked sufficient armor to defend against IEDs, and it took a long time to order and ship over more armor. Casualties mounted, and in December 2004 Rumsfeld flew to Kuwait to show that he cared for the troops. During a question and answer session, a soldier asked, "Why do we soldiers have to dig through local landfills for pieces of scrap metal . . . to up-armor our vehicles?" The defense secretary replied, "You go to war with the Army you have, not the Army you might want or wish to have at a later time." Although by this time everyone knew that the administration had been planning the war for at least six months before the invasion, Rumsfeld told the soldiers to "suck it up, you have what you have."

Troops in Iraq and commentators in America were outraged with Rumsfeld's remarks as soldiers took what many considered were unnecessary and preventable casualties. In the first year of the insurgency,

IEDs were responsible for about one-third of American deaths and about two-thirds of the wounded. During the next years, IEDs became the biggest killers of U.S. troops, and by 2006 the enemy exploded over 4,700 IEDs. The constant threat had a numbing effect on some soldiers. "You quit looking," said an army captain in charge of a bomb squad. "You almost feel like you're part of the walking dead."

Car bombs also were a constant threat, as one army lieutenant described:

> A sedan comes barreling toward us. The headlights are out. The car is not slowing down. Maybe the driver can't see the line of soldiers in the street. Maybe he doesn't notice the headlights of two Humvees facing him. Maybe he's extremely drunk. Maybe the car is filled with a hundred pounds of explosives. We wave our flashlights at the car. But he keeps coming. We scream, yell, and wave our arms. But he keeps coming. The car is close enough now that I can see the outline of the three passengers inside the cabin. But he keeps coming. I think about the fact that last week, another Squad lit up a car and killed a little girl. The .50-cal rounds blew her head clear off her body. She was wearing a little blue dress. I saw the pictures. But the driver keeps fucking coming. Just a few weeks ago, four American soldiers were killed ten blocks away when a car loaded with explosives ran a checkpoint. One of the soldiers had five kids. Another was nineteen years old and had just gotten married. We fire rounds into the ground feet in front of the bumper. But he keeps coming. There are no alternatives left. The vehicle is close enough that I can see dents in the orange hood.
>   What would you do?

As Americans fought the 360° war, they continued the task of rebuilding Iraqi security forces. It was difficult because it depended on trust, of which there was little between occupation forces and Iraqis. Moreover, constant U.S. troop rotation hurt the effort. "All the relationships an adviser has established, all the knowledge he has built up, goes right with him" when he leaves, one expert remarked. "We should put out a call for however many officers and NCOs we need, and give them six months of basic Arabic. In the course of this training we could find the ones suited to serve there for five years." Nor had the Pentagon sent enough inter-preters; throughout 2005, the typical U.S. company of about 150 soldiers only had one or two who could speak Arabic.

Lieutenant General Petraeus was in command of training the new Iraqi security forces—army, national guard, border patrol, and police—and the task was slow and laborious. "In less than six months we have gone from zero Iraqis providing security to their country to close to a hundred thousand Iraqis," Rumsfeld had claimed in Octo-ber 2003. Where the secretary got those numbers was not known, and Bremer informed the president that such figures were "flat-out mis-leading." In reality, desertion rates were in the stratosphere, and one of Bremer's advisers told him the "Army is sweeping up half-educated men off the streets, running them through a three-week training course, arming them, and then calling them 'police.' It's a scandal, pure and simple."

Training Iraqi security forces would take years. Petraeus placed more emphasis on embedding U.S. advisers with Iraqi units, but it was difficult to train reliable Iraqi troops, mostly because of a lack of loyalty to the central government. Recruitment usually was based on political party militias, sects, tribes, and local politicians; recruits usually remained loyal to their benefactors—not to the Iraqi government. Con-sequently, two years later a diplomat reported that of the 115 army battal-ions, "60 are Shiite, 45 are Sunni Arab, and nine are Kurdish." While the administration called them Iraqi troops, Sunnis usually felt Shiite troops were "not fighting for Iraq but for a pro-Iranian Shiite-dominated polit-ical order." The U.S. Army also paid local leaders to keep their unem-ployed men from joining the insurgency, so during summer 2004 brigade commanders were distributing between $50,000 and $100,000 a month. By January 2005, Iraq listed 120,000 in their security forces, but the coalition calculated that only 5,000 could be effective in combat; 13 months later in February 2006, American generals admitted that out of 98 Iraqi battalions not one was capable of fighting insurgents without help from the U.S. Army.

As training limped along in Iraq, the American presidential campaign was in full swing with the main issues being terrorism and the war. The eventual Democratic Party nominee, Senator John Kerry of Massachusetts, accused Bush of "deliberately misleading the American people" into Iraq. During the first presidential debate, the Democrat blasted the president on the "colossal blunder," the decision to go to war in Iraq. "I think we can do better . . . and Iraq is not even the center of focus of the war on terror." The president responded, "The world is better off without Saddam Hussein," later adding, "Iraq is a central part on the war on terror. That's why Zarqawi and his people are trying to fight us. Their hope is that we grow weary and we leave." The United States had to "stay the course," Bush repeated many times, and even the Democrat did not call for withdrawal, for that would be irresponsible. "We have to succeed," said Kerry. "We can't leave a failed Iraq."

Bush focused on national security and presented himself as a decisive leader. "I will never relent in defending America," he pledged, "whatever it takes." The president claimed that Kerry was a "flip-flopper," a politician who had voted for the October 2002 resolution and now opposed the war. That was Kerry's dilemma, and he helped the president when he made an incredible statement concerning funding the war: "I actually did vote for the $87 billion before I voted against it." Kerry, a media critic wrote, was "proving a genius at self-destruction, handing the White House loaded weapons with which to mow him down."

The November 2004 election was unusual, but not as much as the 2000 contest. The president won 50.7 percent while Kerry won 48.3. Of 121 million votes cast, Bush's margin of victory of just over 3 million votes was the smallest of any incumbent in U.S. history. Bush won a second term, the Republicans increased their control of both houses of Congress, as a slight majority of voters decided to "stay the course."[5]

Four days after Bush's reelection, General Casey ordered U.S. Marines to launch the second battle of Fallujah in an attempt to eliminate that insurgent safe haven before the January 2005 Iraqi elections. Zarqawi's men and additional foreign fighters had arrived to supplement the Sunni insurgents, which alarmed the government in Baghdad. "We have asked Fallujah residents to turn over Zarqawi and his group," declared Prime Minister Allawi, and his national security chief said he hoped the local residents would kick out foreign fighters, "otherwise we are preparing to crush them." Casey sent a message for civilians to evacuate. Most did, and the general had received the assurances from the Iraqi Governing Council that they would make public statements supporting military action.

The American force was three times larger than the one in April and it included Iraqis led by U.S. commanders, so when the attack began some 8,000 Americans and 2,000 Iraqis stormed the city to fight about 2,000 insurgents. The combat was intense. After mortars and artillery had softened areas, the marines advanced in a block-by-block clearing movement supported by snipers and air strikes. The enemy was determined, and with no place to escape they fought suicidally for the next ten days until U.S. forces captured the city. At least 1,000 insurgents died, including only about 15 foreign fighters; Zarqawi escaped. Americans lost 54 with 425 wounded, while Iraqis lost 8 with 43 wounded. By the end of November, it had become the bloodiest month of the occupation: 137 Americans were dead and 1,350 wounded.

Then came the hard part—the clearing phase. Troops had to enter nearly every room of each building, about 25,000 structures, to look for wounded, prisoners, weapons, bombs. It was grueling, searching hundreds of buildings each day, engaging in firefights, and killing the enemy, often at close range. In one encounter, a marine burst into a room and saw an AK-47 barrel pointed at his head, jumped just in time to avoid the blast and unloaded a burst into the insurgent's chest. During the next six weeks, American troops discovered about 25 bomb factories and over 450 weapons caches.

The battles for Fallujah and earlier in Najaf were significant because they took away safe havens for the enemy. "Every time the insurgents decided to stand and fight instead of hit and run, the normal roles switched," recalled a marine lieutenant. "We became the hunters, and our enemies became the hunted." After Fallujah, insurgents avoided conventional battles with the heavily armed Americans and reverted to guerrilla warfare, moving into territory that was unguarded, attacking and melting back into the population. Fallujah also further alienated Sunnis. "When we devastated Fallujah," wrote a freelance journalist, "al Qaeda grew like a tumor." A poll conducted later showed that 88 percent of Sunni Arabs approved of attacks on U.S. troops (versus 41 percent among Shia and 16 percent for Kurds), and that Osama bin Laden had higher approval ratings in the Middle East than George Bush; 98 percent of Egyptians had an unfavorable view of the United States.

The battles did, however, secure enough of the nation so the militias could not stop national elections on January 30, the first of three elections held in 2005. The first elected a National Assembly that would appoint a Transitional Government to write a constitution; the second on October 15 was a referendum on the new constitution; and the third on December 15 was for a permanent Iraqi parliament, the Council of Representatives, which would serve until the next national elections were held in March 2010.

Just holding the first election was a success that January. Leaflets in the capital threatened to "wash the streets of Baghdad with the voters' blood." But relatively speaking, there was little violence, meaning that nine suicide bombers killed only 35 in Baghdad. Throughout the nation, 130,000 Iraqi troops guarded more than 5,700 polling stations so more than 8 million could vote, marking a success for the new Iraqi security forces.

In America and Britain, Bush and Blair declared that Iraq was on the road to democracy, but the election divided an already sequestered nation. Sunnis were strongly opposed to the election, irritated that Fallujah was rubble and fearing that the Shia majority would take control of Iraq. Sunnis boycotted, meaning that about 20 percent of the electorate voluntarily disenfranchised themselves and only about 58 percent of Iraqis voted. The main Shiite party, the United Iraqi Alliance (UIA) backed by Grand Ayatollah Sistani, won 48 percent, or as one local declared, "it's a Sistani tsunami." The UIA also was supported by the bloc of Muqtada al-Sadr, which won 23 seats. Combined, the UIA and Sadr's block won a majority, 140 of the 275 seats, and to hold the coalition together Sadr's supporters received two cabinet positions. The Kurdish Alliance was second with about 27 percent, or 75 seats. Prime Minister Ayad Allawi's Iraqiyya, the only secular party and the hope of the Bush and Blair governments, came in third with about 14 percent, only 40 seats, and he refused to participate in the new government. The Shiites and Kurds negotiated until April to form a government. Jalal Talabani, a Kurd, became president and he appointed Shiite Ibrahim al-Jaafari to be prime minister with the secular Shia Ahmed Chalabi as deputy prime minister. Although the Sunni Arabs had won only 6 percent, 17 seats, a prominent Sunni in Iraqiyya, Hachem al-Hassani, was elected speaker of parliament. The new government began writing a constitution, and on October 15 a majority of the electorate, but not the Sunnis, ratified the new federal constitution of Iraq.

The January election was a disaster for the Bush and Blair administrations. Regardless of the spin about Iraqis having the first free election in decades, the new Shiite government looked east to Iran, the enemy of the United States since the hostage crisis of 1979. The election also refuted the president's most recent claims for the invasion—that the U.S. was developing a Western democracy in Iraq. In fact, when given a choice the Shiites did not vote for a secular, liberal democracy but for their own Islamists. In Shia provinces the UIA won between 70 and 80 percent of the vote, while in Kurdistan the Kurdish Alliance achieved over 90 percent.

Shiites wrote the eventual constitution. It made Iraq a federalized nation with a weak central government that had power only over foreign, fiscal, and defense policy. The document avoided important questions about Baghdad's powers over the provinces and who controlled the nation's oil, especially in Kurdistan. The Kurds supported the constitution because it gave their region quasi-independence; they continued to maintain security in their provinces with their Peshmerga militia, while they established their own assembly and even flew their own flag.

Dissatisfaction with the election was quietly acknowledged when the Bush administration recalled Ambassador John Negroponte and appointed a new envoy, Zalmay Khalilzad, an American of Afghani (Pashtun) descent. Fluent in Arabic, he was a Sunni Moslem who had been U.S. Ambassador to Afghanistan from 2003 to 2005. Since the election had demonstrated the triumph of the new Shia order over the old Baathist Sunni, which would encourage civil war, Khalilzad worked to repeal the results by encouraging Sunnis to return to the political process and reduce the insurgency.

Back in Washington, Cheney announced on May 30, 2005, that the violence was in decline. "I think they're in the last throes, if you will, of the insurgency." In reality, however, the opposite was true. Bad went to worse. Throughout 2005, Sunni insurgents launched vicious assaults on Shia civilians and holy places. Shiites responded with their own attacks, while Zarqawi's terrorists intensified their violence toward Shiittes, the government, and U.S. forces. In 2004, the various enemies launched over 26,000 attacks; during 2005, that rose to more than 34,000, and by the end of the year bomb attacks soared to 1,800 a month. During summer 2005, over 100 insurgent groups were proudly claiming responsibility for

attacking Americans or new Iraqi security forces; an average of ten policemen or soldiers were slain each day. Kidnapping soared—more than
5,000 in just the first two years of the occupation—as the slaughter continued. At least 40 bodies a day turned up at Baghdad's morgue, and on
one day 50, all murdered, washed up on the banks of the Tigris. To get
into the Green Zone a visitor had to go through eight security checks,
and insurgents continually lobbed mortars into the area. "No one was
safe anywhere," wrote a freelance journalist. "Iraq belonged to militias,
the resistance, terrorists, any man with a gun. The roads leading to Baghdad were a terror zone. The streets of Baghdad were war zones. . . . Iraqis
continued to live in a republic of fear."

Americans in the war zone and at home grew frustrated. "On the
current course we will have two options," said a marine lieutenant colonel leading combat troops. "We can lose in Iraq and destroy our army, or
we can just lose." Later in 2005, the Democratic Congressman and Vietnam vet John Murtha added, "We cannot continue in our present
course. . . . It's a flawed policy wrapped in an illusion," and two months
later retired General William Odom, former head of National Security
Agency, called Iraq "the greatest strategic disaster in American history."[6]

"As Iraqis stand up," Bush responded, "we will stand down," but
Iraqification would have to be accelerated, since by summer 2005 there
was an increasing number of signs that U.S. land forces were in crisis.
As the war's death toll moved toward 2,000, young men and women no
longer were enlisting. Rumsfeld already had announced the "stop-loss"
program, which prevented thousands of soldiers from leaving the service and added months onto their tours beyond their enlistment contracts. Throughout 2005, the National Guard missed its recruiting
goals and at the end of September the army announced that for the
fiscal year it missed its recruiting target by the widest margin since
1979. To encourage enlistments, the government began paying up to
$40,000 bonuses, while nearly all soldiers and marines in the war
zones received a $15,000 bonus for reenlisting. In 2006, the retention
bonuses cost the taxpayer $600 million. Immigrants in the U.S. armed
forces got the bonuses and were put on fast track toward citizenship;
about 25,000 became citizens during the first three years of the war. In
addition, the Pentagon increased the number of "moral waivers" for
potential recruits, meaning that by 2007 one in ten had been convicted

of serious misdemeanors and even felonies. By that year, the army was exhausted, and its 38 available combat units were deployed, returning home, or preparing to go to Iraq at a time when additional troops were needed because of the Taliban resurgence in Afghanistan. Moreover, levels of desertions, suicides, and divorces spiked. "People aren't designed to be exposed to the horrors of combat repeatedly," said General Casey, "and it wears on them."

But not all Americans were worn down, for the all-volunteer armed forces meant that relatively few citizens were affected by the war. By the end of 2006, over five years after the U.S. invaded Afghanistan, only about one in every 230 Americans had been deployed either to that country or to Iraq. "The fatal flaw was when right after September 11 the president asked everyone to go on with their lives," said a special forces sergeant. "That set the stage for no one sacrificing. That's why they aren't behind it, because they don't have a stake in this war." Soldiers in Iraq had a common saying: "The military went to war. America went to the mall."

Still, Iraq was hard to ignore and support declined. For the first time, pollsters reported in June 2005 that a majority of citizens believed that the administration had "intentionally misled" the nation into war, that the conflict wasn't "worth it," and that it had not made America "safer." Gallup found that 59 percent wanted to withdraw some or all U.S. troops from Iraq, and two months later those who approved of Bush's handling of the war plunged to 34 percent. That disaffection appeared in a personal way on August 6. While the president vacationed at his Crawford ranch, Cindy Sheehan of California, a mother who lost her son Casey in a Sadr City battle in April 2004, began camping outside of his ranch, demanding a meeting with the president. He avoided her. She bought five acres and attracted other antiwar activists who for the next two years occupied her land, "Camp Casey."

Sheehan reinvigorated the antiwar movement and kept the president inside his ranch until another force of nature slammed into the Gulf Coast—Hurricane Katrina. The massive storm clobbered New Orleans and eventually killed over 1,800. Governors along the coast lamented that the war in Iraq had stripped the National Guard of personnel and equipment needed to provide security at home, and a critic wrote that the storm "administered the coup de grace to the Bush presidency."

Bush's approval rating took another beating, dropping to the lowest so far, 40 percent, while a new high of 55 percent disapproved.

Katrina opened the floodgates of criticism at home, while the administration quietly began to revise their policies toward Iraq. Throughout the year, the new Secretary of State, Condi Rice, differed with Rumsfeld over how to wage the war in Iraq. Rumsfeld was convinced that the correct way was to have Iraqi leaders take control of their country, and if they could not, it was their problem and U.S. troops should withdraw; he opposed nation-building. During 2005, Rice came to the conclusion that Rumsfeld was wrong, that the United States could not leave a failed, chaotic Iraq, which might spread to other fragile nations in the Middle East. The administration had to have a more comprehensive approach, leading her to accept the strategy of counterinsurgency.

Counterinsurgency already was being practiced by some commanding officers in Iraq. More difficult to defend against than conventional warfare, insurgency aimed at insecurity, confusion, disruption—all which were cheap to create and expensive to prevent. "Classic counterinsurgency . . . is not primarily about killing insurgents," stated one expert, "it is about controlling the population and creating a secure environment in which to gain popular support." Colonel H. R. McMaster agreed: "Every time you treat an Iraqi disrespectfully, you are working for the enemy." McMaster was the commanding officer of the army regiment that pacified the old city near the Syrian border, Tal Afar. He banned his soldiers from using the term "*haji*" as a slang description because it was disrespectful of the Moslem religion, had his officers check out books on Iraqi history and culture, and had one of every ten of his soldiers receive a short course in conversational Arabic. The colonel admitted previous mistakes to the locals, was conciliatory, and willing to listen, all of which weakened the insurgency and especially the position of foreign fighters who advocated more violence. He ordered his Iraqi counterparts to survey the local population and ask questions. How were they being treated? What were their problems? How could coalition forces help? With this approach, local officials quickly recruited 1,400 police who helped 2,000 Iraqi troops patrol the city, while the mayor and city council worked to rebuild the infrastructure. Tips poured in, even from locals using their cell phones to call American troops and report insurgents planting IEDs.

Hearing of this success, Secretary Rice dispatched one of her aides to talk with Colonel McMaster, who described his strategy as "Clear, Hold, Build." In October, the secretary clarified this policy in the Senate: "Our political-military strategy has to be . . . to clear areas from insurgent control, to hold them securely and to build durable Iraqi institutions." Rumsfeld was furious, demanding that he run the show in Iraq, but two weeks later the president supported Rice by declaring U.S. policy now was to "Clear, Hold and Build."

That meant a long war, which was confirmed in November, when General Casey returned to Washington and testified to Congress. He declared that a study of more than 50 insurgencies around the world during the past century demonstrated that the average one took nine years to win, "and there's no reason that we should believe that the insurgency in Iraq will take any less time." Shortly thereafter, Wolfowitz and Feith left the Pentagon, meaning that neocon ideology was diluted, freeing the military to tackle the task at hand—winning the war in Iraq.

Casey returned to Iraq and in 2006 established the COIN Academy, the acronym for counterinsurgency, at a big base north of Baghdad. The general made attending its intensive one-week course a prerequisite to commanding a unit in Iraq. In California, the army erected a mock Iraqi village, complete with 400 Arabic speakers who played shopkeepers, police, and insurgents. "Because the Army won't change itself," the general told his subordinates, "I'm going to change the Army here in Iraq."

Army Lieutenant General Petraeus was on that team and so were Marine Lieutenant Generals James Mattis and James Amos. After the initial invasion in 2003, Petraeus had been in charge of the northern city of Mosul, where he avoided an insurgency by reaching out to the people, holding immediate local elections, and minimizing de-Baathification, which kept people employed and public services and businesses running. After training Iraqi security forces in 2004, Petraeus was rotated back to Fort Leavenworth, Kansas, where he and a team began revising the army and marine field manual on counterinsurgency. Petraeus ordered the officers in classes at the Command and General Staff College to study counterinsurgency, and by December 2006 the U.S. Army published the new field manual, which was quickly reviewed, even by *Jihadi* websites. Fort Leavenworth posted the manual on its website and it was downloaded two million times in the next two months.

The manual was an attack on how the Pentagon had been fighting the war while it signaled the approach Petraeus would take if he was given the command:

-An operation that kills five insurgents is counterproductive if collateral damage leads to the recruitment of fifty more insurgents.
-Treat detainees professionally and publicize their treatment. . . . At no time can Soldiers and marines detain family members or close associates to compel suspected insurgents to surrender or provide information.
-The *cornerstone* of any COIN effort is establishing security for the civilian population.

That was a major shift in focus. For three years the army had been living on secure bases, going out on patrols to kill insurgents and returning to base, instead of making the civilian population secure. David Kilcullen, an adviser to Petraeus, advocated "a residential approach—living in your sector, in close proximity to the population, rather than raiding into the area from remote, secure bases. Movement on foot . . . establish links with the locals, who see you as real people they can trust and do business with, not as aliens who descend from an armored box."

Counterinsurgency was a gamble, of course, and one part of the strategy was "to enhance the host government's legitimacy," wrote an expert. "But what if the government isn't good or brave or wise?"[7]

That was a problem in Baghdad, and to bring about Iraq's first permanent government and Council of Representatives that was to govern for more than the next four years, Iraqis went to the polls in December 2005. Realizing that boycotting elections was counterproductive, the Sunnis participated, resulting in almost 80 percent turnout of eligible voters, about 11 million. There was little violence, making it a hopeful scene for a weary nation. Out of 275 seats, the Shiite UIA won 128, the Kurdistan Alliance took 53, and the Sunni Iraq Accord Front won 44. The basic geometry remained the same; the Shia Islamic parties were dominant and had to share power for a majority. It took months to form a government, and in April 2006, after pressure from the Bush administration, Prime

Minister Jaafari stepped aside and the office was given to a less divisive Shiite politician, Nouri al-Maliki. He had a government assembled the next month. The Kurd Jalal Talabani remained as president, and Shiite Adil Abdul-Mahdi and Sunni Tariq al-Hashemi became vice presidents. To placate the Sunnis, one was named to head the Defense Ministry, while a Shiite was named minister of interior. The losers in the election were the former prime minister Ayad Allawi's Iraqiyya, by now a secular, cross-sectarian coalition, which lost 40 percent of its seats, and Ahmed Chalabi, whose party did not win one seat. A "major step forward in achieving our objective," declared Bush, of "having a democratic Iraq." Others were not so sure. "The steady grind of this guerrilla war is going to go on," said the Islamic expert Juan Cole. "The elections are not relevant to it."

What was relevant was who controlled the government ministries. "We pretend there is a national government," said the intelligence specialist Anthony H. Cordesman, "but it's a coalition in which ministries have been divided among the political parties." In fact, "ministries have become spoils, and since there is no civil service they hardly run at all." The Health and Education Ministries were controlled by Muqtada al-Sadr's Shiite party, protected by his Mahdi Army; the Interior Ministry was under control of the Supreme Council for the Islamic Revolution in Iraq, a main Shiite party, guarded by their Badr militia. Sunni death squads often dressed in Iraqi police or security uniforms and attacked the Shia ministries, while the Shiite-dominated government settled scores and ran a campaign of intimidation, abductions, and assassinations against innocent Sunnis. American troops in Baghdad found a "secret" prison located in a government building with over 200 starving detainees, mostly Sunnis, many with torture scars. The sight of Interior Ministry officials and police was unwelcome in Sunni areas of Baghdad because it was common knowledge that the city's 60,000 policemen were affiliated with Shia militias. "That's how the civil war worked," wrote an American journalist in Baghdad, "death squads became official."

Consequently, services suffered while corruption ran rampant. Just during the first year of the occupation, the special investigator for reconstruction, Stuart Bowen Jr., announced the CPA "lost" $8.8 billion. There was little or no oversight. In the city of Hillah, one American contracting officer later pleaded guilty to stealing more than $2 million. Thieves were encouraged because most of the funds were in cash. "Fresh new, crisp, unspent, just-printed $100 bills," said an American official. "It was the Wild West."

More corruption infected the Iraqi government. "You can't get the smallest contract from the government," said an Iraqi businessman, "without bribery at every level." The former minister of defense, his adviser, and other high-ranking officials stole approximately $2 billion from the arms procurement budget before they fled the nation. The heist, according to the head of the Iraqi Integrity Commission, was "possibly the largest robbery in the world." Oil corruption was out of control; the source of over 90 percent of the nation's revenue, petroleum fraud probably reached $4 billion in 2005 out of a GDP of about $30 billion. A U.S. report noted that "about 10 percent of refined fuels are diverted to the black market, and about 30 percent of imported fuels are smuggled out of Iraq and sold for a profit," some of the funds ending up in the hands of the insurgents. "It's the money pit of the insurgency," said an American officer. In September 2006, Prime Minister Maliki issued 88 arrest warrants for former government officials, including 15 former ministers, but over 60 of them already had fled the country.

Corruption affected reconstruction, which was painfully slow. In October 2003, Congress had allocated over $18 billion for reconstruction projects but when the United States handed over the country to Iraqis in June 2004 only 2 percent of those funds had been spent, only about 100 of 2,300 projects had been started. By that summer it was too dangerous to continue building projects. "Security trumps everything," said the mission director for USAID. "It does us little good to build a school if parents are afraid to send their children to that school because they may not come home." Three years after the invasion, the large construction firm Bechtel, which had received $2.3 billion from the U.S. government to rebuild power, water, and sewage plants, pulled out of Iraq after the death of 52 employees. Security concerns and corruption affected basic services. During Saddam's era, Baghdad usually had electricity 24 hours a day; although the Bush administration allocated $7.7 billion in contracts to rebuild power stations, three years after the invasion that supply only was 6–8 hours. As for restoring oil production, the United States committed $1.7 billion in mostly no-bid contracts to corporations such as Halliburton, but production dropped from 2.6 million barrels a day at the start of the war to 1.1 million barrels by the end of 2005, mostly because of graft and sabotage of pipelines.[8]

The corruption that plagued the government was minor compared to the violence unleashed after February 22, 2006, when radical Sunni insurgents blew up one of Shia's holiest sites, the shrine of the Two Imams in Samarra, collapsing its magnificent golden dome. "The war could really be on now," said a Shiite street peddler. "This is a strike at who we are." The Grand Ayatollah Sistani, who had urged his Shia to be restrained, no longer could control his sect and they took to the streets in a rage of revenge. "Shiite militia members flooded the streets of Baghdad," reported a journalist, "firing rocket-propelled grenades and machine guns at Sunni mosques as Iraqi Army soldiers—called out to stop the violence—stood helpless nearby. By the day's end, mobs had struck 27 Sunni mosques in the capital, killing three imams and kidnaping a fourth." Shia militias attacked Sunnis in a half-dozen central and southern Iraqi cities and quickly slaughtered nearly 1,300 people. "If the government can't protect us," declared one Shia leader on Sharqiya TV, "then we will have to do it ourselves."

They did. Up to then, the Sunni insurgency was the greatest threat to U.S. plans for a peaceful Iraq, but that was supplanted by Shia militias unleashing sectarian killings. In March, suicide bombings killed about 170 while sectarian murders sacrificed another 1,300. Executions rose from about 200 in January to more than 700 in March, a month in which eight times as many Iraqis died by murder than from insurgents' bombings. By June, an average of 100 civilians a day were killed. In July, 1,666 bombs exploded, the most ever, while over 3,400 were butchered, marking the deadliest month of the war for Iraqi civilians.

The Bush administration refused to call the violence a "civil war," but chaos reigned as Shia and Sunni militias and death squads roamed the streets of many towns, especially Baghdad, which suffered at least 2,500 killings in the ten weeks after the Samarra bombing. Neighborhood militias quickly materialized and each evening they rolled out barriers to curtail attacks. On one Sunday in May, bombs killed at least 30 while 45 men were murdered in the capital, most tortured by electric drills before they were shot in the head. Shiites began roaming districts asking to see young men named Omar and Bakr, popular Sunni names, while bakeries became favorite targets of Sunni gunmen because the cooks usually were Shiites. People could be killed simply because of their sect or if they were Kurds, Turkmen, or Christians. Thousands of families began to leave integrated neighborhoods and move to exclusively Shia or Sunni areas; a map of Baghdad soon looked like the Shiites lived on the east and Sunnis the west of the Tigris River. By November about 500,000 people, threatened in mixed cities like Baghdad, Mosul, along with Babil, Diyala, and Salahaddin provinces, had fled their homes. Nearly 1,000 Iraqis were displaced while 1,000 left for Jordan and 2,000 moved to Syria—*each day*. This flight resulted in a massive refugee problem for those countries, or as one expert declared, "the fastest-growing humanitarian crisis in the world." In Baghdad, the owner of a downtown business reported that each month he was visited by a gang of armed men demanding $300 for protection. "I just pay," he said. "We all pay."

"Here on the streets of Baghdad, it looks like hell," wrote a reporter. "Corpses, coldly executed, are turning up by the minibus-load. Mortar shells are casually lobbed into rival neighborhoods. Car bombs are killing people wholesale, while assassins hunt them down one by one." No one was safe; in the months following Samarra at least 311 teachers—and 64 pupils under the age of 12—were murdered. "Is it civil war?" asked a journalist, to which the scholar Farid Khazen answered, "In Iraq it is no longer a matter of definition—'civil war,' or 'war' or 'violence' or 'terrorism.' It is all of the above."

Iraqis blamed the occupier. "There is anger," said a Shiite cleric. "You can hear it in the slogans at Friday prayers: 'Death to America.' They're burning American flags. They're saying, 'The American won't leave except by the funerals of their sons.'" In fact, a U.S. report found that "the Iraq conflict has become the 'cause celebre' for jihadists, breeding a deep resentment of U.S. involvement in the Muslim world and cultivating supporters for the global jihadist movement." Bush's war in Iraq, a National Intelligence Estimate concluded, had increased the threat from terrorism by "shaping a new generation of terrorist leaders and operatives." When the Pentagon surveyed Iraqi public opinion in 2003 it found that 14 percent of Sunnis supported the insurgency; by September 2006, that figure had soared to 75 percent, the highest ever, a time when over 70 percent wanted the United States to withdraw and 77 percent thought the Americans intended to keep permanent military bases in Iraq.

In the middle of this chaos were U.S. troops, many of whom felt there was no way out. "It sucks," said one soldier. "Honestly, it feels like we're driving around waiting to get blown up." His squad leader added, "No one wants to be here . . . personally, I want to fight in a war like World War II."

In Baghdad, London, and Washington, political leaders were paying the price. "We've been told over and over that the political process is going to make us safer," said a Baghdad resident disillusioned with Prime Minister Maliki. But "all we see are parties fighting over ministries so they can get jobs and money for themselves."

In London, approval ratings for Prime Minister Tony Blair dropped to a new low, around 30 percent. Commonly called "Bush's poodle," pressure mounted for his resignation, and in September 2006 he announced that he would be stepping down within a year. "I would have preferred to do this in my own way," he admitted. When he resigned the following June his approval rate was only 25 percent, and his replacement, Gordon Brown, quickly announced that British troop levels in Iraq would be reduced to only 4,500 by the end of the year.[9]

In Washington, critics went on the attack. At a press conference one month after Samarra, the veteran journalist Helen Thomas said to the president, "Every reason given, publicly at least, has turned out not to be true. My question is, why did you really want to go to war? . . . what was your real reason?" Stunned, Bush commenced on a long defense, "I didn't want war. . . . The Taliban provided safe haven for al Qaeda . . . I was hoping to solve this problem diplomatically." While Fox News commentators called Thomas "out of bounds," the question alone demonstrated the lack of trust the mainstream media and more of the public had with the president, which was revealed in opinion polls. During the first months of 2006, pollsters found that Americans felt the war was the "nation's top problem," about 60 percent thought the war was a mistake, only a third approved of Bush's handling of the conflict, and just 20 percent believed U.S. forces would win. By the end of the year, over 70 percent disapproved of Bush's handling of the conflict, including, for the first time, a majority of the troops. Even conservatives lamented. William F. Buckley wrote that Bush had to "cope with failure" while George Will carped that "all three components of the 'axis of evil'—Iraq, Iran, and North Korea—" now were "more dangerous than they were when that phrase was coined in 2002."

The Bush administration fought back. "Iraqis have shown the world they want a future of freedom and peace," the president declared in March, later adding, "Americans have never retreated in the face of thugs and assassins, and we will not begin now." By August, Bush vowed, "We're not leaving so long as I'm president," and then, strangely, acknowledged in a press conference that Iraq had "nothing" to do with 9/11. Rumsfeld called war critics "quitters" who "blame America first" and give "the enemy the false impression Americans cannot stomach a tough fight," and Cheney added that "terrorists are encouraged" by those debating the wisdom of the war.

The administration did receive some good news on June 8: Zarqawi was killed. U.S. planes dropped two 500-pound bombs on a safe house where he had been spotted, about 30 minutes northeast of Baghdad, but like Saddam's capture, the terrorist's death did not stop the violence that raged throughout 2006. In July, Shiites appeared in a Sunni neighborhood near the Baghdad airport and set up a roadblock, went into homes, and slaughtered about 50. Retaliation quickly followed, as Sunnis exploded two large car bombs in Sadr City, killing at least 30, and the next day gunmen attacked a Shiite bus station and murdered 22 more. More than 3,000 Iraqis were slain every month from June to September. Then, "Red October." The UN estimated that an unprecedented 3,709 Iraqi civilians were slaughtered as Sunnis and Shiites conducted "a merciless campaign of revenge killings." Death squads connected to the Mahdi Army, as well as to other Shia and Sunni groups, captured and executed civilians in cold blood, sometimes dragging them out of hospitals or government ministries. In one 24-hour period, 110 bodies were found in Baghdad. The next month, Sunni militants carried out their deadliest attack to date as multiple car bombs killed more than 200 people in Sadr City.

The violence was overwhelming, and U.S. forces no longer patrolled many areas, such as Sadr City, labeled "No Go Zones." "If the war in Iraq is not a civil war," the *Houston Chronicle* editorialized, "it is only because the conflict has come to resemble something worse: complete and total anarchy."

During the anarchy of 2006, President Bush began to understand that his "stay the course" policy was not working. "What are you hearing from people in Baghdad? What are people's daily lives like?" he asked his deputy national security adviser, Meghan O'Sullivan. "It's hell, Mr. President." By August, Bush conceded to his advisers, "The situation seems to be deteriorating," and by October, the president was more frustrated. He told National Security Adviser Stephen J. Hadley to begin a full strategy review—one that did not ask advice from Rumsfeld's Pentagon. Congress already had begun its review with the bipartisan Iraq Study Group.

During the Iraqi violence, the American people went to the polls for the November midterm elections. In a press conference two weeks earlier the president again repeated his familiar theme of holding the Iraqi government to "benchmarks," a term he used 13 times, and declared that he wasn't satisfied with the situation but the U.S. effort would last "as long as it takes." Under a barrage of sharp questions the president clung to his faith, using the word "believe" 21 times. "I believe that the military strategy we have is going to work, that's what I believe." Later in the campaign he went on the attack. "The stakes are high," he declared. "The Democrats are the party of cut and run."

Actually, almost everyone was ready to cut and run. Republican senators were calling for a new approach; many, along with some foreign policy experts, demanded that the United States cut Iraq into three pieces—Kurdish north, Sunni west, and Shia south—and then withdraw. Neocons played the blame game; thoroughly discredited, they cast blame on others in the administration. As for the president, he had lost credibility, especially with the middle, liberals, and youth. Lambasted every night on Comedy Central's *Daily Show with Jon Stewart* and Stephen Colbert's *Colbert Report*, he also was the target of the new video sharing website, YouTube. A week before the election Bush proclaimed, "we've never been 'stay the course'" in Iraq, and in six days there were 96 entries on YouTube, videotapes showing Bush using the phrase over and over again.

The electorate no longer was listening to Bush. At the polls, voters handed a massive defeat to him, his party, and his administration's policies toward Iraq—the most important issue in November 2006. Bush called it "a thumpin." Democrats picked up 31 seats and captured the House and also gained six seats and control of the Senate. Next day, Bush accepted Rumsfeld's resignation and nominated former CIA director and Texas A&M University President Robert M. Gates. An arrogant ideologue had been replaced by a thoughtful pragmatist. When Gates was asked at his confirmation hearings who was responsible for 9/11, he responded "Osama bin Laden." When asked who represented a greater threat to the U.S., he repeated, "Osama bin Laden." And when asked if the United States was winning in Iraq, he said, "No, sir." "Goodness Gracious!" exclaimed the *New York Times* columnist Maureen Dowd. "The Truth!"

Weeks after Rumsfeld left the Pentagon, on December 30, the Iraqi government executed Saddam Hussein. A video of the execution was surreptitiously taken on a cell phone camera, exposing a bizarre scene. Shiites mocked the former Sunni dictator as he was pushed up the stairs to the platform, hands tied behind his back. The noose was put around his neck, and he said something back to the crowd, when someone yelled, "Go to Hell." The trapdoor released, Saddam fell, snapping his neck. Shortly thereafter, the video of the sordid affair was circulating on the Internet, demonstrating that the Iraqi government was so incompetent that they couldn't even conduct a hanging with any dignity, and they even made Saddam a martyr to many Sunnis.[10]

Concerning the Sunnis, the U.S. Army was experimenting during autumn 2006 with a security plan involving Awakening Councils, which were Sunni tribal militias in Anbar Province. Earlier that year the provincial capital Ramadi had been reduced to rubble. Bombs went off continually, and were often set by indigenous Islamic insurgents calling themselves al Qaeda in Mesopotamia, a group associated with al Qaeda in Iraq. The terrorists controlled large parts of the city and province and imposed their unpopular fundamentalist brand of Islam on the local populations. They attacked anyone who had relations with Americans. Anbar's governor had survived 29 attempts on his life, but others were not so lucky. His predecessor and his deputy had been shot to death; his secretary beheaded.

"Since 2003, there has been no law here in Ramadi," said Anbar's governor, "no order—only chaos. The tribal leaders are looking for a way to protect themselves." That way appeared in September when al Qaeda killed family members of a sheikh in Ramadi; he called for a meeting, which attracted over 50 sheikhs. Although U.S. officials blamed al Qaeda for only about 10 percent of attacks on coalition forces in Iraq, they were savage ones, killing many Sunnis in Anbar. That prompted

Ramadi sheikhs to sign on to Awakening Councils, and during September so did 25 of the 31 tribes throughout Anbar. Soon, fresh recruits appeared for local police forces, first called Concerned Local Citizens and eventually Sons of Iraq. They provided more intelligence for American forces, while denying insurgents operating bases to attack the government or U.S. forces. The Sons of Iraq also helped with the unemployment problem, since the Americans paid the men $10 a day, about $300 a month. In other words, American commanders began paying former insurgents who had fought and killed U.S. troops. As one sergeant said, "We're paying them not to blow us up."

Former Sunni insurgents became temporary, paid allies of the U.S. military. "Once a tribal leader flips" against al Qaeda in Iraq, said Colonel Sean MacFarland, "attacks on American forces in that area stop almost overnight." Soon, local Sunnis were ambushing al Qaeda. In 2006, Anbar Province was the most lethal place for U.S. troops, with one soldier killed almost every day, but by mid-2007 a month might go by without losing an American.

Sons of Iraq was one new U.S. military strategy adopted during autumn 2006, while another was percolating in the minds of some senior officials and officers back in the United States—the surge.

Retired General Jack Keane and two of his protégés, Lieutenant Generals David Petraeus and Raymond Odierno, had become convinced that year that the United States was going to lose the war unless they changed strategy. They believed that adding 20,000 to 30,000 new troops would provide security so they could begin counterinsurgency, protect the population, build Iraqi security forces, and stabilize the government. The old policy of using overwhelming force, attacking insurgents in cities, and withdrawing to bases had failed. "We've taken Samarra four times, and we've lost it four times," said an army officer. "We need a new strategy."

Yet changing strategy was not favored at the Pentagon—until Rumsfeld was fired. That opened the door for new ideas, and the Iraq Study Group, published in December, suggested a whopping 79 changes in policy toward Iraq. The president was unpopular, frustrated, and finally open to new ideas and possible solutions. The White House invited the retired generals Keane and Barry McCaffrey, along with Professor Eliot Cohen and defense expert Stephen Biddle to a meeting.

"Mister President, I'm going to be very blunt," Cohen began. "I don't mean to cause offense, but this is wartime, and I feel I owe it to you." For the next hour the experts laid it on the line to Bush and Cheney. "Time is running out," declared Keane. "We need more troops. For the first time, we will secure the population, which is the proven way to defeat an insurgency." While all the experts did not agree on the surge, they did agree on who should be the commanding officer—David Petraeus. Other meetings were held, and the result appeared on January 10, 2007, when the president addressed the nation. This time, Bush made no claims of progress in Iraq. "The situation in Iraq is unacceptable to the American people, and it is unacceptable to me. . . . Where mistakes have been made, the responsibility rests with me." He continued, stating that the United States needed a new command structure and a change in strategy. He then announced his "New Way Forward," which quickly was dubbed "the surge," sending almost 30,000 more troops.

Thus, after almost four years at war in Iraq, the commander-in-chief admitted that his administration's strategy of deploying a relatively small force to kill and capture the enemy was a failure. It would now be replaced with a new one—surge and counterinsurgency—and this included a change in emphasis: protect the Iraqi population.

About 70 percent of Americans opposed sending more troops, and so the surge unleashed a firestorm of debate. "By surging troops and bringing security to Baghdad and other areas," the Republican senator John McCain wrote, "we will give the Iraqis the best possible chance to succeed." Most other politicians were not so sure. "I am not persuaded that 20,000 additional troops in Iraq is going to solve the sectarian violence there," said the Democratic presidential contender Senator Barack Obama. "In fact, I think it will do the reverse." The Republican senator Chuck Hagel was scathing, calling the plan "the most dangerous foreign policy blunder in this country since Vietnam."

Democrats did not try to stop the surge. In control of Congress, they spent the next two years setting "benchmarks" of progress for Iraq, advocating troop withdrawal, and occasionally holding hearings and grilling General Petraeus. Some Democrats advocated impeaching Bush, but they did not have the 60 votes for conviction in the Senate; most were in a holding pattern anticipating victory in the 2008 elections and they were tired of Iraq. "Like it or not," said the Senate majority leader Harry Reid of Nevada, "George Bush is still the commander-in-chief, and this is his war."

During that time, the president sent a new team to Iraq. In December 2006, Lieutenant General Ray Odierno arrived to take over daily operations of the U.S. Army. In January, the White House announced that General Petraeus would become the top officer in Iraq as commander of Multi-National Force-Iraq, and in March the State Department sent a new U.S. Ambassador, Ryan Crocker, a Middle East expert fluent in Arabic and a former ambassador to Pakistan. The new war managers worked well together and tried to avoid confrontation while still being brutally honest.

That honesty appeared in January when General Petraeus addressed the Senate Armed Services Committee. Unlike many previous upbeat assessments from the Pentagon or military commanders, he announced the "deteriorating situation . . . increase in the level of violence, fueled by the insurgent and sectarian fighting." In that tough situation the Iraqi government had "found it difficult to gain traction." And the general leveled when describing the challenge ahead: "insurgents, international terrorists, sectarian militias, regional meddling, violent criminals, governmental dysfunction, and corruption."[11]

As Petraeus and Odierno were setting up in Baghdad, violence continued unabated during the first half of 2007. On January 16, bombs were detonated at a Baghdad university, killing over 60, and six days later more bombs exploded at a street bazaar, slaughtering 80. In February, insurgents detonated a ton of explosives in a Shiite market, killing 125 and wounding 300, and when Ambassador Crocker arrived in March he labeled the violence "monstrous. Sunnis and Shiites were slaughtering each other with guns and knives and power drills. Roadside bombs were picking off American soldiers by the dozens." In April, the tally for just one day across the country was 289, while May was bloodier. On average, sectarian murders claimed the lives of 22 people *each day* in Baghdad. "It is hell," said a fleeing Baghdad resident, and a Shiite businessman added, "Now we regret that Saddam Hussein is gone, no matter how much we hated him."

The surge that began in Baghdad was a complex strategy. "Three-dimensional chess in the dark," said one general, "and I believe that's an understatement." American commanders were faced with the tasks of securing the population, confronting the insurgents and militia who controlled neighborhoods, while fighting off terrorists such as al Qaeda in Iraq. The surge had to clear, hold, and build, so Generals Petraeus and Odierno ordered their troops to make a visible commitment. That meant moving from large, secure Forward Operating Bases into the lawless capital, where they set up smaller posts, 35 to 100 troops, called Joint Security Stations or Command Posts (COPS). They increased the number of interpreters and formed partner companies with Iraqi security forces; the same number of U.S. and Iraqi troops worked together, which increased trust and prevented abuses of civilians. Eventually, these units moved into every neighborhood in the city, established 75 outposts manned 24/7, and began patrolling on foot, first through eastern Baghdad, then the western part of the city, and then spreading out into the southern sector. Since the Iraqi security forces were made up mostly of Shiites, the U.S. commanders pressured the Maliki government to allow the Sons of Iraq to work with both U.S. and Iraqi forces in the city's Sunni neighborhoods, and eventually 25,000 helped with security. In extremely violent Sunni areas bordering Shia ones, 12-foot concrete walls were erected to divide and protect residents; one wall ran for three miles, and after a wall was erected in the Adhamiyah neighborhood, civilian deaths declined by two-thirds. Moreover, the surge came with a new American attitude—humility. After four years of telling Iraqi civilians what to do, U.S. troops now held respectful interviews, listened to them, and attempted to solve their problems. Most Iraqis wanted to know one thing: "Are you staying?"

"We surged," declared Major General Rick Lynch. "He surged." The response was vicious. "This is a period in which it gets harder before it gets easier," Petraeus said in May. When U.S. troops appeared, they were attacked by militias in almost every district who controlled the area or by vengeful terrorists. Enemy attacks on U.S. and Iraqi forces increased 40 percent in the first half of 2007, to almost 1,600 in June. That year became the deadliest one of the war—904 U.S. troops were killed in action—bringing the total mortality toll to 3,907 by the end of December. It was the price paid for moving from big, safe bases to smaller outposts among the people—and the enemy.

Spring and summer 2007 was the toughest time. The enemy now employed much more powerful roadside bombs—ones capable of flipping over the 25-ton Bradley Fighting Vehicles. Only the size of a coffee can, these new EFPs, "explosively formed penetrators," were manufactured in Iran, brought across the border, and used almost exclusively by Shiite militias. Fighting intensified; casualties soared. Between mid-June and mid-July almost 600 unidentified bodies were found dumped in different parts of Baghdad. The violence had an impact on infrastructure; during the incredible heat of July the capital was receiving an average of only one hour of electricity a day. Nearly 70 percent of Iraqis said that the surge had worsened their lives, while an astonishing 26 percent of Iraqis told pollsters that a family member or relative had been murdered.

As in the previous year, the surge and subsequent violence took a toll on the U.S. Army. As comrades died, morale plummeted. For the first time, the percentage of troops who thought victory in Iraq was likely decreased to 50 percent, a drop of 30 percent in two years. For older officers, the war was reminding them of Vietnam. "There are no good guys, and there are no bad guys," declared one colonel. "Everybody is gray." Frustration mounted. "I love the Army," said a 12-year veteran, "but I hate this war."

So did many Americans back home, where attacks on the president became brutal; Bush felt the pressure. "I never wanted to be a war president," he told an audience in July, and then he shifted to Iraq and ad libbed, "By the way, al Qaeda is doing most of the spectacular bombings, trying to incite sectarian violence. The same people that attacked us on September 11 is the crowd that is now bombing people, killing innocent men, women and children." Liberal commentators pounced. Eugene Robinson denounced the president's "cognitive dissonance," Maureen Dowd reminded the president that al Qaeda in Iraq "did not exist before 9/11." "Was nothing real? Was nothing true?" wrote Leonard Pitts Jr. "No, nothing was." MSNBC's Keith Olbermann was more vicious— and personal: "This, sir, is your war. . . . Go there and fight, your war. Yourself."[12]

The last surge troops arrived in June 2007, bringing the U.S. troops level in Iraq to 156,000, while Iraqi security forces had improved and increased to 400,000. Petraeus told his soldiers it was "hard but not hopeless," which seemed accurate because by late summer and autumn the military could see the first promising results. Security in sections of

Baghdad slowly improved. In August, after two Shia militias drew weapons and left 49 people dead, Muqtada al-Sadr ordered a "freeze" on action by his Mahdi Army. Attacks on American and Iraqi forces in country decreased from a high of almost 1,600 in June to 600 by December; during 2008 they dropped to under 200 a month. In Baghdad, by the end of 2007 there was a 90 percent reduction in murders, 80 percent decrease of attacks on citizens, and a 70 percent decline of vehicle bombs. By that time, a journalist reported that life in the capital was calmer. "Some shops stay open until late into the evening. Children play in parks, young women stay out after dark, restaurants are filled with families, and old men sit at sidewalk cafes playing backgammon and smoking sheesha pipes."

As Baghdad's security improved, the U.S. and Iraqi forces began spreading to cities and towns outside of the capital. Partnering was building trust between Americans and Iraqi forces. "They have always come when I am in trouble," said a U.S. captain clearing the town of Baqubah. "They never back down." That meant that the U.S. military could begin handing over security tasks in the provinces to Iraqi troops. In the north, the Kurdish security forces always had maintained control in their provinces and had worked with U.S. troops. The first Shia province turned over was Najaf, home of Grand Ayatollah Ali al-Sistani, in December 2006, but the process lagged until 2008. In February, the marines yielded control of Hit to the Iraqi security forces, and by September the Iraqis had primary responsibility for maintaining security in 11 of its 18 provinces. That included the first Sunni province, Anbar, where attacks against U.S. and Iraqi forces had dropped 90 percent. During the ceremony in Ramadi, the American commanding officer said to his Sunni and Shia audience, "There are two things that are desperately needed that security forces cannot provide here, trust and friendship amongst all of you and between the province and the rest of Iraq."

The Iraqis themselves would have to provide that trust, and naturally there were suspicions and setbacks. Although distrust remained deep between Malaki's Shiite-led government and the Sunni forces, the Sons of Iraq, after the U.S. Army cut funds, the Maliki government continued paying the Sunni militia and integrated some of them into Iraqi security forces, the government, and reconstruction projects. Paying the former militiamen decreased violence, so early in 2008 U.S. forces began paying Shia men $300 a month to work in public service jobs. That also improved security. The Shiite-dominated Iraqi Army was another problem because they were distrusted by the Sunni and Kurd populations. Decreasing suspicion would take time, but to appease Sunnis' fears the Iraqi Parliament passed a bill allowing for the reinstatement of low-level Sunni Baath Party members for certain government jobs and a pension for former higher level Baathists.

Reconciliation was a long and slow process, and the Shiite Prime Minister Maliki had to demonstrate that he could be not just a Shia political boss but an Iraqi leader. He began in March 2008 by ordering the Iraqi Army to take control of Basra, which was in the hands of Shiite militias, including Sadr's Madhi Army. The British had evacuated the city and no longer patrolled the streets. "By late 2007," said expert Anthony Cordesman, "the British position in Basra had eroded to the point of hiding in the airport."

Maliki had problems taking Basra. Some 1,300 Iraqi forces and police refused to fight or deserted instead of facing off with the Mahdi Army. The prime minister fired them, and after a slow start the army proved itself against the insurgents with U.S. air support; a cease-fire was negotiated, and government forces gained control of Basra. Sadr had threatened a million man march on the capital but became conciliatory as other politicians in the government supported the prime minister. That boosted the position of Maliki and decreased the political power of the Shiite militias. It brought the second-largest city and main seaport back under control of the central government. Basra also was a statement to Iran to stop meddling in Iraq, and it eventually increased the Iraqi government's prestige. Visiting Basra a couple months later a professor saw a "city wall covered with pro-Maliki graffiti. Commerce is returning to the city center . . . the Mahdi army's unchallenged hold has ended."

In May, Maliki took charge of a military operation to rout al Qaeda in Iraq from Mosul, which many officials described as the terror group's last major stronghold. Also that month, Maliki made an agreement with Sadr to allow the Iraqi Army and police to enter Sadr City and take over security. "Iraqi soldiers are smiling and saying hi to everybody," noted one resident. "Our children love the Iraqi soldiers because the children know these soldiers belong to Iraq, not to America." So, by June 2008, the government had confronted both Shia and Sunni militias in the south and north and won control of its three largest cities: Baghdad, Basra, and Mosul.[13]

The surge ended in July 2008 with the additional U.S. troops returning home, bringing down the total to 147,000. Baghdad and many cities were much more secure, allowing 160,000 contractors to work on reconstruction projects throughout the country. During the year electricity production reached preinvasion levels, and oil almost grew to that level; there were no attacks on pipelines. American employees were embedded in Iraqi ministries helping to increase efficiency and cut corruption. Businesses reopened, including coffee shops, restaurants, and kebab stands, and people went out at night. In July, the Iraq national football team returned to Baghdad for the first time in seven years and the next month 40,000 Iraqis crowded al-Shaab stadium to see the soccer finals of their national league. For the first time since 1990, the stadium was filled, with thousands more outside on the street. During 2008, almost 40,000 displaced families returned to Baghdad, while the next year the national government took primary responsibility for maintaining security in the remainder of its provinces.

"There was no question that under Petraeus, the U.S. military had regained the strategic initiative, an extraordinary achievement," wrote the military correspondent Tom Ricks. The surge and counterinsurgency stopped the country from falling further into civil war and curtailed the insurgents and militias, while it stabbed deep into the heart of al Qaeda in Iraq. It worked because there were enough U.S. troops to partner with the newly trained Iraqi troops and to protect, respect, and live with the population, because Americans were putting more unemployed men—many former militiamen—to work, and because most Iraqis had tired of the violence, the deaths, and many were becoming repulsed by terrorist groups. The surge also worked to give the Maliki government time to demonstrate that it could govern.

"Rather than retreating," declared President Bush in February 2008, "we sent 30,000 new troops into Iraq, and the surge is succeeding." True, violence had decreased. But so had American aims, which had become much more realistic. Administration rhetoric had ended about democracy flowering in Iraq and spreading throughout the Middle

East. "In terms of what it is that we are trying to achieve," General Petraeus told Congress in April, "I think simply it is a country that is at peace with itself and its neighbors . . . that can defend itself, that has a government that is reasonably representative and broadly responsive to its citizens . . . we're not after Jeffersonian democracy. We're after conditions that would allow our soldiers to disengage."

In September, Petraeus disengaged from Iraq and became commander of CENTCOM. After Secretary Gates and others gave Petraeus a standing ovation in Baghdad, command in Iraq was transferred to General Ray Odierno, who cautioned, "We must realize that these gains are fragile and reversible, and our work here is far from done."

It also was far from done in Afghanistan, where the situation had been deteriorating. "I think it's a mistake to look at Afghanistan as sort of one eight-year war," recalled Secretary Gates. "We had a war in 2001, 2002, which we essentially won. And the Taliban was kicked out of Afghanistan. Al Qaeda was kicked out. . . . And then things were very quiet in Afghanistan." Gates continued that the second war began in late 2005 and early 2006 and the United States did not get "its head into this conflict" until 2008. While the administration focused on Iraq, the Taliban and al Qaeda allies returned. In autumn 2003, only 20,000 U.S. troops were in country, meaning that battalions with 800 soldiers were trying to secure provinces the size of Vermont. Fighting intensified. While only about 30 U.S. troops died there in 2002 and in 2003, three times that were killed in 2005, and over 150 in 2008; by that year Afghanistan was more dangerous to the 31,000 U.S. troops stationed there than Iraq. Just months before the president left office, a National Intelligence Estimate warned Afghanistan was heading into a "downward spiral," which was critical because the more territory the Taliban controlled, the more money it could make from narcotics; by 2008 the country had again become the world's largest grower and exporter of opium.

The reemergence of the Taliban reminded Americans of the original aims of Bush's war on terror—capture or kill al Qaeda and its leader, Osama bin Laden. Seven years had passed since 9/11 and the world's number one terrorist remained at large. In that sense, Bush failed to win his war on terror. His supporters declared that his administration had kept America safe, that al Qaeda and other groups had not launched another massive attack on U.S. soil. True, the government was much more efficient attacking terrorist networks, derailing numerous attempts to strike at American interests at home and abroad.

Many times since declaring his war on terror the president had declared, "We don't do torture," yet he was contradicted by numerous reports, many from former detainees and interrogators. In 2006 the administration held about 14,000 detainees beyond the reach of U.S. law in various detention centers. Captured on battlefields, pulled from beds at night, grabbed off streets as insurgent suspects, U.S. forces had about 13,000 Iraqis held at Camp Cropper near Baghdad airport, Camp Bucca in the south, and Fort Suse in the north. UN Secretary-General Kofi Annan declared the arbitrary detention inconsistent with international law, Maliki said it violated Iraqis' rights, and in June 2006 the U.S. Supreme Court struck down military tribunals to try detainees. The president and his supporters struck back; in October, Congress passed and the president signed the Military Commissions Act, relabeling noncitizens as enemy combatants, stripping from them the right of habeas corpus and access to U.S. courts. Two years later, a divided Supreme Court for the third time sent a stinging rebuke to the president's antiterror policies. "The laws and Constitution are designed to survive, and remain in force," wrote Justice Anthony Kennedy in the majority opinion, "in extraordinary times."

That decision, however, did not mean that the 270 men remaining at Guantanamo would be released or even tried. The rest had been sent home or to third countries who would take them, while only 19 had been charged with a war crime. Instead, the administration would do the same with the war on terror as Afghanistan and Iraq—give the problem to the next president.

The last year of the Bush presidency was a struggle. In January 2008, two nonprofit journalism organizations released a report that in the two years following 9/11 the president and his top officials made "935 false statements" which were "part of an orchestrated campaign that effectively galvanized public opinion and . . . led the nation to war under decidedly false pretenses." For the remainder of the year, Bush's approval ratings hovered around 30 percent, bottoming out at 28 percent, and for the first time in the six decades of modern polling, surveys found that a whopping 76 percent disapproved of how Bush was handling his job, making him the most unpopular president. Vice President

Cheney's approval rating skidded to only 18 percent. In November, again for the first time, Gallup found that 50 percent "strongly disapproved" of Bush, surpassing the previous record holder President Richard Nixon when he resigned because of the Watergate scandal. The wars in Iraq, Taliban resurgence in Afghanistan, mixed with the beginning of the Great Recession in September, resulted in only 12 percent thinking that the nation was "headed in the right direction." After Bush's last State of the Union address the previous January, a year before he left office, a *USA Today* reporter said the president's message was, "I'm still here," and another quipped, "Out of Gas."

Before the tank was empty, however, the administration during 2008 negotiated the U.S.-Iraq Status of Forces Agreement. While Bush had desired 58 U.S. bases in Iraq, Maliki and his cabinet refused, saying that was "unacceptable." In July, the Iraqi prime minister became involved in the U.S. presidential campaign between the Democratic senator Barack Obama and the Republican senator John McCain by declaring that Obama's plan to withdraw all U.S. troops from his country in 16 months was "realistic," and if security improved he wanted all troops out by the end of 2010.

It was the beginning of the end of Bush's war in Iraq. By November, the administration had dropped its demand for bases, and the Iraqi government signed the Status of Forces Agreement. It stipulated that American troops would withdraw from Iraqi cities by June 2009 and that all U.S. forces would be out of the country by the end of 2011.

As the president was preparing to leave office, the journalist Bob Woodward, who had held several interviews with and written four books about Bush, conducted Bush's final interview at the White House. Woodward asked the president about his successor, "What are you going to say to the new leader about what you are handing off in Iraq?" Bush responded, "Don't let it fail."[14]

Epilogue: Obama

"Tonight, I am announcing that the American combat mission in Iraq has ended. Operation Iraqi Freedom is over. . . . And, next July, we will begin transition to Afghan responsibility."
— President Barack Obama, August 31, 2010

President Bush held a press conference in March 2006 and was asked about the crisis in Iraq. Frustration was mounting in the nation, and in the White House; he responded if and when the United States withdrew would be "decided by future presidents and future governments of Iraq."

So would the war on terror. In 2009 federal prosecutors charged more suspects with terrorism than in any year since the 9/11 attacks. Experts said a rise in plots was spurred by Internet recruitment, the spread of al Qaeda internationally, and the shifting tactics of terror leaders. One expert commented that the wide range of cases showed that al Qaeda "is in it for the long haul and we need to be as well." That year plots were uncovered in Illinois, North Carolina, Texas, and New York City. On Christmas, the Nigerian Umar Farouk Abdulmutallab attempted to blow up an airplane bound for Detroit, for which Osama bin Laden claimed responsibility. "Our attacks against you will continue as long as U.S. support for Israel continues," declared the terrorist. "It is not fair that Americans should live in peace as long as our brothers in Gaza live in the worst conditions."

Federal agencies had improved detecting and thwarting attacks, but little had transpired concerning Obama's campaign pledges to abandon antiterror laws of the Bush years. The new president discontinued the use of torture and announced support for international law, but he showed little interest in changing warrantless surveillance and it proved more difficult to amend the Patriot Act or close the detention center at Guantanamo. Congress debated a new law on terrorism but eventually passed a bill extending the Patriot Act, putting off that issue while it passed an economic stimulus plan to ease the recession and conducted long debates and eventually passed bills to reform health care and Wall Street. The administration—and the nation—continue to search for the appropriate balance between civil liberties and national security in the age of terrorism.

Guantanamo raised another issue: where to house the detainees? The previous administration sent them either to nations that would take them or to Saudi Arabia for its "terrorist-rehab" program, which had about an 80 percent success rate for returning men to normal lives. The Obama administration wrestled with Congress over the detention center, and eventually announced that it would like to transfer about half of the remaining 180 to a high-security facility, Thompson Correctional Center in rural Illinois. But Congress blocked bringing the detainees to U.S. soil or closing Guantanamo. Consequently, if, when, and where they would be tried—in military tribunals or civilian courts—was mired in legal limbo.[1]

The administration presented more clarity with its policy toward Iraq. In August 2008, during the presidential campaign, Senator Obama outlined his plans toward Iraq and Afghanistan in a speech to the Veterans of Foreign Wars. To him, the "biggest beneficiaries" of Bush's decision to attack Iraq were "al Qaeda's leadership, which no longer faced the pressure of America's focused attention; and Iran, which has advanced its nuclear program, continued its support for terror, and increased its influence in Iraq and the region." He declared that the "long-term solution in Iraq is political—the Iraqi government must reconcile its differences and take responsibility for its future." As he had advocated during his campaign, he again stated that the United States should remove combat brigades during summer 2010. Ending the war in Iraq would allow America "to finish the fight against al Qaeda and the

Taliban in Afghanistan and the border region of Pakistan," which he called "the central front in the war on terrorism."

To date, President Obama has been relatively true to his plans. He, Secretary of State Hillary Clinton, and Secretary of Defense Robert Gates have worked to stabilize Iraq and to confront the deteriorating situation in Afghanistan.

Yet massive problems remain on both fronts. Although greatly reduced from previous years, violence continued. The two main terrorist groups, al Qaeda in Iraq and Islamic State of Iraq, attacked the population and targeted government workers and buildings in an attempt to undermine faith in the government and derail the democratic process. Suicide bombers launched scattered attacks, the worst one in October 2009, when they struck the Justice Ministry, killing over 155 people and leaving about 500 wounded in a scene "filled with bloody human flesh."

Obviously, al Qaeda remained a lethal enemy, and that was demonstrated on March 7, 2010, when Iraq held its second parliamentary election since the fall of Saddam. Terrorists attempted intimidation, setting off numerous morning bombs in Baghdad, killing 36 and wounding 89 in the capital. "We mourn the tragic loss of life today," declared Obama, "and honor the courage and resilience of the Iraqi people who once again defied threats to advance their democracy."

Besides the violence, the election proceeded rather smoothly. Political posters covered walls and buildings, politicians held rallies, and more than 6,200 candidates grouped in five main groups vied for office in one of the most democratic elections held in the Arab Middle East. This time the parliament had been enlarged to 325 seats, with the mandate that 82 be filled by women, another first in the Arab world. Iraqi forces maintained good security throughout the country, and over 62 percent of eligible voters turned out. There "is no doubt that the outcome," said the chairman of Iraq's electoral commission, "will pave the way for a new era of democratic system and peaceful rotation of power."

That was the hope, and to help bring about more stability two main political coalitions sought support from both Shia and Sunni voters. In October 2009, Maliki met with Sunni and Shia political leaders and they announced the birth of the State of Law coalition. The prime minister attempted to recast himself as a secularist with multisect support, as did the former secular Shiite prime minister Ayad Allawi, who led the Iraqiyya alliance. By the March elections, Maliki also was running on improved security. "I would like to ask," he said during the campaign, "were things going smoothly two years ago?" Moreover, two weeks before the election, and as a gesture of reconciliation, his government reinstated 20,000 mostly Sunni army officers who had been dismissed after the 2003 invasion.

The State of Law and Iraqiyya coalition fared well in the elections, as a surprising number of Sunnis voted for the secular Shiite Allawi, whom they saw as more independent of ties to Iran than Maliki. Iraqiyya won 91 seats and State of Law picked up 89. The Iraqi National Alliance, a Shia bloc, which included Muqtada al-Sadr and the inveterate political survivor Ahmed Chalabi, won 70 seats, and the Kurds had 43. A fractured Iraqi electorate split the country's 18 provinces among four political groups. As expected, Maliki won Baghdad and six predominantly Shia provinces south of the capital, Allawi won or ran virtually even in five provinces north and west, while the Kurds swept their northern provinces.

The election was a hopeful sign, and there were others. On January 1, 2010, General Ray Odierno announced, "December was the first month that the U.S. had zero battle casualties in Iraq." The Iraqi government reported that 3,454 Iraqis died in violence in 2009, the lowest level since the war began. Attacks dropped from more than 200 a day at the end of 2007 to about 15 a day at the end of 2009. "In 2002, when I flew over Baghdad," Odierno continued. "I remember looking down on a city cloaked by darkness and gripped in fear. Today, when I fly over Baghdad, I see hope, with bright lights and busy traffic." To reflect the reduced American role in Iraq during 2010, the Obama administration announced the name of the U.S. mission was being changed from Operation Iraqi Freedom to Operation New Dawn, and in August the general ordered the withdrawal of the last U.S. combat troops, leaving less than 50,000 support and training soldiers. Those remaining were slated to leave throughout 2011, formally ending the American occupation of Iraq that began in March 2003.

While Iraqis hoped for the best, America lost interest. "On the streets," said a Baghdad resident, "ordinary Iraqis vow they will never allow a return to the days of 2005–07, when Sunnis and Shiites were slaughtering one another." If the slaughter did reappear, "If Iraq were to fall backward into some kind of chaos," said a senior administration official, "I don't think there'd be any great appetite for going back in."

Naturally, numerous complications remain for the Iraqis. The government has not resolved the tough problems facing the country: an effective oil law proportioning the nation's reserves; the status of petroleum and the militia in semi-independent Kurdish lands; and Kirkuk's designation as a mixed, Arab, or Kurdish city. Although the U.S. troop surge gave the government necessary breathing space to try to resolve these issues, little has been accomplished. "We have failed to build a state of institutions, of law and order," said an Iraqi lawmaker. "Our institutions are based on ideological, sectarian and ethnic foundations. They are dangerous, they are shaky and they could collapse at any moment." Iraqis have shown great resilience in holding elections, but the vote has not solved many problems. The first election helped to unleash civil war; another approved a flawed Constitution; a third created a shaky and corrupt government; and a fourth in March 2010 continued that situation, hardly a sign of an emerging democracy. "Iraq has proven under U.S. tutelage that it can organize elections and develop this political culture," said an International Crisis Group worker. "But I've still seen no evidence that any government can govern."

Nor does it seem that they can govern their economy. The Iraqi government provides jobs, directly or indirectly, for about 50 percent of the workforce so it is in constant need of revenue, of which over 90 percent comes from petroleum. The nation possesses the world's third-largest proven oil reserves, but in 2009 it was the 13th-largest producer. Only about 17 of the nation's 80 known fields were in production, many of those in the semiautonomous Kurdistan region. In 2002 the country produced about 2.8 million barrels a day, but that dropped to 1.3 million after the invasion; by 2009 production finally was close to prewar amounts, with a record export of over 2 million barrels per day. That year, the government finally held auctions for its best undeveloped oil fields, and awarded international companies development rights to seven fields that within a few years could substantially increase production.

In the oil sector, and throughout the economy, however, red tape and corruption remained rampant. In 2010, setting up a business required 11 procedures at 11 different ministries, took an average of 77 days and cost about $2,800 in fees. A World Bank study measured the cost and ease of starting a business in 183 nations; Iraq scored close to the bottom at 153. As for corruption, in a 2009 survey by Transparency

International, Iraq ranked fifth from the bottom, making it one of the most corrupt countries in the world. Survey data in Iraq demonstrate that many small businesses paid 20 to 40 percent of all their costs in bribes. A UN audit in 2008 found that one of the Oil Ministry's subsidiaries, the North Oil Company, could not account for almost 700,000 barrels, and the next year U.S. Special Inspector Stuart Bowen Jr. wondered about Iraq's corruption investigation agency, the Commission on Public Integrity (CPI). "It remains an open question whether the CPI is rooted firmly enough in the Iraqi political structure to survive the eventual withdrawal of U.S. support."

It also remained an open question of what will transpire in the future for the Improbable Country. The "basic questions" in Iraq remain unanswered, said the veteran correspondent Tom Ricks. "How do you share oil revenue? What's the relationship between Sunni, Shiite and Kurd? Will Iraq have a strong central government or be a weakened federation? What is the disposition of the Kurdish cities like Kirkuk? What's the role of Iran? Will the Kurds maintain pseudo-sovereignty in Kurdistan; will the Sunnis in Anbar? Will the Kurdish and Shia provinces share the oil wealth with Anbar?" All those questions led to violence in the past. Will they be resolved in the future?

No matter what happens, Bush's war involved Iraq and the United States in a long, hard road that will continue for years. "The Iraq story post-2003, this is still chapter one," said the former ambassador Ryan Crocker. "This is a very long book."[2]

So is America's role in the Graveyard of Empires. When Obama became president the Taliban was retaking Afghanistan, making a bad situation worse and increasingly complex. Pashtuns in Pakistan were aiding the Taliban and the government in Islamabad was offering little cooperation in preventing their Pashtuns from helping militants in Afghanistan. By the end of 2009, the Taliban had expanded operation into 33 of 34 provinces while increasing their attacks on NATO forces. During that year they mounted over 7,200 IED attacks, compared to about 80 in 2003, with much more powerful devices that could "flip a heavy armored vehicle like a toy." With few troops in country, the Pentagon relied on air strikes, which killed innocent Afghan civilians and enraged the populace. NATO floundered, without a clear mission, avoiding combat missions, and not training enough soldiers for the Afghan

National Army (ANA). President Hamid Karzai's government, local officials, and police were so corrupt that they drove their people toward warlords or the Taliban. As the security situation declined, NGOs withdrew their personnel, ending rural development projects and leaving people unemployed. "Afghanistan's war is not a sideshow," the *New York Times* had warned. "It is the principal military confrontation between America and NATO and the forces responsible for 9/11 and later deadly terrorist attacks on European soil. Washington, NATO and the governments of Pakistan and Afghanistan must stop fighting it like a holding action and develop a strategy to win. Otherwise, we will all lose."

Obama held many conversations with his advisers during autumn 2009 discussing if his administration should make a similar move in Afghanistan as Bush had done in Iraq in 2007—the surge and counterinsurgency. Though the U.S. Ambassador to Afghanistan, former General Karl Eikenberry, was opposed, it was supported by CENTCOM commander General Petraeus and the top commander in that country, General Stanley McChrystal. The president floated the idea of adding more troops and opinion polls found only 32 percent approved. Many wondered, "How can American forces protect the population, let alone help build a functioning nation," wrote the columnist Frank Rich, "in a tribal narco-state consisting of some 40,000 mostly rural villages over an area larger than California and New York combined?"

Nevertheless in November, the president announced the policy he had declared a year earlier to the VFW on the campaign trail. "After eight years—some of those years in which we did not have, I think, either the resources or the strategy to get the job done—it is my intention to finish the job. . . . I feel very confident that when the American people hear a clear rationale for what we're doing there and how we intend to achieve our goals, that they will be supportive." The commander in chief announced that he was sending 30,000 additional U.S. troops, increasing it to over 90,000. NATO said it would add 7,000 soldiers to the 40,000 non-American allied troops already in Afghanistan. By summer 2010, General Petraeus, who replaced McChrystal in Afghanistan, commanded 100,000 troops assigned to the NATO International Security Assistance Force.

Obama began the surge in Afghanistan: clear, hold, build. Like the first four years in Iraq, the first eight years of Operation Enduring

Freedom saw U.S.-led NATO forces mount large military operations to clear towns and cities of Taliban insurgents. They then moved on, never leaving behind enough troops to hold. The Taliban returned, and Americans began the same process, which soldiers derisively called "mowing the grass." The Taliban paid insurgents about $100 a month to fight, and many had joined not because of religious zealotry but because they were angry at government officials and police, were pressured from tribe members, or simply because they were broke. The Obama administration had an answer. "Counterinsurgency," said Secretary of State Clinton. "We found out how to do it in Iraq." The aims were complex, she continued: "getting international donors to have a comprehensive approach to stabilize the nation militarily, train Afghan forces, and lure the people away from the Taliban with offers of participating in society, paying them if necessary, having a job and a future that is better than the Taliban offers."

Naturally, there were skeptics, including Ambassador Eikenberry. "President Karzai is not an adequate strategic partner," wrote the ambassador. He "continues to shun responsibility for any sovereign burden, whether defense, governance or development." One result was massive corruption. In 2009, Transparency International ranked Afghanistan the second most corrupt nation in the world and that same year the UN reported that half of all Afghans paid at least one bribe to cut through red tape or get help from the government. In a country where the average per capita income was about $500 a year, the average bribe cost a hefty $160. Bribes were demanded by virtually anyone in power, from senior politicians to police to clerks issuing drivers licenses, even from teachers in public schools and doctors in public hospitals. "The Afghans say it is impossible to obtain a public service without paying a bribe," said a UN official. This "tax" robbed the nation of the equivalent of a quarter of the nation's gross domestic product. Nearly 60 percent of Afghans regarded corruption as their biggest worry. "Corruption is a stronger threat than terrorism for Afghanistan," said Finance Minister Omar Zakhilwal. "It is a cancer, a disease. It has destroyed the reputation of Afghanistan." A UN official called on the Karzai government "to make fighting corruption its highest priority."

In a national economy based largely on opium, smuggling also was rampant. Every day in 2009 an estimated $10 million was smuggled out of Afghanistan, mostly through Kabul International Airport. Much of the money came from drug cartels and flowed to the Taliban insurgents who controlled the poppy fields—funding the insurgency.

To address Afghanistan's problems and discuss ways to proceed, the international community held the London Conference in January 2010. World leaders discussed a comprehensive security plan, one with a "reintegration fund" to lure local Taliban fighters away from al Qaeda and back into society. Soon, international allies pledged $500 million for the so-called "Taliban Trust Fund." Most donors agreed with the U.K. foreign secretary David Miliband, who stated that "the Taliban leadership do not have as their principal aim al Qaeda's violent global jihadist agenda." Other aims of the conference were to encourage better governance from the Karzai administration and to put pressure on Pakistan and Iran to help in a long-term regional solution. The attendees agreed on a timetable for turning over security duties in Afghan provinces in about a year while Karzai warned that training and equipping the Afghan security forces would take 5–10 years. Worse, it would take far longer than that to build a sustainable economy.

A test case for Obama's strategy began in February. The Afghan National Army and U.S. Marines battled the Taliban for the city of Marjah in the southern Helmand Province, an opium-producing region. "I tell the Marines constantly," said USMC Brigadier General Larry Nicholson, "—and they always give me big eyeballs when I say it—we cannot win this war, we cannot possibly win it, but we can help the Afghans win it." Partnering with the ANA, the marines reported that the Afghans were becoming more effective. Unlike the police, who were known for corruption, the ANA soldiers were willing to engage in battle and were "much more proficient than Americans at searching Afghan homes and identifying potential Taliban members."

After the ANA and marines secured Marjah, they remained to protect the population and began the "civilian surge." The Americans paid Afghans for damage to their homes and held meetings with elders to discuss how to help. The local people were skeptical. "I can't say I blame them," a U.S. colonel said. "Trust is earned, not given. We've got to provide." Shortly thereafter, the Americans flew in new, trained, and supposedly dependable Afghan officials, and an ANA general declared, "We want to show people that we can deliver police, and services, and development."

Then they began the next stage, putting people to work on short- and long-term projects. The Americans employed Afghans to build schools, markets, and health clinics. To cut corruption, Americans and the international community oversaw long-term projects. One was an agriculture development program to transplant opium fields into ones of wheat, vegetables, and fruit trees, while establishing plant nurseries and rebuilding irrigation canals.

U.S. troops and the ANA then moved to Kandahar, the spiritual center of the Taliban, in the next attempt to clear, hold, build. All the while they implemented another part of the strategy, employing technology—drone attacks—and convincing Pakistani intelligence to work more closely with the Americans. Drone strikes had been used by the previous administration, of course, but the new administration worked with the Pakistani government so Predator Drones flew from a secret base in that country, controlled by satellite link from the CIA, to attack insurgent hideouts inside Pakistan. Early in 2010 the administration doubled the number of Predators in the area and replaced them with the bigger, faster, more heavily armed Reaper. In the first three weeks of January, the United States launched a drone attack every other day. Overall, 11 strikes killed about 90 suspected militants in North and South Waziristan. The attacks caused panic among militants and forced many of them from Miram Shah, North Waziristan's capital. The next month, American and Pakistan intelligence agents captured three senior Taliban leaders. "The arrests—all three in Pakistan—demonstrate a greater level of cooperation by Pakistan in hunting leaders of the Afghan Taliban," wrote the war correspondent Dexter Filkins, "than in the entire eight years of war." A senior NATO officer added, "The Taliban are feeling a new level of pain."

That pain was a small payback for the terrorist attacks of 9/11. Terrorists in general—and al Qaeda in particular—have learned strategic patience, and will wait out the days by testing defenses and preparing for future targets. As in Vietnam, the enemy trades space for time, waiting for the allies to tire and eventually go home. "You have the watches," one Taliban detainee said to his U.S. interrogators, "but we have the time."

As for Afghanistan and Iraq, in the long run there is only so much the American and NATO allies can do. The rest is up to the Afghans— and to the Iraqis. Both countries will have to build effective central governments and improve relations with their neighbors. They will have to cut corruption and overcome tribal in favor of national identity, and will have to improve the economic lives of their people, keeping men working for their families instead of joining insurgencies against the government. The Western effort at nation-building in both countries is "a major, major challenge" that "will require all instruments of power," said former Ambassador Crocker, "economic, social development, schools and clinics, employment opportunities . . . as well as the proper application of military force, over a long period of time."

"I can't begin to predict what will unfold in Afghanistan," Ambassador Crocker wrote in 2009, "or in Iraq." Predictions always are perilous, but whatever transpires, perhaps the statement that Generals Petraeus and Odierno both made a year apart about the small steps of progress in Iraq could be applied to Afghanistan. "The gains are fragile, and they are tenuous."[3]

Concluding Remarks and Legacies

"Whatever the verdict on my presidency, I'm comfortable with the fact that I won't be around to hear it. That's a decision point only history will reach."

— George W. Bush, *Decision Points*, 2010

Legacies of contemporary history are fraught with peril. "One way or another," the journalist James Fallows wrote in 2006, "future Americans will speak about the 'Lessons of Iraq.' We just can't tell what lessons those will be." It will take years, perhaps decades, to sort out the lessons and legacies of Bush's Wars.

Nevertheless, it is a historian's responsibility to make a premature attempt and to evaluate the Bush administration. "I'm fully prepared to accept any mistakes that history judges to my administration," said President Bush during the second presidential debate in October 2004, "because the president makes decisions, the president has to take the responsibility."

That statement seemed strange because by that time his administration already had begun revising why and how the nation became involved in Iraq. As we have seen, revisionism began shortly after WMDs—the proclaimed reason for the war—were not found in Iraq. In May 2003, Bush had changed finding WMDs to discovering "facilities to produce" WMDs, and in September a journalist began a question to Rumsfeld, "Before the war in Iraq, you stated . . . they would welcome us with open arms." Rumsfeld cut him off quickly: "Never said that. Never did." In fact, Rumsfeld said that on February 20 on PBS *News Hour*, and when he was asked in October about his earlier statements that Saddam had extensive stocks of WMDs, Rumsfeld replied, "The UN reported extensive stocks. That is where that came from." In fact, it came from Rumsfeld, for the UN Investigator Hans Blix reported before the invasion that he and his large team had not found WMDs. Revisionism continued throughout the second term. On November 12, 2005, Bush responded to critics: "When I made the decision to remove Saddam Hussein from power, Congress approved it with strong bipartisan support," which really was not what Congress had approved in the October 2002 Resolution. "While it's perfectly legitimate to criticize my decision or the conduct of the war, it is deeply irresponsible to rewrite the history of how that war began." Ten days later, Vice President Cheney was more incensed, charging that "any suggestion that prewar information was distorted, hyped or fabricated by the leader of the nation is utterly false. . . . This is revisionism of the most corrupt and shameless variety."[1]

Revisionism will continue for some time as will debate about a significant question: Why did the president and his administration invade Iraq?

After 9/11, the president wrote, "We had to take a fresh look at every threat in the world. There were state sponsors of terror. There were sworn enemies of America. There were hostile governments that threatened their neighbors. There were nations that violated international demands. There were dictators who repressed their people. And there were regimes that pursued WMD. Iraq combined all those threats."

So Bush went to war because he thought we were threatened—not because of an attack on an ally or on the United States. In modern times presidents responded to aggression, such as German U-boats sinking American ships in 1917 or Pearl Harbor in 1941, and then asked Congress for a Declaration of War. World Wars I and II clearly were in our national interest, if not survival, and in the cold war we attempted to contain communist expansion. Truman and Johnson responded to aggression from North Korea and North Vietnam and their Vietcong allies. After the end of the cold war, George H. W. Bush responded to Saddam's preemptive attack on Kuwait: "This will not stand, this aggression against Kuwait." The senior Bush assembled a large international force and received mandates from Congress and the United Nations. Then September 11, and Bush responded by attacking the Taliban regime that was shielding al Qaeda. That was entirely justifiable, supported by almost all nations of the world. Yet the next step, attacking Iraq, was a radical departure from previous presidential behavior, and not justifiable—even if Saddam had WMDs. He was no threat to U.S. security, as Secretary of State Powell and National Security Adviser Rice said in spring 2001; he was "contained." True, as Bush wrote, Saddam was a "homicidal dictator," but the world is full of such leaders, and the United States has avoided full-scale wars against thugs because we dislike them, from Fidel Castro to Hugo Chavez to the military dictators in Myanmar—including the dictators who enslave Iran and North Korea.

Being threatened was not a sufficient casus belli, but this was an unusual time in which the trauma of 9/11 facilitated the strike on Saddam. "The rush to war was accelerated by—in fact could not have happened without—the emotional fallout from 9/11," wrote the Republican Chuck Hagel. The year after the September 11 terrorist attacks was a propitious time. It was the "high tide of imperial self-confidence," wrote the British journalist Patrick Cockburn. The United States had just "won" in Afghanistan, and so the "main motive for going to war," in Iraq, he continued, "was that the White House thought it could win such a conflict very easily."

The immediate post-9/11 era was an emotive time for most Americans, and the president used emotional appeals, especially those concerning "terror" and "evil." Bush laced his speeches on Saddam with various forms of "terror" when in fact it had little to do with the origins of the war in Iraq; in the post-9/11 years the use of the term "terrorism" almost became equivalent to the use of "communism" during the long cold war. In the evening of the 9/11 attack, the president told the public, "Today, our nation saw evil," a term he used three more times in the four-minute address. Three days later he told the audience at the National Cathedral, "Our responsibility to history is already clear: to answer these attacks and *rid the world of evil.*" The president apparently saw the world in terms of good and evil, and as a born-again Christian he was sure, as he told Congress, "God is not neutral."

During 2002 and 2003 the administration stated many reasons to go to war—Saddam was evil, he had supported terrorists, he had violated international sanctions, had secret relations with al Qaeda—but the one reason they eventually came to believe and promote was WMDs. "The truth is that, for reasons that have a lot to do with the U. S. government bureaucracy," admitted Paul Wolfowitz, "we settled on the one issue that everyone could agree on which was weapons of mass destruction as the core reason" to go to war. Years later in his memoirs, Bush admitted that he was "shocked and angry . . . when we didn't find the weapons. I had a sickening feeling every time I thought about it. I still do."

Naturally, there also were ideological factors prompting the administration toward war. We invaded Iraq, wrote Chuck Hagel, because of the "triumph of the so-called neoconservative ideology, as well as Bush administration arrogance and incompetence that took America into this war of choice." The British political scientist Toby Dodge added, "The Bush doctrine is the attempt to collapse three distinctly separate problems—terrorism, weapons of mass destruction, and the weakness of postcolonial states—into one policy. It was Saddam Hussein's regime that provided the vehicle for this aspiration." The neocons, more than most Americans, felt that the United States should use its might, not just to keep the peace, but to spread democracy. "I think democracy is a universal idea," said Wolfowitz, an idea accepted by Bush.

Others contend that Bush and his top neocon subordinates created their own "reality." In summer 2002, the reporter Ron Suskind was invited to the White House, where he held a discussion with a high-ranking presidential adviser. The official declared that journalists are in the "reality-based community," but that's "not the way the world really works anymore. We're an empire now, and when we act, we create our own reality. And while you're studying that reality—judiciously, as you will—we'll act again, creating other new realities." Such beliefs, Suskind later wrote, led Cheney after 9/11 to develop the "one percent doctrine." "It's not about our analysis, or finding a preponderance of evidence," Cheney said. "It's about our response." Cheney's doctrine signaled a shift in policy making. In the past, administrations conducted foreign policy based on firm intelligence and analysis, which directed them toward a certain action. In the Bush administration, if there was just a one percent chance that there might be another terrorist attack, response would be immediate. "As to 'evidence,'" wrote Suskind, "the bar was set so low that the word itself almost didn't apply."

One reality in Iraq that everyone could agree on was that the nation had enormous proven oil reserves. Before the war, the United States bought nearly one quarter of its imported oil from the Persian Gulf, including about $10 billion annually from Saddam. Just one month into the Bush administration, it had drawn up maps of Iraq's oil fields and was listening to advice from Ahmed Chalabi. His vision for that nation's petroleum coincided with the ideas of Ariel Cohen of the conservative Heritage Foundation, who advocated privatizing Iraq's nationalized industry, complementing the neocon ideology. In September 2002, the president met with Republican leaders and told them Saddam was "a brutal, ugly, repugnant man who needs to go. . . . And our planning will make sure there is no oil disruption; we are looking at all options to enhance oil flow." After the invasion a reporter asked Wolfowitz why Iraq was invaded instead of a more threatening nuclear power such as North Korea. "Let's look at it simply," said the deputy defense secretary. "The most important difference between North Korea and Iraq is that economically, we just had no choice in Iraq. The country swims on a sea of oil." Petroleum was a fundamental prerequisite for the invasion. "I'm saddened that it is politically inconvenient to acknowledge what everyone knows," wrote Alan Greenspan in 2007. "The Iraq war is largely about oil."

The war also was a result of the president's beliefs and character. "I'm gonna make a prediction. Write this down," Bush told Republican officeholders in September 2002. "Afghanistan and Iraq will lead that part of the world to democracy. They are going to be the catalyst to change the Middle East and the world." The president mixed this theme with religion. "I believe the United States is *the* beacon for freedom in the world," the president said to Bob Woodward. "Freedom is God's gift to everybody in the world. I believe that." That being the case, the president announced before the invasion a "new regime in Iraq would serve as a dramatic and inspiring example of freedom for other nations in the region." "Not until well into my time as press secretary," recalled Scott McClellan, "did I realize that the dream of a democratic Middle East was actually the most powerful force behind President Bush's drive to war." That complemented the president's desire to leave a mark on history. "As I have heard Bush say," McClellan continued, "only a wartime president is likely to achieve greatness. . . . In Iraq, Bush saw his opportunity to create a legacy of greatness."

The president also saw an opportunity for revenge. In 1993, Saddam had tried to assassinate Bush's father in Kuwait. "The SOB tried to kill my dad," declared Bush on at least two different occasions, and at another time, "I was a warrior for George Bush."

Some commentators have added that the president felt competition with his father. In 1998, Governor Bush told a family friend: "Dad made a mistake not going into Iraq when he had an approval rating in the nineties. If I'm ever in that situation, I'll use it—I'll spend my political capital." That sense of competition extended into electoral results. "The president had promised himself that he would accomplish what his father had failed to do by winning a second term in office," wrote Scott McClellan. "And that meant operating continually in campaign mode: never explaining, never apologizing, never retreating. Unfortunately, that strategy also had less justifiable repercussions: never reflecting, never reconsidering, never compromising. Especially not where Iraq was concerned."

Although educated at some of the finest institutions in America, Bush had limited knowledge of the cultural diversity of the world. "Moral truth is the same in every culture, in every time, and in every place," he told West Point cadets in 2002. Actually, as he learned, the world was much more complex. Western cultures, along with most Islamic ones, don't flog men and women for "mingling" together, don't cut off hands for theft, and don't stone to death adulterers—all punishments assigned in fundamental Islamic tribal areas of Pakistan and Afghanistan. Nor do people in Western cultures turn themselves into suicide bombs, and think that they are headed for eternal salvation. In January 2003, the president met with three Iraqi Americans who had to explain Sunnis and Shiites. "So two months before he ordered U.S. troops into the country," wrote the former diplomat Peter Galbraith, "the president of the United States did not appear to know about the division among Iraqis that has defined the country's history and politics. He would not have understood why non-Arab Iran might gain a foothold in post-Saddam Iraq. He could not have anticipated U.S. troops being caught in the middle of a civil war between two religious sects that he did not know existed."

Sadly, and like President Lyndon Johnson expanding the U.S. commitment in Vietnam, the Bush administration was filled with cultural bravado and ignorance. Neocons talked about bringing democracy and more moderate forms of Islam to Iraq and the Middle East, prompting Chuck Hagel to write, "The hubris of such assumptions—to bring democratic changes and affect the course of religious history at the point of a gun in Iraq—is breathtaking."

Most likely, one of the reasons Bush went to war in Iraq involved his own unreflective nature, which surprised his biographers. The president told Robert Draper, as they were conducting the first of six interviews, "I really do not feel comfortable in the role of analyzing myself. I'll try. But I don't spend a lot of time." When Bob Woodward interviewed him in August 2002, Bush mentioned a dozen times "instincts" or his "instinctive" reactions, adding, "I'm not a textbook player, I'm a gut player." "The president doesn't have second thoughts," his press secretary admitted in 2008, and that same year Woodward held his last interviews with Bush. "President Bush often displayed impatience, bravado and unwavering personal certainty about his decisions. Perhaps most troubling to some in his administration, the result sometimes was a delayed reaction to realities and advice that ran counter to the president's gut instincts." Fearful of defeat, and apparently of looking weak, the president told Draper: "And they look at me—they want to know whether I've got the resolution necessary to see this through. And I do. I believe—I know we'll succeed." Many times in his second term, and in his memoirs, he compared himself to other wartime leaders—Truman, Lincoln, Washington, even Winston Churchill. All too often, it seemed that his bravado—"wanted, dead or alive," "bring 'em on"—was aimed to appear tough instead of facing the nation's problems and providing pragmatic solutions.[2]

For all those reasons the president got his nation involved in a war of choice, an unnecessary attack on and occupation of Iraq, which allowed the Taliban to reemerge in the original site of Bush's war on terror—Afghanistan. Since 2004 and the British Butler Review, the U.S. Senate Report of Pre-war Intelligence on Iraq, and *The 9/11 Report*, citizens have known that the Bush administration misled the nation into war in Iraq. Whether officials did it based on poor intelligence or "cherry picked" what they wanted to believe will be debated for years.

So will two other questions about Iraq. Was the war "worth it"? Not to most Americans. When Obama announced that the combat mission was over, 70 percent of those asked said the war was not worth the financial costs and the loss of American lives, 60 percent said the United States should have never take military action in the first place. "The problem with this war," said Secretary Gates, "is that the premise on which we justified going to war proved not to be valid." There were no WMDs. Thus, he continued, the outcome "will always be clouded by how it began." Finally, was going to war the right decision? That depends on how the reader answers one question: was the price in blood and treasury worth getting rid of Saddam?

To some, the answer is an emphatic yes. "Neocons, including myself, were commonly accused of wanting to spread democracy by the sword," wrote Douglas Feith. "But I saw no evidence of that. . . . In my view, the reason to go to war with Iraq was self-defense." Karl Rove wrote that the administration went to war because of "faulty intelligence." "So, then, did Bush lie us into war? Absolutely not." And Bush recalled, "For all the difficulties that followed, America is safer without a homicidal dictator pursuing WMD and supporting terror at the heart of the Middle East."

Supporters and opponents of the war in Iraq made different historical comparisons. Neocons like Wolfowitz compared it to World War II. Bush was acting like Franklin Roosevelt and saving the United States from evil—the Third Reich or Imperial Japan—and the preemptive strike against Iraq saved the nation from another Pearl Harbor. Critics scoffed at such ideas, and instead they saw the war in terms of Vietnam. President Johnson fudged the facts to get Congress to pass the Gulf of Tonkin Resolution that supposedly gave him legal justification to expand the conflict in Southeast Asia. Bush acted the same concerning Iraq, using only intelligence that supported his goal of a preemptive attack to get public support for his war. "We invaded a country on false premises, preemptively," stated journalist Tom Ricks, "perhaps, the worst decision in the history of American foreign policy. And Americans, I think, still don't grasp just what a terribly expensive decision that was, not just in money, but also in blood and moral credibility."

Those expenses are legacies of Bush's war in Iraq. The administration's policies resulted in soaring monetary cost. By the end of 2009, it cost $1 million a year *per soldier* in Afghanistan. By autumn 2010, the National Priorities Project estimated that Iraq had cost U.S. taxpayers about $750 billion, while Afghanistan was over $350 billion, meaning that together they surpassed $1 trillion. "By our accounting," wrote the Nobel Prize winner Joseph Stiglitz and Linda Bilmes, "the U.S. has already spent $1 trillion on operations and related defense spending, with more to come—and it will cost perhaps $2 trillion more to repay the war debt, replenish military equipment and provide care and treatment for U.S. veterans back home."

Those expenses do not include reconstruction and subsequent corruption committed by U.S. and Iraqi contractors. The Pentagon admitted in 2008 that it had not followed usual spending rules, resulting in massive graft. Mysterious payments were made to the United Kingdom for $68 million, Poland for $45 million, and South Korea for $21 million, all with no explanation. "It sounds like the coalition of the willing is the coalition of the paid," said one congressman, "they're willing to be paid." Other payments to contractors totaled over $8 billion without the usual paperwork, meaning that in the first three years of the war almost 95 percent of the payments were made without proper documentation. By March 2010, Congress had appropriated $53 billion for reconstruction projects in Iraq and $51 billion for reconstruction in Afghanistan. Also by that time, 58 Americans had been convicted of fraud and corruption in Iraq, many more had been indicted, and the government had announced large fines against many contractors, including Xe Services (formerly Blackwater USA) and KBR. Louis Berger Group admitted massive overcharges and was fined over $69 million, the largest fine against a contractor in U.S. history. Shady practices, flawed documentation, corruption—all at taxpayer expense— brought into question the administration's unprecedented reliance on outsourcing a war to private enterprise.

The war in Iraq had an impact on Bush's war on terrorism—it increased those attacks. Richard Clarke and other terror experts had predicted that Western Christian troops in the Islamic Middle East would only inspire jihad, and that is what has transpired. Terrorists launched major attacks in Riyadh and Istanbul. Their bombs in a Western nightclub in Bali killed 200 mostly young Australian tourists, and devices on four commuter trains in Madrid killed 196. In July 2005, a series of bombs detonated in the London transportation system, killing 52 and wounding hundreds, and two weeks later local terrorists again attacked, but fortunately none of the devices exploded. The RAND corporation found that in the 12 months after March 2004, terrorists' attacks killed over 5,300 people worldwide, double the rate before Bush invaded Iraq in March 2003. Specialists feared an "endless war" or at least a "long siege" against terrorists far into the twenty-first century, and one expert added, "The public has to have the resolve to face the reality there will be other incidents."

Bush's Wars also have had an impact on the U.S. Armed Forces. In August 2000, Dick Cheney charged that "Clinton and Gore have extended our military commitments while depleting our military power. . . . George W. Bush and I are going to change that. . . . I can promise them now, help is on the way. Soon, our men and women in uniform will once again have a commander in chief they can respect, one who understands their mission and restores their morale." Basically, however, the opposite happened to the U.S. Armed Forces. By autumn 2010, over 4,400 had died in Iraq, and over 1,200 in Afghanistan, with almost 35,000 wounded. Multiple tours had resulted in stretching troops to the breaking point. In 2009, one in four returning vets were diagnosed with some type of mental health problem, while post-traumatic stress and suicide rates were higher than after Vietnam. One vociferous critic has been former commander Lieutenant General Sanchez. "The Iraq War became a national nightmare with no end in sight. The initial plans of the military were micromanaged by the Bush administration, as were many of the individual battles, troop deployments, and strategic operations." Like post-Vietnam, "It will take at least a decade to repair the damage."

The endless wars in Afghanistan and Iraq decreased morale in the U.S. Armed Forces. Some 1.7 million have served in those two theaters and many are on their third, even fourth tours of duty. In summer 2010 a war correspondent in Afghanistan asked an American sergeant, "Is this a fight you can win?" "Beats me," he replied, and his colleague added, "I guess winning to me is going home, really, after our deployment's done." The sergeant added, "Going home alive." The correspondent asked, "That's how you measure success in Afghanistan?" a question also appropriate to Iraq, and the soldier answered, "Yes sir."

Afghans and Iraqis, of course, have received some benefits from Bush's Wars. The U.S. invasion of Afghanistan ended the harsh Taliban regime. Afghans, especially women, have much more freedom today than during the years of Mullah Mohammed Omar. Bush's invasion of Iraq ended the brutal rule of Saddam Hussein. No one knows how many of his own citizens the dictator imprisoned, tortured, and murdered, or how many Iranians and Kuwaitis died because of his invasions. Few disagreed when President Bush declared that "there's no doubt the world is a safer, freer place" without Saddam. The invasion also brought about what General Petraeus called an "Iraqacy, not necessarily democracy, but in that region that is still something that is quite unique."

Yet both the Karzai government and the Iraqacy are "fragile and reversible" and probably are the best-case scenario for the future. The worst case for the Graveyard of Empires is a return of a Taliban regime linked with al Qaeda and the worst for the Improbable Country is a return of a dictator who is aligned with a nuclear armed Iran.

Iraqis also have paid a heavy price for Bush's Wars. In October 2006, over 3,700 Iraqis perished—a record for one month. The number of deaths since the invasion has been disputed, with the Iraq Body Count organization estimating between 95,000 and 104,000 deaths due to violence while the Associated Press's figures exceed 110,000. Both estimates, however, exclude the thousands of people who are missing and civilians who were buried in the chaos of war without official notice. Added to that are about 150,000 civilians who were wounded, or the approximately 2 million Iraqis who fled to Syria, Jordan, Iran, and Egypt, with the same number displaced in their own country. Those tragic realities raise an emotional question for the relatives of the casualties: was getting rid of Saddam and the establishment of Iraqacy worth the price?

U.S. national credibility also paid a price. Bush's war on terror was a natural response to 9/11; his government sought to protect America. But the question soon arose: what was protection and what was violation of individual liberties? The administration took the hard line at home and abroad. The FBI picked up suspects, held them for weeks without charging them, and the CIA picked up foreigners and kept them in "black sites" or secret prisons. The administration went to "the dark side," as Cheney called it, and employed torture. Cheney and Karl Rove contended that such actions "saved lives," and although Bush declared many times during his presidency, "We don't do torture," in his memoirs he admitted approving waterboarding; he claimed that the technique resulted in capturing at least five al Qaeda operatives and preventing possible attacks. These tactics, however, also decreased the international standing of the United States, and the legal reasoning behind detention without habeas corpus was challenged and the Supreme Court eventually ruled against it. Before he died in 2007, the distinguished historian Arthur Schlesinger Jr. stated that the "Bush administration's extralegal counterterrorism program presented the most dramatic, sustained and radical challenge to the rule of law in American history." He continued, "No position taken has done more damage to the American reputation in the world—ever."

Moreover, there are ancillary costs from Bush's Wars. In 1991 the United States became the world's sole superpower. The economy in the last half of that decade roared; the Clinton administration not only balanced the federal budget but was paying down the national debt. Then September 11, and the Bush administration responded not only with his war on terror and the necessary invasion of Afghanistan, but also with tax cuts and an unnecessary war in Iraq. The administration failed to secure Afghanistan, fought a fierce enemy in Iraq, and became the policeman of the world against terrorism. That cost over a trillion dollars, and sank the nation deeper in debt; total federal debt doubled during the Bush years from about $5.5 to about $11 trillion. That precarious economic situation was one of many causes in 2008 for the beginning of the Great Recession and the subsequent slow recovery. All the while, the other two Axis of Evil nations—Iran and North Korea—pursued their aggressive WMD and nuclear programs, and became much greater threats to the world and to America. Moreover, the economic positions of the European Union, Japan, India, and especially China, vis-à-vis the United States, steadily improved. By summer 2010 China had surpassed Japan and had become the second-largest economy in the world, and some economists predicted that Chinese Gross Domestic Product could overtake that of the United States by 2020. No one can predict the future, of course, but if the second decade of the twenty-first century witnesses an additional decline of American economic and diplomatic influence, future scholars probably will conclude that the origin of that demise was linked to the war in Iraq—a conflict that hurt the U.S. economy, diminished American stature in the world, and failed to bring about religious toleration or democracy in the Middle East.

Furthermore, the war to remove Saddam had an unforeseen impact on the Middle East. The dictator had been a counterweight to Iran in the continuing battle for supremacy in the Persian Gulf region. A relatively weak Iraq boosted Iran's power and influence, and that situation certainly was not in the national interest of the United States.

How will historians judge President Bush? Just think for a moment: what if Bush had not attacked Iraq? He would have been remembered as the man who saved the nation from additional terror attacks after 9/11, and who focused on denying al Qaeda and the Taliban control of areas in Afghanistan and Pakistan. Most likely, sometime in his second term, U.S. and NATO troops would have secured Afghanistan, ending the conflict in the Graveyard of Empires. But that was not to be.

"History will render its verdict on his presidency in the fullness of time," wrote Karl Rove, "and I have little doubt that verdict will be kind." That assessment was more favorable than Bush gave himself in 2010, when he admitted that the president has "to make the calls. I got some right. I got some wrong." He was more positive in his memoirs. "History can debate the decisions I made, the policies I chose, and the tools I left behind. But there can be no debate about one fact: After the nightmare of September 11, America went seven and a half years without another successful terrorist attack on our soil. If I had to summarize my most meaningful accomplishment as president in one sentence, that would be it."

Others were not so positive. During the second term authors penned numerous books on his administration with titles such as *Broken Government*, *Anatomy of Deceit*, *A Tragic Legacy*, and *Takeover: The Return of the Imperial Presidency and the Subversion of American Democracy*. Insults even came from former allies. The conservative commentator Richard Viguerie published *Conservatives Betrayed*, the former House Republican majority leader Dick Armey called the Bush presidency a "bitter disappointment," while the first prime minister of post-Saddam Iraq, Ayad Allawi, labeled Bush's policies in his country an "utter failure."

Nor have historians been positive, who obviously are not waiting for Bush's death before they make their judgments. The president's legacy, of course, will be linked with the future outcomes in Afghanistan and Iraq. Nevertheless, historians were discussing Bush's "failed presidency" by the end of 2006, and it is probable that his eventual ranking will be in that category with a few other administrations, such as James Buchanan, Andrew Johnson, Warren Harding, and Richard Nixon. Others were even more critical. The Columbia University professor Eric Foner wrote, "It is impossible to say with certainty how Bush will be ranked in, say, 2050. But somehow, in his first six years in office he has managed to combine the lapses of leadership, misguided policies and abuse of power of his failed predecessors. I think there is no alternative but to rank him as the worst president in U. S. history."[3]

America's fate is now intertwined with the Graveyard of Empires and the Improbable Country. No one witnessing the 2000 presidential campaign could have foreseen the long and agonizing road the president would take in creating Bush's Wars—a road leading from Kabul to Guantanamo and to Baghdad.

"Just as war defines a nation," wrote Bob Woodward as the Texan was preparing to leave office, "a president's leadership in war defines him." As for his presidency, the journalist concluded, in the long run Bush will be a "man defined by his wars."

Notes

Presidential statements are not cited because they can be found on the Internet. I used whitehouse.gov during the Bush years. I also consulted the Government Printing Office's gpo access at www.gpoaccess.gov/pub-papers/search.html, which is the electronic version of *Public Papers of the Presidents of the United States*. ProQuest Newspapers is an important database providing full text of over 500 domestic and international newspapers; it was an invaluable resource. Of course I also simply used the search engine Google to find many quotes, as could any reader.

Full book citations are in the Bibliography.

ABBREVIATIONS USED IN THE ENDNOTES

AP	Associated Press
CSM	*Christian Science Monitor*
CT	*Chicago Tribune*
HC	*Houston Chronicle*
IHT	*International Herald Tribune*
LAT	*Los Angeles Times*
McC	*McClatchy Newspapers*
MT	*McClatchy-Tribune*
NPR	National Public Radio
NSA	National Security Archive, George Washington University. www.gwu.edu/~nsarchiv/
NYT	*New York Times*
PBS	Public Broadcasting Service
WP	*Washington Post*
WSJ	*Wall Street Journal*

PREFACE

1. Draper, *Dead Certain*, x; Woodward, *Bush at War*, 205; and Feith, *War and Decision*, 223–24.

INTRODUCTION EAST

1. Scholar is Madelung, *Muhammad*. Maude and Bell in Ellen Knickmeyer, "Ghosts of Iraq's Birth," *WP* Weekly Edition, March 13–19, 2006. Mackey, *Reckoning*, 107. Much of this background is based on Mackey and on Dodge, *Inventing Iraq*.

2. For Afghanistan crisis of 1979 see Leffler, *Soul of Mankind*, 329–333; Westad, *Global Cold War*, 316–26; and Meyer, *Dust of Empire*, 125–37. Churchill in Ellen Knickmeyer, "Ghosts of Iraq's Birth," *WP* Weekly Edition, March 13-19, 2006, and 1945 British Report and Faisal's British training in Mackey, *Reckoning*, 149–51. Qassim also is spelled Qasim and Kassem. Ike and Anderson in Little, *American Orientalism*, 27–28, 61. CIA in Roger Morris, "A Tyrant Forty Years in the Making," *NYT*, March 14, 2003, and David Morgan, "Ex-U.S. Official Says CIA Aided Baathists," Reuters, April 20, 2003. Killing continued in Eppel, *Iraq*, 206, and see Coughlin, *Saddam*, 40.

INTRODUCTION WEST

1. Saddam's background is in Coughlin, *Saddam*, chapters 1–5.

2. Iraqi defense minister, and support of shah in Schulzinger, *U.S. Diplomacy*, 305–9. Making of oil embargo, see Little, *American Orientalism*, 65–69. Arab oil and Stalin in Coughlin, *Saddam*, 108, 174. Baghdad throbbed in Mackey, *Reckoning*, 9, and killing off political opposition in Robert Fisk, "He Takes His Secrets to the Grave," *The Independent* (London), December 31, 2006.

3. American dog in Little, *American Orientalism*, 221, and butcher Saddam in Mackey, *Reckoning*, 248–50. On Saddam obtaining weapons, see Coughlin, *Saddam*, 126–31, and on using them on his own people, John F. Burns, "Hussein's Voice Speaks in Court in Praise of Chemical Atrocities," *NYT*, January 9, 2007, and Mackey, *Reckoning*, 262.

4. Strategic defeat for the West, chemical weapons on almost a daily basis, and just another way of killing people is in Gregory Elich, "Selective Justice and the Execution of Saddam Hussein," information clearing house (http://www.informationclearinghouse.info/article16036.htm), December 31, 2006, which includes many sources. On United States providing Iraq with materials, see Donald W. Riegle, "The Riegle Report," United States Senate, May 25, 1994, and NSA, "Shaking Hands with Saddam Hussein." Our SOB is from Little, *American Orientalism*, 227.

5. Beirut bombing and hostages, see "20 Years Later, Lebanon Bombing Haunts," CNN.com, October 23, 2003, and Joel Greenberg, "Hezbollah Fugitive Killed," *CT*, February 14, 2008. Saddam's statements and behavior in Khadduri and Ghareeb, *War in the Gulf*, 105–14, and for Glaspie see Little, *American Orientalism*, 254–55, and Galbraith, *End of Iraq*, 38–39.

6. Cheney to the president in Bush and Scowcroft, *World Transformed*, 323–24, and Saddam's curious statement in Coughlin, *Saddam*, 256. Kennedy and Cheney from Little, *American Orientalism*, 258–60. Powell, *American Journey*, 495, and Schwarzkopf, *Autobiography*, chapters 22 and 23.

7. Distrust of Americans in Jones, *Crucible*, 330, and for other examples of revenge, see Galbraith, *End of Iraq*, 46–60. Cheney interviewed by American Enterprise Institute, April 15, 1994; Bush and Scowcroft, *World Transformed*, 489–92; and Schwarzkopf, *Autobiography*, 579. Boutros-Ghali in *Newsweek*, January 7, 1991, 22. Saddam's obstruction, UNICEF, and INC, see Coughlin, *Saddam*, 284–93.

8. Saddam got the point, from Clarke, *Enemies*, 83–84. Clinton, *My Life*, 834, and Blumenthal, *Clinton Wars*, 546, 566. Desert Fox, Lott, and Zinni in Ricks, *Fiasco*, 19–21. Four thousand . . . children in Patrick Cockburn, "UN Aid Chief Resigns over Iraq Sanctions," *The Independent* (London), October 1, 1998, and seasoned journalist is Mackey, *Reckoning*, 371.

9. Dropped on Japan in Benjamin and Simon, *Sacred Terror*, 7. Immigration flaws, who are these guys, and Yousef in Clarke, *Enemies*, 77–78, 148. War on God from Wright, *Looming Tower*, 260, and CNN's May 10, 1997, interview with bin Laden, reproduced in Bergen, *Osama bin Laden I Know*, 181–84. No matter what it takes from Blumenthal, *Clinton Wars*, 460.

10. On antiterrorism act and PDD-39, see Benjamin and Simon, *Sacred Terror*, 228–30, 248. Aggressive intelligence program is Bamford, *Pretext for War*, 205–6; authorized killing in Blumenthal, *Clinton Wars*, 656–57; and Berger in *Sacred Terror*, 260. Boots on the ground from Clarke interview, NPR, *Fresh Air*, September 22, 2004; no brainer in Tenet, *Storm*, 115–16; and Zawahiri's response in Wright, *Looming Tower*, 285–86. Tenet's PDB and warnings in *Storm*, 105, 124–25, and Berger in Clarke, *Enemies*, 211–12. Sheehan and Pickering in Barton Gellman, "Clinton's War on Terror," *WP*, December 19, 2001, and Pickering also in *Sacred Terror*, 268–80. Contacts with Taliban, see NSA, "The Taliban File Part IV" and Kean and Hamilton, *9/11 Report*, 263–64. USS *Cole* in *Looming Tower*, 319–20, *Storm*, 130, and Clinton, *My Life*, 925, 803–5.

CHAPTER 1

1. Full speed ahead and Cheney to Cohen in Woodward, *Plan of Attack*, 28, 9. Cheney's energy task force in Michael Abramowitz and Steven Mufson, "Papers Detail Industry's Role in Cheney's Energy Report," *WP*, July 18, 2007, and see Neil Mackay, "Official: US Oil at the Heart of Iraq Crisis," *The Sunday Herald* (Scotland), October 2, 2002. NSC meetings from Suskind, *Price of Loyalty*, 72–75, 84–86, and CBS News, "Bush Sought 'Way' to Invade Iraq," January 11, 2004.

2. Two neocons are Robert Kagan and William Kristol, "Toward a Neo-Reaganite Foreign Policy," *Foreign Affairs*, July–August 1996. For claims, see Mylroie, *A Study of Revenge*, and rebuttal is Peter Bergen, "Armchair Provocateur: The NeoCons' Favorite Conspiracy Theorists," *Washington Monthly* (December 2003). For more background, see Mann, *Rise of the Vulcans*, and for their articles, see Ehrenberg et al., *The Iraq Papers*, chapter 1.

3. Berger to Rice in Barton Gellman, "A Strategy's Cautious Evolution," *WP*, January 20, 2002. Clarke to Rice, January 25, 2001, is from NSA, posted 2/21/2007, and his warnings in Clarke, *Enemies*, 227–36. Bob Woodward, "Two Months before 9/11, an Urgent Warning to Rice," *WP*, October 1, 2006, her response is *NYT*, October 2, and a slightly different recount is Tenet, *Storm*, 145–54. Kerrick in Blumenthal, *Clinton Wars*, 796, and see Daniel Benjamin, "Clarke Wasn't Alone in Warning of al-Qaida," *HC*, April 1, 2004. Some senior officials, *Storm*, 104–5, and 44 reports from Clarke interview, NPR, *Fresh Air*, September 22, 2004. Presidential briefing in Kean and Hamilton, *9/11 Report*, 375–76, and August 6 briefing in *AP*, April 10, 2004, and in Bamford, *Pretext for War*, 242–44.

4. Missile shield in Barton Gellman, "A Strategy's Cautious Evolution," *WP*, January 20, 2002. September 4 meeting in Clarke, *Enemies*, 237–38, and Tenet, *Storm*, 160. Clarke emphasized and blinking red from Kean and Hamilton, *9/11 Report*, 307 and chapter 8. Hayden and zero hour in Bamford, *Pretext for War*, 247–49, and see Woodward, *Bush at War*, 4.

5. Attackers and quotes from Kean and Hamilton, *9/11 Report*, chapter 1, or 3–23, 60–62, 67, 70, and INS commissioner in Bamford, *Pretext for War*, 245.

6. Clarke, *Enemies*, 30–33, and Rumsfeld from Bamford, *Pretext for War*, 285, and Kean and Hamilton, *9/11 Report*, 479. Feith, *War and Decision*, 15, confirms that in a September 13 NSC meeting the president and Rumsfeld stated their interest in attacking Iraq, and so do the British, see Campbell, *The Blair Years*, 566–69. Tenet, *Storm*, 163–69, Benjamin and Simon, *Sacred Terror*, xi, and see Drumheller, *On the Brink*, 31. Franks, *American Soldier*, 240. *Storm*, 306, and see PBS, *Frontline*, "The Dark Side," January 2, 2007. Bush's *Decision Points* does not mention Clarke.

7. Brzezinski in *WP*, March 25, 2007. "We Are Not the Enemy: Hate Crimes against Arabs, Muslims . . . after September 11," Human Rights Watch, November 2002, 3, 11, 23. Patriot Act; see "A Crack in the Stone Wall," *NYT* editorial, November 30, 2006, and David Savage, "Supreme Court Rejects Wiretap Suit," *LAT*, February 20, 2008.

8. At least 1,200 from "We Are Not the Enemy," Human Rights Watch, November 2002, 27, and see Nina Bernstein; "U.S. Is Settling Detainee's Suit in 9/11 Sweep, *NYT* February 29, 2006, and statement of Inspector General Glenn A. Fine, "The September 11 Detainees: A Review of the Treatment of Aliens . . . after September 11," Senate Committee on the Judiciary, June 25, 2003. Wolfowitz in Kean and Hamilton, *9/11 Report*, 479, and Powell in Woodward, *Plan of Attack*, 25. September 17 presidential finding in Bamford, *Pretext for War*, 287, permission to kill from "CIA Holds Terror Suspects in Secret Prisons," *WP*, November 2, 2005, and Dana Priest, "A CIA Mistake, Uncovered," *WP Weekly Edition*, December 12–18, 2005. Black in Tenet, *Storm*, 208, and Blair and Bush reported by *AP*, April 5, 2004. No evidence, Murray Wass, "Key Bush Intelligence Briefing Kept from Hill Panel," *National Journal*, November 22, 2005, and see George Piro interview, CBS, *60 Minutes*, January 27, 2008: Saddam felt bin Laden was a "fanatic . . . a threat to him and his regime."

9. Family background in Wright, *Looming Tower*, chapter 3, and 338, 146. Islamic customs from Leor Halevi, "The Torture of the Grave: Islam and the Afterlife," *IHT*, May 4, 2007, and see his *Muhammad's Grave*, and Ibn Warraq, "Virgins?

What Virgins?" *Guardian*, (London) January 12, 2002. Taliban regime in Seierstad, *Bookseller*, 19–21, 43–44, 79–83, and also interesting is Khaled Hosseini's novel, *A Thousand Splendid Suns*.

10. Heads on pikes from Schroen, *First In*, 38, and Crumpton in Sims and Gerber, *Transforming US Intelligence*, 168–70, and see chapter 3; Tenet, *Storm*, 187; and Franks, *American Soldier*, 297. No one clean from PBS, *Frontline*, "Campaign against Terror," September 8, 2002, and killing each other in Briscoe et al., *Weapon of Choice*, 158. Payments from Schroen, *First In*, 36–37, and Woodward, *Bush at War*, 139–43, and Franks in *American Soldier*, 312. And see Stephen Biddle, "Afghanistan and the Future of Warfare: Implications for Army and Defense Policy," Strategic Studies Institute, November 2002.

11. See Mary Anne Weaver, "Lost at Tora Bora," *NYT*, September 11, 2005. BLU-82 in Berntsen, *Jawbreaker*, 290–98, 306–9, and Franks claimed on PBS, *Frontline*, "Campaign against Terror." Berntsen's response in interview with Tim Russert, CNBC, http://www.leadingauthorities.com/24282/Gary_Berntsen.htm. Mattis in Weaver, above, and Delta Force from CBS, *60 Minutes*, "Elite Office Recalls Bin Laden Hunt," October 5, 2008. Definitely not from Suskind, *One Percent Doctrine*, 58–59. Toll in *Jawbreaker*, 289, and meals in Briscoe et al., *Weapon of Choice*, 213–26. One expert is Weaver. Crumpton in Sims and Gerber, *Transforming US Intelligence*, 168, and for defense of the strategy see Feith, *War and Decision*, 135–37.

12. Black sites in Scott Shane et al., "Secret U.S. Endorsement of Severe Interrogations," *NYT*, October 4, 2007. For enemy combatants and extraordinary rendition see Mayer, *Dark Side*, 85–87, chapter 6. ACLU in Andrew Buncombe, "US Tribunals to Allow Hearsay in Terrorist Trials," *Independent* (UK), December 29, 2001. For torture, see Joby Warrick, "CIA Tactics Endorsed in Secret Memos," *WP*, October 15, 2008; Ali H. Soufan, "What Torture Never Told Us," *NYT*, September 6, 2009; and for the administration's view, see Feith, *War and Decision*, 159–65. Bounty payments, see Tom Lasseter's five-part series, "Guantanamo: Beyond the Law," *MT*, June 2008, and another investigation is Corine Hegland, "Guantanamo's Grip," *National Journal*, February 3, 2006. And see Margulies, *Guantanamo*, chapter 4; Sherry Jones's documentary, "Torturing Democracy"; and Greg Miller and Josh Meyer, "CIA Interrogation Memos: Obama Unseals Justice Department Documents," *CT*, April 17, 2009.

13. Karzai and troops from Briscoe et al., *Weapons of Choice*, 179, 207–11, and Berntsen, *Jawbreaker*, 303. *Jordan Times*, October 5–6, 2001; for the letter and a picture, see http://www.theflagpole.com/uss_winston_churchill.htm.

CHAPTER 2

1. Bush is stupid and Franks on posturing in Woodward, *Plan of Attack*, 94, 58; Pearl Harbor from Draper, *Dead Certain*, 147; and Skelton in Ricks, *Fiasco*, 35. War planning from *Plan of Attack*, 1–3, 30, and Franks, *American Soldier*, 315. Schroen, *First In*, 359, and Cheney on CNN in Rich, *Story Ever Sold*, 58.

2. Niger from Isikoff and Corn, *Hubris*, chapter 5, and Wilson, *Fair Game*, chapter 7, and Wilson, *Politics of Truth*, 2–3, 21–24, chapter 16. European response in Steven Erlanger, "A Nation Challenged: The Allies," *NYT*, February 13, 2002.

Blair in *Daily Telegraph*, March 4; *Observer*, March 10, both 2002. Crawford ranch in Woodward, *Plan of Attack*, 119–20, and fundraiser and Rumsfeld in Suskind, *One Percent Doctrine*, 99, 121. Elisabeth Bumiller, "U.S. Must Act First to Battle Terror, Bush Tells Cadets," *NYT*, June 2, 2002, and McClellan, *What Happened*, 134.

3. Decisions were made in Tenet, *Storm*, 309–10, and McClellan, *What Happened*, chapter 8. Ricketts in Isikoff and Corn, *Hubris*, 27. Memo in *The Times* (London), May 1, 2005, and see *LAT*, May 12, and *NYT*, May 20, both 2005, and Campbell, *Blair Years*, 630. Roche in John Barry and Michael Hirsh, "A Warrior Lays Down His Arms," *Newsweek*, November 20, 2006, and Powell dinner composed from DeYoung, *Soldier*, 401–2, Draper, *Dead Certain*, 179–80, and Woodward, *Bush at War*, 332–34. Poll, CBS News, September 7, 2002.

4. McClellan, *What Happened*, 142, our campaign and stagecraft from 120–25. Card from NPR, *Morning Edition*, "Commentary: Bush Administration's Marketing of the Possible War against Iraq," September 17, 2002. Cheney and CIA in Bamford, *Pretext for War*, 316–20; "crap" quoted in Murray Waas, "Key Bush Intelligence Briefing Kept for Hill Panel," *National Journal*, November 22, 2005; and Tenet, *Storm*, 348. On Miller, see Rich, *Story Ever Sold*, 40, and Ricks, *Fiasco*, 35. Daschle and Armey in Isikoff and Cord, *Hubris*, 21–25, and Woodward, *Plan of Attack*, 168–72.

5. Governors meeting in McClellan, *What Happened*, 139–41, and Rove in Isikoff and Cord, *Hubris*, 21–25. Nelson in Bamford, *Pretext for War*, 330–31, and Newbold from Hagel, *America*, 59. Zinni, October 10, 2002, to the Middle East Institute, Washington, DC, and in Dodge, *Inventing Iraq*, 157. Hagel on CBS News, *Face the Nation*, August 4, 2002, and see his *America*, 38–40, 55–57. Conservative support, see Glenn Greenwald, "Selective Amnesia," *The American Conservative*, January 15, 2007, and Bob Drogin, "John McCain Is Betting Big on Iraq" *LAT*, March 23, 2008.

6. Tenet, *Storm*, 307–39; on tubes, see Wilson, *Fair Game*, 122–23; Isikoff and Corn, *Hubris*, on the Atta fabrication, chapter 6, and other examples of administration pressure on CIA is Suskind, *One Percent Doctrine*, 189–91. "Stop the bullshit" in Isikoff and Corn, *Hubris*, 105, and Thielmann in PBS, *Frontline*, "Truth, War & Consequences," October 9, 2003. For other CIA statements about the NIE, see PBS, *Frontline*, "Bush's War," March 24, 2008. Hagel, *America*, 38, and later report is John Prados, "U.S. Intelligence and Iraq WMD," NSA, August 22, 2008.

7. About regime change from Sidney Blumenthal, "2 CIA Officers: Bush Knew Saddam Had No Weapons of Mass Destruction," *Salon*, September 6, 2007. On al-Libi's treatment, see Isikoff and Corn, *Hubris*, 119–24, and on him as a source, Lawrence B. Wilkerson, "An Oversight Hearing on Pre-War Intelligence Relating to Iraq," June 26, 2006, given to the U.S. Senate, and Michael Isikoff and Mark Hosenball, "Al-Libi's Tall Tales," *Newsweek*, November 10, 2005. Numerous prisoners were tortured to support the administration's case: see Jonathan Landay, "Report: Abusive Tactics Used to Seek Iraq-al Qaida Link," *McC*, April 22, 2009. Wilson, *Fair Game*, 106–7. Curveball in Drumheller, *On the Brink*, chapter 6; Isikoff and Corn, *Hubris*, 129–32; Tenet, *Storm*, 375–83; and see Drogin, *Curveball*, chapters 20–21. Goodman, *Failure*, 253, and for British failed intelligence, see BBC News, "Serious

Flaws in Iraq Intelligence," and "At-a-Glance: Butler Report," July 14, 2004, on *The Butler Report*.

8. David Kirkpatrick, "Response to 9/11 Offers Outline of McCain Doctrine," *NYT*, August 17, 2008. Hagel, *America*, 55–58. Steven Erlanger, "Bush-Hitler Remark Shows U.S. as Issue in German Election," *NYT*, September 20, 2002. CBS News, "Rumsfeld: It Would Be a Short War," November 15, 2002. Stunned Hagel from Draper, *Dead Certain*, 184. Feith, *War and Decision*, 339–43, and Thomas E. Ricks and Karen DeYoung, "Ex-Defense Official Assails Colleagues over Run-Up to War," *WP*, March 9, 2008.

9. Slam dunk from Woodward, *Plan of Attack*, 249–50, and Tenet, *Storm*, chapter 19, and marketing on 362. Shinseki in Fontenot et al., *On Point*, 29. Awful . . . outraged in Bamford, *Pretext for War*, 333–35. ElBaradei's statement to the UN, "The Status of Nuclear Inspections in Iraq," January 27, 2003, and see Blix, *Disarming Iraq*, 135–41. January 31 Bush-Blair meeting from Richard Norton-Taylor, "Blair-Bush Deal before Iraq War Revealed in Secret Memo," *Guardian* (London), February 3, 2006, and Don Van Natta Jr., "The Reach of War: Leaders; Bush Was Set on Path to War, Memo by British Adviser Says," *NYT*, March 27, 2006. Lawrence B. Wilkerson, "An Oversight Hearing on Pre-War Intelligence Relating to Iraq," June 26, 2006, given to U.S. Senate, and see Isikoff and Corn, *Hubris*, 180–81, and 170 on Niger claim. Drogin, *Curveball*, chapter 25, and *LAT*, November 20, 2005. Powell, terrible in *NYT*, September 9, 2005, and also see DeYoung, *Soldier*, 435–52.

10. Children laugh in Napoleoni, *Insurgent Iraq*, 117; Scheuer in Isikoff and Corn, *Hubris*, 123, and see Scheuer, *Marching*, 122. Media critic is Frank Rich, "In Defense of the 'Balloon Boy' Dad," *NYT*, October 25, 2009, and on how easily the press was duped, see his "The Ides of March 2003," *NYT* March 18, 2007. Veteran reporter is PBS, *Bill Moyers Report*, April 25, 2007. Pillar and study in *Hubris*, 196–99, and Schwarzkopf in Ricks, *Fiasco*, 83. Byrd in Ehrenberg et al., *Iraq Papers*, 102–5. *Tehran Times* in Bodansky, *Secret History*, 251, and for international reaction to war see *Iraq Papers*, chapter 3. Straw from Campbell, *Blair Diaries*, 67. Woodward, *Plan of Attack*, 329, and see Franks, *American Soldier*, 428–31. Adam Cowell, "Threats and Responses," *NYT*, March 19, 2003.

CHAPTER 3

1. The military campaign is from Franks, *American Soldier*, chapters 11–12; Ricks, *Fiasco*, chapter 7; and Fontenot et al., *On Point*, chapter 3. For Broadhead see *On Point*, 128–31; Petraeus and Iraqi general in *Fiasco*, 125; darkest, blackest night from interview with USMC Colonel Jerry Smith, March 11, 2010. DeLong, *Inside CentCom*, 83; Wallace and thunder runs in Murrey and Scales, *Iraq War*, 206–10. Iraqi information minister in *On Point*, 347, and detailed fall of Baghdad also in Gordon and Trainor, *Cobra II*, chapters 19–21.

2. Adelman in *WP*, April 10, 2003, FOX News comments in Jim Hightower, "Words to Remember," *The Texas Observer*, May 5, 2006, and James Zogby, "Holding the Media Accountable for Iraq," June 22, 2007, huffingtonpost.com. Franks, *American Soldier*, 854. Hoar in *NYT*, April 2, 2003, and Faleh A. Jabar, "Post-Conflict Iraq: A Race for Stability, Reconstruction, and Legitimacy," *Special Report 120*,

United States Institute of Peace, May 2004, 6, and McKiernan in Ricks, *Fiasco*, 122–23. Zinni and Rumsfeld in Gordon and Trainor, *Cobra II*, 435, 4, 105. Mackey, *Reckoning*, 29, and army study in Record, *Dark Victory*, 117. Lieutenant is Rieckhoff, *Chasing Ghosts*, 53; Garrels in Hoyt et al., *Reporting Iraq*, 25–26; and Fallujah in *Cobra II*, 462.

3. Reconstruction plans and ORHA, Jay Garner, in Feith, *War and Decision*, 348–, Isikoff and Corn, *Hubris*, chapter 11. February meeting see Packer, *Assassins' Gate*, 121–23 and Ricks, *Fiasco*, 101–3, and on ORHA personnel see Rajiv Chandrasekaran interview, *Frontline*, "The Lost Year in Iraq," June 2007. Chalabi's fighters see DeLong, *Inside CentCom*, 78, and Tenet, *Storm*, 398–99. Feith-Garner see Ricks, *Fiasco*, 154, 104–7, and for more animosity see *Assassins' Gate*, 128, and Bodine and Di Rita on 132–33. DeLong, *Inside CentCom*, 83. Assumptions from Michael Gordon, "The Conflict in Iraq . . ." October 19, 2004, "A Prewar Slide Show Cast Iraq in Rosy Hues," February 15, 2007, both *NYT*, and Gordon and Trainor, *Cobra II*, 142, 463; Bodine in Ferguson, *No End in Sight*, 88. Economic expert is Allawi, *Occupation of Iraq*, 121–23. Lack of plans see *Fiasco*, 109–11 and *Assassins' Gate*, chapter 4.

4. Price of metal in Gordon and Trainor, *Cobra II*, 468; electrical survey from "Bechtel Calls It Quits after More Than 3 Years in Iraq," *LAT*, November 3, 2006, and on looting, see interviews in Ferguson, *No End in Sight*, chapter 4. Polk and Schuster, *Looting of the Iraq Museum*, 1–3, and one tank is Hoyt et al., *Reporting Iraq*, 29. Rumsfeld in CNN.com, April 12, 2003, and Garrels in *Reporting Iraq*, 30–31. Weapons looting from Sanchez, *Wiser in Battle*, 173, and legal adviser and looting calculation in Packer, *Assassins' Gate*, 138–39. Tombstone from Rieckhoff, *Chasing Ghosts*, 64–65. Tariq Panja, "Three Charged in Record British Theft," *AP*, March 2, 2006, and Guy Gugliotta, "Looted Iraqi Relics Slow to Surface," *WP*, November 8, 2005. Carjackings, *Cobra II*, 473–73; CPA official and April 28 meeting in *Assassins' Gate*, 144.

5. Rumsfeld and Fleischer from Isikoff and Corn, *Hubris*, 214, and Saddam from Gordon and Trainor, *Cobra II*, 118, 134–37. Looking for WMDs, see Prados, *Hoodwinked*, 264–72, Elvis sightings from Drogin, *Curveball*, 185, and Ford in *Hubris*, 214–15 (italics added). Polish journalist in Rich, *Story Ever Sold*, 96. Fleischer in "Bush: 'Bring on' Attackers of U.S. Troops," *USA Today*, July 2, 2003, and Bush interview with Diane Sawyer, December 16, 2003, *ABC News*. Pillar in *Hubris*, 139–40, and Lawrence B. Wilkerson, "An Oversight Hearing on Pre-War Intelligence Relating to Iraq," June 26, 2006, given to U.S. Senate. "Wolfowitz Comments Revive Doubts over Iraq's WMD," *USA Today*, May 30, 2003.

6. Sawers in *The Guardian*, March 14, 2006. Bremer, *My Year*, 3; Franks, *American Soldier*, 531; junior commanders from Ricks, *Fiasco*, 155–58; and worst decision and scratch from Joe Kline, "Saddam's Revenge," *Time*, September 22, 2005. I'm the CPA and Wallace relieved in Sanchez, *Wiser in Battle*, 178–82, 196–97, and Saddamism from Gordon and Trainor, *Cobra II*, 476. Bitching and Bremer's views in *My Year*, 45, and de-Baath opposition from Chandrasekaran, *Emerald City*, 70–72; *Fiasco*, 159; and *Wiser in Battle*, 148. May 16 meeting from *My Year*, 44–49, and on problems creating the IGC, see Dobbins et al., *Occupying Iraq*, chapter 3. Basra from Dodge, *Inventing Iraq*, 167–68.

7. Garner, intelligence officer, Abizaid, Zinni, and friend in Ricks, *Fiasco*, 154–64, and Hughes in Gordon and Trainor, *Cobra II*, 479–85. Almost everyone

except Bremer and some Pentagon neocons thought Order Number Two was the greatest mistake made by the U.S. occupation, see Ferguson, *No End in Sight*, chapter 6. State-run industries in Dobbins et al., *Occupying Iraq*, 223–27. Western diplomat from Joe Kline, "Saddam's Revenge," *Time*, September 18, 2005; Maguire in Isikoff and Corn, *Hubris*, 225; and State Dept. official in *Fiasco*, 225. Garner and three mistakes from Bob Woodward, "Secret Reports Dispute White House Optimism," *WP*, October 1, 2006.

8. For journalists on CPA briefings see Hoyt et al., *Reporting Iraq*, chapter 3, and Iraqi journalist from Cockburn, *Occupation*, 70. On CPA staffing see Dobbins et al., *Occupying Iraq*, 20–30, and for hiring procedures see Chandrasekaran, *Emerald City*, chapter 1, 91–94, and his interview, PBS, *Frontline*, "The Lost Year in Iraq," October, 2006, and "In Iraq, the Job Opportunity of a Lifetime; Managing a $13 Billion Budget with No Experience," May 23, 2004, and "Ties to GOP Trumped Know-How among Staff Sent to Rebuild Iraq," September 17, 2006, both *WP*. On uneven quality of CPA personnel see Bensahel, *After Saddam*, 116–17, and CPA number from Philips, *Losing Iraq*, 163. Sanchez, *Wiser in Battle*, 193–95. Life in Green Zone is *Emerald City*, 148–49, 56–57, and Chandrasekaran's interview in "Lost Year in Iraq." Media from Allawi, *Occupation of Iraq*, 153–55, rumors in Rosen, *Green Bird*, 57–59, and reconstruction from Packer, *Assassins' Gate*, 241, 225.

9. Sanchez, *Wiser in Battle*, 198, and scary as hell, Rieckhoff, *Chasing Ghosts*, 158–59. Garner in Michael Gordon, "The Conflict in Iraq . . .," *NYT*, October 19, 2004; classic insurgency from Joe Kline, "Saddam's Revenge," *Time*, September 22, 2005, and Democratic response in "Bush: 'Bring on' Attackers of U.S. Troops," *USA Today*, July 2, 2003. Officer in *Chasing Ghosts*, 158; *Wiser in Battle*, 227–31; Abizaid from Ricks, *Fiasco*, 184, and foreign troops, Gordon and Trainor, *Cobra II*, 470–77, and *Wiser in Battle*, 244–45.

10. No Muslim in Rosen, *Green Bird*, 24, and Muqtada al-Sadr in Bremer, *My Year*, 135. In 2005 an associate of al Qaeda, affiliate Abu Musab al-Zarqawi, admitted guilt for bombings of Jordanian embassy, UN headquarters, and death of al-Hakim. See Rod Norland, Tom Masland, and Christopher Dickey, "Iraq: Unmasking the Insurgents," *Newsweek*, February 7, 2005. Sanchez, *Wiser in Battle*, 257, and Bremer, *My Year*, 112–17, 148–52. Intelligence in Ricks, *Fiasco*, 194, and for the enemy see Brian Bennett and Michael Ware, "Life behind Enemy Lines," *Time*, December 15, 2003, Allawi, *Occupation of Iraq*, 176–85, and Anthony H. Cordesman, "Iraq's Evolving Insurgency: The Nature of Attacks and Patterns and Cycles in the Conflict," Center for Strategic and International Studies, 2006. Inevitable insurgency, see Gordon and Trainor, *Cobra II*, 492–96, epilogue, and PBS, *Frontline*, "The Lost Year in Iraq," October 2006. Survey on IGC and other problems of establishing a government see Phillips, *Losing Iraq*, 181, chapter 16, and in retrospect is from Dobbins et al., *Occupying Iraq*, xxiv, 104.

CHAPTER 4

1. Zinni in Herspring, *Rumsfeld's Wars*, 138. Tom Ricks and Vernon Loeb, "Iraq Takes a Toll on Rumsfeld: Criticism Mounts with Costs, Casualties," *WP*, September 14, 2003. One journalist is Packer, *Assassins' Gate*, 241, and Sanchez in Tyler

Marshall, "U.S. General Says Iraqi Rebels Getting Stronger," *LAT*, October 3, 2003. Rumsfeld's slog from Feith, *War and Decision*, 509, and CBS News, December 11, 2003. Bremer, *My Year*, 171. "Report of the International Committee of the Red Cross on the Treatment by Coalition Forces of Prisoners of War and Other Protected Persons by the Geneva Conventions in Iraq during Arrest, Internment, and Interrogation," February 2004. Garrels in Hoyt et al., *Reporting Iraq*, 65, and often terrified is in James Fallows, "Why Iraq Has No Army," *The Atlantic*, December 2005. Coughlin, *Saddam*, 368. Polls and CPA adviser from Diamond, *Squandered Victory*, 25–26, 82.

2. For Fallujah, see Ricks, *Fiasco*, 330–35, Sanchez, *Wiser in Battle*, chapter 18, and Foulk, *The Battle for Fallujah*, chapter 2. Security guards killed in Scahill, *Blackwater*, 101–3, and Rumsfeld's orders and Bush in *Wiser in Battle*, 331–33. New Iraqi Army failures in Bremer, *My Year*, 328, 354, and *Wiser in Battle*, 349–51. Sadr from Jeffrey Bartholet, "How Al-Sadr May Control U.S. Fate in Iraq," *Newsweek*, December 4, 2006, and Shia problems and pep talk, *Wiser in Battle*, 335–50. Coalition troops, critical crisis from *My Year*, 321–33. Bush to Sanchez in *Wiser in Battle*, 357, 360, 371. Mattis in Ricks, *Fiasco*, 342, siren on 345, and no link in *Wiser in Battle*, 454.

3. On torture, see Josh White, "Abu Ghraib Tactics Were First Used at Guantanamo," *WP*, July 14, 2005. No intelligence, to another level, assholes, urinated, and high ground from Ricks, *Fiasco*, 238, 290–96, and just for fun and violated, Sanchez, *Wiser in Battle*, 276–77, 303, and see R. Jeffrey Smith and Josh White, "Wide Latitude: Gen. Sanchez Authorized Aggressive Tactics at Abu Ghraib, Documents Show," *WP Weekly Edition*, June 21–27, 2004. One sheikh in Foulk, *The Battle for Fallujah*, 64. Cancer from Diamond, *Squandered Victory*, 227, and skulls from Cockburn, *Occupation*, 141. For Zarqawi's views, see Dexter Filkins, "U.S. Says Files Seek Qaeda Aid in Iraq Conflict," *NYT*, February 9, 2004; Ehrenberg et al., *The Iraq Papers*, 252–58, and Allawi, *Occupation of Iraq*, chapter 13. Curse them from Daniel Williams, "In Sunni Triangle, Loss of Privilege Breeds Bitterness," *WP*, January 13, 2004, and see Jeffrey Bartholet, "How Al-Sadr May Control U.S. Fate in Iraq," *Newsweek*, December 4, 2006. Paranoid Sunni mind from Rosen, *Green Bird*, 105; Iraqi resistance is Foulk, *The Battle for Fallujah*, 57; and unintended . . . vengeance is Allawi, *Occupation of Iraq*, 456.

4. Bodyguards from Foulk, *The Battle for Fallujah*, 163; $300 from Cockburn, *Occupation*, 154; free-fire zone in Yon, *Moment of Truth*, 11, and charnel house is Packer, *Assassins' Gate*, 258. Blame in Sanchez, *Wiser in Battle*, 394–404; and decoy plane is Galbraith, *End of Iraq*, 145–46. Freedom reign and ineffective is Bremer, *My Year*, 394, 358, and *Wiser in Battle*, 351. Friedman in *NYT*, May 6; Brooks, May 11, both 2004; and see John Tierney, "The World: The Hawks Loudly Express Their Second Thoughts," *NYT*, May 16, 2004. Kean and Hamilton, *9/11 Report*, xvii–xviii, and Chalabi interview, July 2, 2004, *Middle East Quarterly*, summer 2004.

5. 360° from Finkel, *Good Soldiers*, 35–37, and for IEDS see Ricks, *Fiasco*, 217–21; Thom Shanker, "Global Rise in Makeshift Bombs Worries U.S.," *NYT*, October 29, 2009; and NPR, *Morning Edition*, "Battle against IEDs Spreads from Iraq to Afghanistan," October 28, 2009. Walking dead from John Barry, Michael Hastings, and Evan Thomas, "Iraq's Real WMD," *Newsweek*, March 27, 2006, and car bomb

from Rieckhoff, *Chasing Ghosts*, 117–20. Quotes on rebuilding Iraq security forces in James Fallows, "Why Iraq Has No Army," *The Atlantic*, December 2005, and misleading and scandal in Bremer, *My Year*, 209, 183. 60 are Shiite from Galbraith, *End of Iraq*, 187; only 5,000 effective in combat from Herring and Rangwala, *Iraq in Fragments*, 198, and for the problems of building Iraqi security forces see Bensahel, *After Saddam*, chapter 9. Media critic is Rich, *Story Ever Sold*, 133.

   6. Quotes from Foulk, *The Battle for Fallujah*, chapter 18, and see Ricks, *Fiasco*, 398–402, and Wright and Reese, *On Point II*, 344–58. Hunted in Campbell, *Joker One*, 245, and tumor in Yon, *Moment of Truth*, January 2, 2006, survey by WorldPublicOpinion.org, and opinion of U.S. see Philip Kennicott, "An About-Face on America," *WP* Weekly Edition, August 30–September 5, 2004. Voters' blood in Filkin, *Forever War*, 241; tsunami in Cockburn, *Occupation*, 187; and election results from SIGIR, *Hard Lessons*, 206. Complexities of the election and constitution see Allawi, *Occupation of Iraq*, chapters 22 and 23, and Herring and Rangwala, *Iraq in Fragments*, 38–43. Republic of fear is Rosen, *Green Bird*, 227; just lose is in James Fallows, "Why Iraq Has No Army," *The Atlantic*, December 2005; and Murtha and Odom in Cockburn, *Occupation*, 4.

   7. Mark Thompson, "America's Broken-Down Army," *Time*, April 5, 2007, *NYT* editorial, "Moral Waivers and the Military," February 20, 2007, Lolita Baldor, "Troop Buildup in Iraq May Be Hard to Sustain," AP, August 20, 2007, and Casey in *USA Today*, "Deployments Strain Army Recruiting, Retention," February 20, 2008. No stake in the war in Ann Scott Tyson and Josh White, "With Iraq War Come Layers of Loss," *WP*, January 2, 2007, and mall from Yon, *Moment of Truth*, 226. Critic is Rich, *Story Ever Sold*, 197. Counterinsurgency expert in James Fallows, "Why Iraq Has No Army," *The Atlantic*, December 2005, and McMaster in Ricks, *Fiasco*, 420–23, and see PBS, *Frontline*, "End Game," June 19, 2007. Casey in Ricks, *Gamble*, 12, and see 369–71. John A. Nagl, "Foreword" and Sarah Sewall, "Introduction" to the University of Chicago Press Edition, *The U.S. Army, Marine Corp Counterinsurgency Field Manual*. Kilcullen in Finkel, *Good Soldiers*, 46, and expert is Sewall, "Introduction," xxxix.

   8. Cole in Robin Wright, "Experts Cautious in Assessing Iraq Election," *WP*, December 16, 2005, and Cordesman in Walter Pincus, "1,000 Iraqis a Day Flee Violence, U.N. Group Finds," *WP*, November 24, 2006. Death squads is Filkins, *Forever War*, 321. Wild West in CBS News, *60 Minutes*, "Billions Wasted in Iraq," February 9, 2006, and Dobbins et al., *Occupying Iraq*, 177–82. Corruption and fraud see SIGIR, *Hard Lessons*, chapters 20 and 21; bribery is from Cockburn, *Occupation*, 177; and largest robbery in Allawi, *Occupation of Iraq*, 367, and see chapter 20. Money pit is Richard A. Oppel Jr., "In Iraq, Oil Profits Help Feed Insurgency," *NYT/ Le Monde*, March 22, 2008, and USAID is Stephenson, *Losing Golden Hour*, 98.

   9. Peddler and Shia leader in Dan Murphy, "Attack Deepens Iraq's Divide," *CSM*, February 23, 2006, and journalist is Robert Worth, "Blasts Destroys Shrine in Iraq, Setting off Sectarian Fury," *NYT*, February 22, 2006. Farah Stockman and Bryan Bender, "Iraq Militias' Wave of Death," *Boston Globe*, April 2, 2006, and see PBS, *Frontline*, "End Game," June 19, 2007. Walter Pincus, "1,000 Iraqis a Day Flee Violence, U.N. Group Finds," *WP*, November 24, 2006, and humanitarian crisis in Hassan M. Fattah, "Uneasy Havens Await Those Who Flee Iraq," *NYT*,

December 6, 2006. We all pay, fighting over ministries, in Dan Murphy, "Death Squads Deepen Division in Baghdad," *CSM*, May 8, 2006, and corpses and Khazen in Charles J. Hanley, "What Would Iraq Civil War Look Like?" AP, March 15, 2006. Death to America from Cockburn, *Occupation*, 219; NIE in Brian Knowlton, "Bush Makes Public Parts of Report on Terrorism," *NYT/IHT*, September 26, 2006; Jonathan Karl, "Insurgency Gains Alarming Support among Iraq's Sunni Muslims," ABC News, September 20, 2006; and Amit R. Paley, "Most Iraqis Favor Immediate U.S. Pullout, Polls Show," *WP*, September 27, 2006. Joshua Partlow, "Waiting to Get Blown Up," *WP*, July 27, 2006. BBC News, "Tony Blair: Highs and Lows," May 10, 2007.

10. *Military Times*, January 2, 2007, and Will, "Rhetoric of Unreality," *WP*, March 2, 2006. Steven R. Hurst, "Red October," AP, November 23, 2006, and car bombs from Jeffrey Bartholet, "How Al-Sadr May Control U.S. Fate in Iraq," *Newsweek*, December 4, 2006. *HC*, December 2, 2006, and O'Sullivan from Bob Woodward, "Doubt, Distrust, Delay," *WP*, September 7, 2008, and see his *War Within*, 101–2. Tom Ricks, "Bush's Proposal on 'Benchmarks' for Iraq Sounds Familiar," *WP*, October 26, 2006, and cut and run from Draper, *Dead Certain*, 295. Barry Schweid, "Conservatives Challenge Iraq Policy," AP, November 4, 2006, YouTube from Dan Froomkin, "Most Ridiculous Moment?" *WP* October 27, 2006, and Dowd, *NYT*, December 6, 2006

11. See Greg Bruno, "Profile: Al-Qaeda in Iraq (a.k.a. al-Qaeda in Mesopotamia)," *WP*, November 19, 2007, and Anbar's governor is from Dexter Filkins, "US Hands Off Pacified Anbar, Once Heart of Iraq Insurgency," *NYT*, September 2, 2008, and his *Forever War*, chapter 19. Khalid Al-Ansary and Ali Adeeb, "Most Tribes in Anbar Agree to Unite against Insurgents," *NYT*, September 18, 2006; not to blow us up from Andrew J. Bacevich, "Surge to Nowhere: Don't Buy Hawks Hype . . .," *WP*, January 20, 2008. MacFarland in Jim Michaels, "An Army Colonel's Gamble Pays off in Iraq," USAToday.com, May 1, 2007, and need a new strategy from Joe Kline, "Saddam's Revenge," *Time*, September 18, 2005. White House meeting from Ricks, *Gamble*, chapter 3, and Harry Reid is MSNBC, April 25, 2007.

12. Ryan Crocker, "Eight Years On: A Diplomat's Perspective on the post-9/11 World," *Newsweek*, September 14, 2009, Scott Canon, "3rd Month of Surge Sees Iraq Deaths Up," *MT*, May 24, 2007, and Saddam in Sudarsan Raghaven, "4 Years after Hussein's Fall, Regret in Iraq," *WP*, April 9, 2007. Three-dimensional, are you staying, he surged from NPR, *Morning Edition*, "Slow Going for U.S. Forces South of Baghdad," June 28, 2007. Attacks from SIGACTS (CF reports), May 2, 2009, worsen lives from ABC News, September 10, 2007, and family member murdered in Michael E. O'Hanlon and Jason H. Campbell, "Iraq Index: Tracking Variables of Reconstruction & Security in Post-Saddam Iraq," Brookings Institution, April 3, 2008, 54. No good guys from NPR, *Morning Edition*, "Future Iraqi Advisers Face Hard Lessons," March 27, 2007; hate this war in Mark Thompson, "America's Broken-Down Army," *Time*, April 5, 2007.

13. Not hopeless in "On Leadership: Petraeus on Being 'Brutally Honest' with the Public," washingtonpost.com. February 24, 2010; attacks from SIGACTS (CF reports), May 2, 2009, and Liz Sly, *CT*, "Life Returns to Baghdad's Streets as Violence Falls," November 18, 2007. Never back down from Yon, *Moment of Truth*, 131.

Dexter Filkins, "US Hands Off Pacified Anbar, Once Heart of Iraq Insurgency," *NYT*, September 2, 2008, and trust and friendship in Tina Susman, "U.S. Hands Over Control of Anbar to Iraqi Forces," *LAT*, September 2, 2008. Elena Becatoros, "New Program Aims to Give Iraqis Jobs—and Keep Them Away from Militias," AP, January 3, 2008, and Cordesman in Ricks, *Gamble*, 277. Slobodan Lekic, "More Than 1,300 Iraqi Forces Fired for Deserting Mid-Battle," AP, April 14, 2008; professor in Vali Nasr, "Iran on Its Heels," *WP*, June 19, 2008; and Raviya H. Ismal, "Iraqi Forces Enter Sadr City Alone," *MT*, May 21, 2008.

14. Ricks, *Gamble*, 294, and Petraeus to Congress, 164. Odierno in Thom Shanker and Stephen Farrell, "Odierno Succeeds Petraeus in Iraq," *NYT*, September 16, 2008. Elisabeth Bumiller, "Gates' Trip Hits Snags in Two Theaters," *NYT*, December 12, 2009, and downward spiral in Pamela Hess, "Intel Report: Afghanistan Facing Downward Spiral," AP, October 10, 2008. Devlin Barrett, "2009 Year of Terror Charges in US," AP, January 17, 2010, and see Patrick Quinn, "U.S. Wartime Prison System Network Grows into Legal Vacuum for 14,000," AP, September 18, 2006. Voice of America News, "US High Court Says Guantanamo Detainees Can Challenge Detention," June 12, 2008. "Study: False Statements Preceded War," *NYT*, January 23, 2008, and all comments in Dan Froomkin, "Out of Gas," *WP*, January 29, 2008. Leila Fadel, "US Seeks 58 Bases in Iraq," *MT*, June 10, 2008, and Tina Susman and Ned Parker, "Iraq Prime Minister Nouri Maliki Demands Firm Withdrawal Date," *LAT*, August 26, 2008. Bob Woodward, "A Portrait of a Man Defined by His Wars," *WP*, September 10, 2008.

EPILOGUE

1. Devlin Barrett, AP, "2009 Year of Terror Charges in US," January 17, 2010. Tamara Walid, Reuters, "Bin Laden Claims U.S. Plane Attempt, Vows More Attacks," January 24, 2010.

2. Scene filled with bloody is Timothy Williams, "Bombings in Iraq, Deadliest since 2007, Raise Security Issue," *NYT*, October 26, 2009; Iraqi electoral chairman from Aljazeera.net, "Patience Urged in Iraq Vote Count," March 7, 2010. Odierno from Michael Hastings, "December First Month without US Combat Deaths in Iraq," *WP*, January 1, 2010, and Liz Sly, "December First Month without U.S. Deaths; Forces Renamed," *CT*, January 2, 2010. Days of 2005 from Liz Sly, "In Hopeful Sign, More Iraqis Looking to Move beyond Sectarianism," *CT*, November 1, 2009, and not going back in Karen DeYoung, "As Iraq Votes, U.S. Content to Keep Its Distance," *WP*, March 7, 2010. Shaky institutions and can govern from Anthony Shadid, "Unity Elusive as Iraq Grasps Trappings of Democracy," *NYT*, March 5, 2010. For the economy, red tape, and bribes, see NPR, *Morning Edition*, December 9, 2009; "Iraq's Shaky Economy Poses Threat to Future," UPI.com; "Iraq Oil Sales up but Plans Unrealistic," March 5, 2010. Oil corruption is from Timothy Williams, "As Iraq Seeks Oil Investors, They See an Uncertain Bet," *NYT*, October 14, 2009, and CPI from SIGIR, *Hard Lessons*, 213–14. NPR, *Fresh Air*, interview with Ricks, January 27, 2010, and Crocker from Lindsay Wise, "Former Iraq Diplomats Say Success Will Not Come Soon," *HC*, November 5, 2009.

3. Flip like a toy in Laura King, "War Toll Likely to Get Even Worse," *LAT*, January 1, 2010, and *NYT*, "Afghanistan on Fire," August 21, 2008. Tribal narco-state is Frank Rich, "Obama at the Precipice," *NYT*, September 27, 2009. Mowing from Dexter Filkins, "Afghan Offensive Is New War Model," *NYT*, February 13, 2010, and Clinton from NPR, *Morning Edition*, "International Community Reach Out to Taliban" January 29, 2010. Eikenberry from Eric Schmitt, "U.S. Envoy's Cables Show Worries on Afghan Plan," *NYT*, January 25, 2010. Corruption, see Alex Rodriguez, "Corruption Robs Afghans of a Quarter of Nation's GDP, Report Says," *LAT*, January 20, 2010, and Sylvia Hui, AP, "UN: Afghans Forced to Pay Billions in Bribes," January 20, 2010. Cancer is in Tony Perry, "$10 Million Is Smuggled Out of Afghanistan Daily, Official Says," *LAT*, December 7, 2009, and Miliband in Paul Reynolds, "Moving from War to Peace," *BBC News*, January 28, 2010. Nicholson in NPR, *All Things Considered*, "In Marjah, Rooting Out the Taliban Is Only the Start," March 15, 2010, and ANA soldiers in C. J. Chivers, "Military Analysis: Marines Do Heavy Lifting as Afghans Lag in Battle," *NYT*, February 20, 2010. Trust is earned in C. J. Chivers, "After Push in Marja, Marines Try to Win Trust," *NYT*, February 28, 2010; McChrystal and Afghan general from Dexter Filkins, "Afghan Offensive Is New War Model," *NYT*, February 13, 2010. Caused panic in Scott Shane and Eric Schmitt, "CIA Deaths Prompt Surge in U.S. Drone Strikes," *NYT*, January 23, 2010, and Dexter Filkins, "In Blow to Taliban 2 More Leaders Are Arrested," *NYT*, February 18, 2010. Watches, time from Jones, *Graveyard of Empires*, 325. Ryan Crocker interview, C-Span.org, January 27, 2010, and Crocker, "Eight Years On: A Diplomat's Perspective on the Post-9/11 World," *Newsweek*, September 14, 2009.

CONCLUDING REMARKS AND LEGACIES

1. Bush, *Decision Points*, 477. Fallows, *Blind into Baghdad*, 223. Eric Rosenberg, "Rumsfeld Retreats, Disclaims Earlier Rhetoric," *Hearst News*, November 9, 2003.

2. Bush, *Decision Points*, 228; Hagel, *America*, 51; and Cockburn, *Occupation*, 2. Bush and Religion, see Daalder, *American Unbound*, 87–88. "Wolfowitz Comments Revive Doubts over Iraq's WMD," *USA Today*, May 30, 2003, and Bush, *Decision Points*, 262. Hagel, *America*, 51, and Dodge, *Inventing Iraq*, xvii. Ron Suskind, "Faith, Certainty, and the Presidency of George W. Bush," October 17, 2004, *NYT Magazine*, and his *One Percent Doctrine*, 62. Bush and oil in McClellan, *What Happened*, 139; George Wright, "Wolfowitz: Iraq Was About Oil," *Guardian*, June 4, 2003; and Greenspan, *Age of Turbulence*, 463. Prediction from McClellan, *What Happened*, 140, and beacon from Woodward, *Plan of Attack*, 88–89. McClellan, *What Happened*, 131. SOB from Bamford, *Pretext for War*, 260, and spend capital in Draper, *Dead Certain*, 173, and campaign mode, 210. Galbraith, *End of Iraq*, 83; Hagel, *America*, 51; Draper, *Dead Certain*, x; Woodward, *Bush at War*, 342; and Maureen Dowd, "Spock at the Bridge," *NYT*, February 28, 2009.

3. Dalia Sussman, "Polls: Much Skepticism about Iraq, *NYT*, August 31, 2010, and Nancy A. Youssef and Sahar Issa, "Gates: Iraq Outcome 'Will Always Be Clouded by How It Began,'" *McC*, September 3, 2010. Feith, *War and Decision*, 234; Rove, *Courage*, chapter 21, 340; and Bush, *Decision Points*, 267. NPR, *Fresh Air*, interview with Ricks, January 27, 2010. Christopher Drew, "High Cost Weigh on Troop

Debate for Afghan War," *NYT*, November 15, 2009, and Linda J. Bilmes and Joseph Stiglitz, "The U.S. in Iraq: An Economics Lesson," *LAT*, July 2, 2009. James Glanz, "Iraq Spending Ignored Rules, Pentagon Says," *NYT*, May 23, 2008, and his "New Fraud Cases Point to Lapses in Iraq Projects," *NYT*, March 13, 2010. http://www.defense.gov/NEWS/casualty.pdf. Charles J. Hanley, "When Will the Terror Attacks End? 'I don't think it's even started yet,' Expert Says," AP, July 9, 2005. Sanchez, *Wiser in Battle*, 454–55, and war correspondent and sergeant from CBS News, *60 Minutes*, "IEDs in Afghanistan: The Deadliest Weapon," May 30, 2010. John Signoriello, "Gen. Petraeus on Iraq, Iran, Al Qaeda," *NY Military Headlines Examiner*, February 4, 2010, www.defense.gov/NEWS/casualty.pdf and iCasualties.org. Waterboarding in Bush, *Decision Points*, 168–71, and Schlesinger in Mayer, *Dark Side*, 8. Rove, *Courage*, 520, and "Bush Begins His Memoir with a Sober Decision," *HC*, May 26, 2010, and Bush, *Decision Points*, 181. Emily Cahn, "Dick Armey Unloads Both Barrels on the Presidency of George W. Bush," *HC*, June 17, 2010. Khalid al-Ansary, "U.S.-Installed Iraqi ex-PM Says Bush 'Utter Failure,'" Reuters, January 3, 2009. Eric Foner, "He's the Worst Ever," *WP*, December 3, 2006, and see Sean Wilentz, "The Worst President in History?" *Rolling Stone*, April 21, 2006. Bob Woodward, "A Portrait of a Man Defined by His Wars," *WP*, September 10, 2008.

Bibliography

To date, a search of books on the wars on terror, in Afghanistan, and in Iraq will yield a few hundred titles. Thus, this is a select bibliography.

Agresto, John, *Mugged By Reality: The Liberation of Iraq and the Failure of Good Intentions* (New York: Encounter Books, 2007).

Al-Khalil, Samir, *Republic of Fear: The Inside Story of Saddam's Iraq* (New York: Pantheon, 1998).

Ali, Tariq, *Bush in Babylon: The Recolonisation of Iraq* (London: Verso, 2003).

Allawi, Ali A., *The Occupation of Iraq: Winning the War, Losing the Peace* (New Haven, CT: Yale University Press, 2007).

Anderson, Jon Lee, *The Fall of Baghdad* (New York: Penguin, 2004).

Anonymous, *Imperial Hubris: Why the West Is Losing the War on Terror* (Washington DC: Brassey's, 2004).

Auerswald, Philip, *Iraq, 1990–2006: A Diplomatic History through Documents*, 3 vols., Cambridge: Cambridge University Press, 2009).

Bacevich, Andrew, *The Limits of Power: The End of American Exceptionalism* (New York: Metropolitan Books, 2008).

Ball, Howard, *Bush, the Detainees, and the Constitution: The Battle over Presidential Power in the War on Terror* (Lawrence, KS: University Press of Kansas, 2007).

Bamford, James, *A Pretext for War: 9/11, Iraq, and the Abuse of America's Intelligence Agencies* (Garden City, NJ: Doubleday, 2004).

Beckett, Francis, and David Hencke, *The Survivor: Tony Blair in Peace and War* (London: Aurum Press, 2005).

Benjamin, Daniel, and Steven Simon, *The Age of Sacred Terror* (New York: Random House, 2002).

Bensahel, Nora, et al., *After Saddam: Prewar Planning and the Occupation of Iraq* (Santa Monica, CA: Rand, 2008).

Bergen, Peter L., *Holy War, Inc: Inside the Secret World of Osama bin Laden* (New York: Free Press, 2001).

——, *The Osama bin Laden I know: An Oral History of al-Qaeda's Leader* (New York: Free Press, 2006).

Berntsen, Gary, and Ralph Pezzullo, *Jawbreaker: The Attack on bin Laden and al-Qaeda: A Personal Account by the CIA's Key Field Commander* (New York: Crown, 2006).

Blair, Tony, *A Journey: My Political Life* (New York: Knopf, 2010).

Blix, Hans, *Disarming Iraq: Search for Weapons of Mass Destruction* (London: Bloomsbury, 2004).

Blumenthal, Sidney, *The Clinton Wars* (New York: Farrar, Straus and Giroux, 2003).

Bodansky, Yossef, *Bin Laden: The Man Who Declared War on America* (Santa Ana, CA: Forum, 1999).

——, *The Secret History of the Iraq War* (New York: ReganBooks, 2004).

Borjesson, Kristina, ed., *Feet to the Fire: The Media after 9/11: Top Journalists Speak Out* (New York: Prometheus Books, 2005).

Bremer, L. Paul, III, with Malcolm McConnell, *My Year in Iraq: The Struggle to Build a Future of Hope* (New York: Simon and Schuster, 2006).

Briscoe, Charles H., Richard L. Kiper, James A. Schroder, and Kalev I. Sepp, *Weapon of Choice: U.S. Army Special Operations Forces in Afghanistan* (Fort Leavenworth, KS: Combat Studies Institute Press, 2003).

——, Kenneth Finlayson, Robert W. Jones Jr., Cherilyn A. Walley, A. Dwayne Aaron, Michael R. Mullins, and James A. Schroder, *All Roads Lead to Baghdad: Army Special Operations Forces in Iraq* (Fort Bragg, NC: USASOC History Office, n.d.).

Bush, George, and Brent Scowcroft, *A World Transformed* (New York: Knopf, 1998).

Bush, George W., *Decision Points* (New York: Crown, 2010).

Buzzell, Colby, *My War: Killing Time in Iraq* (New York: Putnam, 2005).

Campbell, Alastair, and Richard Stott, *The Blair Years: Extracts from the Alastair Campbell Diaries* (London: Hutchinson, 2007).

Campbell, Donovan, *Joker One: A Marine Platoon's Story of Courage, Leadership, and Brotherhood* (New York: Random House, 2009).

Carroll, Andrew, ed., *Operation Homecoming: Iraq, Afghanistan, and the Home Front, in the Worlds of U.S. Troops and Their Families* (New York: Random House, 2006).

Chandrasekaran, Rajiv, *Imperial Life in the Emerald City: Inside Iraq's Green Zone* (New York: Knopf, 2006).

Chehab, Zaki, *Inside the Resistance: The Iraqi Insurgency and the Future of the Middle East* (New York: Nation Books, 2005)

——, *Iraq Ablaze: Inside the Insurgency* (London: I.B. Tauris, 2006).

Clarke, Richard, *Against All Enemies: Inside America's War on Terror* (New York: Free Press, 2004).

Clinton, Bill, *My Life* (New York: Knopf, 2004).

Cockburn, Patrick, *The Occupation* (London: Verso, 2006).

Coll, Steve, *Ghost Wars: The Secret History of the CIA, Afghanistan, and bin Laden, from the Soviet Invasion to September 10, 2001.* (New York: Penguin, 2004).

Cordesman, Anthony H., *The Iraq War: Strategy, Tactics, and Military Lessons* (Washington, DC: CSIS Press, 2003).

Coughlin, Con, *Saddam: The Secret Life*, rev. and updated ed. (London: Pan Books, 2005).

Crawford, John, *The Last True Story I'll Ever Tell: An Accidental Soldier's Account of the War in Iraq* (New York: Riverhead, 2005).

Crile, George, *Charlie Wilson's War* (New York: Grove Press, 2003).

Daalder, Ivo H., and James M. Lindsay, *America Unbound: The Bush Revolution in Foreign Policy* (Washington, DC: Brookings Institution Press, 2003).

Danner, Mark, *The Secret Way to War: The Downing Street Memo and the Iraq War's Buried History* (New York: New York Review Books, 2006).

———, *Torture and Truth: America, Abu Ghraib, and the War on Terror* (New York: New York Review Books, 2004).

DeLong, Michael, with Noah Lukeman, *Inside CENTCOM: The Unvarnished Truth about the War in Afghanistan and Iraq* (Washington, DC: Regnery Publishing, 2004).

DeYoung, Karen, *Soldier: The Life of Colin Powell* (New York: Knopf, 2006).

Diamond, Larry, *Squandered Victory: The American Occupation and the Bungled Effort to Bring Democracy to Iraq* (New York: Times Books, 2005).

Dobbins, James F., *After the Taliban: Nation-Building in Afghanistan* (Washington, DC: Potomac Books, 2008).

———, Seth G. Jones, Benjamin Runkle, and Siddharth Mohandas, *Occupying Iraq: A History of the Coalition Provisional Authority* (Santa Monica, CA: Rand, 2009).

Dodge, Toby, *Inventing Iraq: The Failure of Nation Building and a History Denied* (New York: Columbia University Press, 2003).

Donnelly, Thomas, *Operation Iraqi Freedom: A Strategic Assessment* (Washington, DC: AEI Press, 2004).

Draper, Robert, *Dead Certain: The Presidency of George W. Bush* (New York: Free Press, 2007).

Drogin, Bob, *Curveball: Spies, Lies, and the Con Man Who Caused a War* (New York: Random House, 2007).

Drumheller, Tyler, with Elaine Monaghan, *On the Brink: An Insider's Account of How the White House Compromised American Intelligence* (New York: Carroll & Graf, 2006).

Duelfer, Charles, *Hide and Seek: The Search for Truth in Iraq* (New York: Public Affairs, 2009).

Ehrenberg, John, J. Patrice McSherry, Jose Ramon Sanchez, and Caroleen Marji Sayej, eds., *The Iraq Papers* (New York: Oxford University Press, 2010).

Engel, Richard, *War Journal: My Five Years in Iraq* (New York: Simon and Schuster, 2008).

Eppel, Michael, *Iraq from Monarchy to Tyranny: From the Hashemites to the Rise of Saddam* (Gainesville: University of Florida Press, 2004).

Ewans, Martin, *Afghanistan: A Short History of Its People and Politics* (New York: HarperCollins, 2002).

Exum, Andrew, *This Man's Army: A Soldier's Story from the Frontlines of the War on Terrorism* (New York: Gotham, 2004).

Fallows, James, *Blind into Baghdad: America's War in Iraq* (New York: Vintage, 2006).

Farouk-Sluglett, Marion, and Peter Sluglett, *Iraq since 1958: From Revolution to Dictatorship* (London: KPI, 1987).

Fassihi, Farnaz, *Waiting for an Ordinary Day: The Unraveling of Life in Iraq* (New York: Public Affairs, 2008).

Feith, Douglas J., *War and Decision: Inside the Pentagon at the Dawn of the War on Terrorism* (New York: Harper, 2008).

Ferguson, Charles H., *No End in Sight: Iraq's Descent into Chaos* (New York: PublicAffairs, 2008).

Ferguson, Niall, *Colossus: The Price of America's Empire* (New York: Viking, 2004).

Filkins, Dexter, *The Forever War* (New York: Knopf, 2008).

Finkel, David, *The Good Soldiers* (New York: Farrar, Straus and Giroux, 2009).

Fisk, Robert, *The Great War for Civilisation: The Conquest of the Middle East* (New York: Knopf, 2005).

Fontenot, Gregory, E. J. Degen, and David Tohn, *On Point: The United States Army in Operation Iraqi Freedom*, vols. 1 and 2 (Fort Leavenworth, KS: Combat Studies Institute Press, 2004).

Foulk, Vincent L., *The Battle for Fallujah: Occupation, Resistance, and Stalemate in the War in Iraq* (Jefferson, NC: McFarland, 2007).

Franks, Tommy, with Malcolm McConnell, *American Soldier* (New York: Reagan-Books, 2004).

Friedman, George, *America's Secret War: Inside the Hidden Worldwide Struggle between America and Its Enemies* (New York: Broadway Books, 2004).

Fukuyama, Francis, ed., *Nation-Building: Beyond Afghanistan and Iraq* (Baltimore, MD: Johns Hopkins University Press, 2006).

Galbraith, Peter, *The End of Iraq: How American Incompetence Created a War without End* (New York: Simon and Schuster, 2006).

Gardner, Lloyd C., *The Long Road to Baghdad: A History of U.S. Foreign Policy from the 1970s to the Present* (New York: New Press, 2008).

Glantz, Aaron, *How America Lost Iraq* (New York: Penguin, 2005).

Goodman, Melvin A., *Failure of Intelligence: The Decline and Fall of the CIA* (Lanham, MD: Rowman & Littlefield, 2008).

Gordon, Matthew S., *The Rise of Islam* (Westport, CT: Greenwood Press, 2005).

Gordon, Michael R., and Bernard E. Trainor, *Cobra II: The Inside Story of the Invasion and Occupation of Iraq* (New York: Pantheon, 2006).

Graham, Bob, with Jeff Nussbaum, *Intelligence Matters: The CIA, the FBI, Saudi Arabia, and the Failure of America's War on Terror* (New York: Random House, 2004).

Greenberg, Karan J., and Joshua L. Dratel, eds., *The Torture Papers: The Road to Abu Ghraib* (New York: Cambridge University Press, 2005).

Greenspan, Alan, *Age of Turbulence: Adventures in a New World* (New York: Penguin, 2007).

Hagel, Chuck, with Peter Kaminsky, *America: Our Next Chapter* (New York: HarperCollins, 2008).

Halevi, Leor, *Muhammad's Grave: Death Rites and the Making of Islamic Society* (New York: Columbia University Press, 2007).

Halper, Stefan, and Jonathan Clarke, *America Alone: The Neo-Conservative and the Global Order* (New York: Cambridge University Press, 2004).

Hammes, Thomas X., *The Sling and the Stone: On War in the 21st Century* (St. Paul, MN: Zenith Press, 2006).

Herring, Eric, and Glen Rangwala, *Iraq in Fragments: The Occupation and Its Legacy* (New York: Cornell University Press, 2006).

Hersh, Seymour, *Chain of Command: The Road from 9/11 to Abu Ghraib* (New York: HarperCollins, 2004).

Herspring, Dale R., *Rumsfeld's Wars: The Arrogance of Power* (Lawrence, KS: University Press of Kansas, 2008).

Hilsman, Roger, *George Bush vs. Saddam Hussein: Military Success! Political Failure?* (Novato, CA: Lyford Books, 1992).

Hiro, Dilip, *Iraq: In the Eye of the Storm* (New York: Nation Books, 2002).

Hosseini, Khaled, *A Thousand Splendid Suns* (New York: Riverhead Books, 2008).

Hoyt, Mike, John Palattella, et al., *Reporting Iraq: An Oral History of the War by the Journalists Who Covered It* (Hoboken, NJ: Melville House Publishing, 2007).

Isikoff, Michael, and David Corn, *Hubris: The Inside Story of Spin, Scandal, and the Selling of the Iraq War* (New York: Crown Publishers, 2006).

Jacobson, Gary C., *A Divider, Not a Uniter: George W. Bush and the American People* (New York: Pearson Longman, 2007).

Jones, Howard, *Crucible of Power: A History of American Foreign Relations from 1945* (Lanham, MD: Rowman & Littlefield, 2009).

Jones, Seth G., *In the Graveyard of Empires: America's War in Afghanistan* (New York: Norton, 2009).

Junger, Sebastian, *War* (New York: Twelve, 2010).

Kean, Thomas H., and Lee H. Hamilton, *The 9/11 Report: The National Commission on Terrorist Attacks upon the United States* (New York: St. Martin's Press, 2004).

Keegan, John, *The Iraq War* (New York: Vintage, 2005).

Khadduri, Majid, and Edmund Ghareeb, *War in the Gulf, 1990–91: The Iraq-Kuwait Conflict and Its Implications* (New York: Oxford University Press, 1997).

Kilcullen, David, *Accidental Guerrilla: Fighting Small Wars in the Midst of a Big One* (New York: Oxford University Press, 2009).

King, R. Alan, *Twice Armed: An American Soldier's Battle for Hearts and Minds in Iraq* (St. Paul, MN: Zenith Press, 2006).

Koontz, Christopher N., ed. *Enduring Voices: Oral Histories of the U.S. Army Experience in Afghanistan*, (Washington, DC: Center for Military History, 2008).

Lambeth, Benjamin S., *Air Power against Terror: America's Conduct of Operation Enduring Freedom* (Santa Monica, CA: Rand Corporation, 2005).

Leffler, Melvyn P., *For the Soul of Mankind: The United States, The Soviet Union, and The Cold War* (New York: Hill and Wang, 2007).

Little, Douglas, *American Orientalism: The United States and the Middle East since 1945* (Chapel Hill: University of North Carolina Press, 2002).

Mackey, Sandra, *The Reckoning: Iraq and the Legacy of Saddam Hussein* (New York: Norton, 2002).

Madelung, Wilfred, *The Succession to Muhammad: A Study of the Early Caliphate* (London: Cambridge University Press, 1997).

Maley, William, *The Afghanistan Wars* (New York: Palgrave Macmillan, 2002).

Maloney, Sean M., *Enduring the Freedom: A Rogue Historian in Afghanistan* (Washington, DC: Potomac Books, 2005).

Mann, James, *Rise of the Vulcans: The History of Bush's War Cabinet* (New York: Viking, 2004).

Margulies, Joseph, *Guantanamo and the Abuse of Presidential Power* (New York: Simon and Schuster, 2007).

May, Ernest R., *The 9/11 Commission Report with Related Documents* (Boston: Bedford/St. Martin's, 2007).

Mayer, Jane, *The Dark Side: The Inside Story of How the War on Terror Turned into a War on American Ideals* (New York: Doubleday, 2008).

McClellan, Scott, *What Happened: Inside the Bush White House and Washington's Culture of Deception* (New York: Public Affairs, 2008).

Meyer, Karl E., *The Dust of Empire: The Race for Mastery in the Asian Heartland* (New York: Public Affairs, 2004).

Meyerowitz, Joanne, ed., *History and September 11th* (Philadelphia: Temple University Press, 2003).

Miller, T. Christian, *Blood Money: Wasted Billions, Lost Lives, and Corporate Greed in Iraq* (New York: Little, Brown, 2006).

Moore, Robin, *The Hunt for Bin Laden: Task Force Dagger* (New York: Random House, 2003).

Mortenson, Greg, and David Oliver Relin, *Three Cups of Tea: One Man's Mission to Fight Terrorism and Build Nations—One School at a Time* (New York: Viking, 2006).

Murray, Williamson, and Robert H. Scales Jr., *The Iraq War: A Military History* (Cambridge, MA: Harvard University Press, 2003).

Mylroie, Laurie, *A Study of Revenge* (Washington, DC: AEI, 2001).

Nagl, John A. *Learning to Eat Soup with a Knife: Counterinsurgency Lessons from Malaya and Vietnam* (Chicago: University of Chicago Press, 2005).

Napoleoni, Loretta, *Insurgent Iraq: Al Zarqawi and the New Generation* (New York: Seven Stories Press, 2005).

Naylor, Sean, *Not A Good Day to Die: The Untold Story of Operation Anaconda* (New York: Berkley, 2005).

Packer, George, *The Assassins' Gate: America in Iraq* (New York: Farrar, Straus and Giroux, 2005).

Pelletiere, Stephen C., *Losing Iraq: Insurgency and Politics* (Westport, CT: Praeger, 2007).

Phillips, David L., *Losing Iraq: Inside the Postwar Reconstruction Fiasco* (Boulder, CO: Westview Press, 2005).

Polk, Milbry, and Angela M. H. Schuster, eds., *The Looting of the Iraq Museum, Baghdad: The Lost Legacy of Ancient Mesopotamia* (New York: Harry N. Abrams, 2005).

Powell, Colin, with Joseph E. Persico, *My American Journey: Colin Powell* (New York: Random House, 1995).

Prados, John, ed., *Hoodwinked: The Documents That Reveal How Bush Sold Us a War* (New York: New Press, 2004).

Rashid, Ahmed, *Taliban: Militant Islam, Oil and Fundamentalism in Central Asia* (New Haven, CT: Yale University Press, 2000).

———, *Descent into Chaos: The U.S. and Disaster in Pakistan, Afghanistan, and Central Asia* (New York: Penguin, 2008).

Record, Jeffrey, *Dark Victory: America's Second War against Iraq* (Annapolis, MD: Naval Institute Press, 2004).

Reynolds, Nicholas E., *Basrah, Baghdad, and Beyond: The U.S. Marine Corps in the Second Iraq War* (Annapolis, MD: Naval Institute Press, 2005).

Rich, Frank, *The Greatest Story Ever Sold: The Decline and Fall of Truth from 9/11 to Katrina* (New York: Penguin, 2006).

Ricks, Thomas, *Fiasco: The American Military Adventure in Iraq* (New York: Penguin, 2006).

———, *The Gamble: General David Petraeus and the American Military Adventure in Iraq, 2006–2008* (New York: Penguin, 2009).

Rieckhoff, Paul, *Chasing Ghosts: A Soldier's Fight for America from Baghdad to Washington* (New York: New American Library, 2006).

Risen, James, *State of War: The Secret History of the CIA and the Bush Administration* (New York: Free Press, 2006).

Ritter, Scott, and Seymour Hersh, *Iraq Confidential: The Untold Story of the Intelligence Conspiracy to Undermine the United Nations and Overthrow Saddam Hussein* (New York: Nation Books, 2005).

Ritter, Scott, and William Rivers Pitt, *War on Iraq: What Team Bush Doesn't Want You to Know* (New York: Context Books, 2002).

Rosen, Nir, *In the Belly of the Green Bird: The Triumph of the Martyrs in Iraq* (New York: Free Press, 2006).

Rove, Karl, *Courage and Consequence: My Life as a Conservative in the Fight* (New York: Simon and Schuster, 2010).

Runion, Meredith L., *The History of Afghanistan* (Westport, CT: Greenwood Press, 2007).

Sanchez, Ricardo S., with Donald T. Phillips, *Wiser in Battle: A Soldier's Story* (New York: HarperCollins, 2008).

Scahill, Jeremy, *Blackwater: The Rise of the World's Most Powerful Mercenary Army* (New York: Nation, 2007).

Scheuer, Michael, *Marching toward Hell: America and Islam after Iraq* (New York: Free Press, 2008).

Schroen, Gary C., *First In: An Insider's Account of How the CIA Spearheaded the War on Terror in Afghanistan* (New York: Presidio Press, 2005).

Schultheis, Rob, *Waging Peace: A Special Operations Team's Battle to Rebuild Iraq* (New York: Gotham, 2005).

Schulzinger, Robert D., *U.S. Diplomacy since 1900* (New York: Oxford University Press, 2002).

Schwarzkopf, H. Norman, with Peter Petre, *The Autobiography: It Doesn't Take a Hero* (New York: Bantam Books, 1993).

Seierstad, Asne, *The Bookseller of Kabul* (New York: Back Bay Books, 2004).

Shenon, Philip, *The Commission: The Uncensored History of the 9/11 Investigation* (New York: Hachette Book Group, 2008).

SIGIR, Special Inspector General, Iraq Reconstruction (Stuart W. Bowen Jr.), *Hard Lessons: The Iraq Reconstruction Experience* (Washington, DC: U.S. Government Printing Office, 2009).

Sims, Jennifer E., and Burton Gerber, eds, *Transforming U.S. Intelligence* (Washington, DC: Georgetown University Press, 2005).

Solomon, Lewis D., *Wolfowitz: Visionary Intellectual, Policymaker, and Strategist* (Westport, CT: Praeger, 2007).

Stephenson, James, *Losing the Golden Hour: An Insider's View of Iraq's Reconstruction* (Washington, DC, Potomac Books, 2007).

Stewart, Rory, *The Price of the Marshes, and Other Occupational Hazards of a Year in Iraq* (New York: Harcourt, 2006).

Strasser, Steven, ed., *The Abu Ghraib Investigations: The Official Reports of the Independent Panel and Pentagon on the Shocking Prisoner Abuse in Iraq* (New York: Public Affairs, 2004).

Suskind, Ron, *The One Percent Doctrine: Deep inside America's Pursuit of Its Enemies since 9/11* (New York: Simon and Schuster, 2006).

———, *The Price of Loyalty: George W. Bush, the White House, and the Education of Paul O'Neill* (New York: Simon and Schuster, 2004).

Synnott, Hilary, *Bad Days in Basra: My Turbulent Time as Britain's Man in Southern Iraq* (London: I.B. Tauris, 2008).

Tenet, George, with Bill Harlow, *At the Center of the Storm: My Years at the CIA* (New York: HarperCollins, 2007).

Tyner, James, *The Business of War: Workers, Warriors, and Hostages in Occupied Iraq* (Aldershot, UK: Ashgate, 2006).

United States, Department of the Army, *The U.S. Army, Marine Corps Counterinsurgency Field Manual*, with forewords by David H. Petraeus, James F. Amos, John A. Nagl, and introduction by Sarah Sewall (Chicago, University of Chicago Press, 2007).

Wahab, Shaista, and Barry Youngerman, *A Brief History of Afghanistan* (New York: Infobase, 2007).

Walker, Martin, ed., *The Iraq War: As Witnessed by Correspondents and Photographers of the United Press International* (Washington, DC: Brassey's, 2004).

West, Bing, *No True Glory: A Frontline Account of the Battle for Fallujah* (New York: Bantam, 2005).

Westad, Odd Arne, *The Global Cold War: Third World Interventions and the Making of Our Times* (New York: Cambridge University Press, 2007).

Wilson, Joseph, *The Politics of Truth: Inside the Lies That Led to War and Betrayed My Wife's CIA Identity* (New York: Carroll & Graf, 2004).

Wilson, Valerie Plame, *Fair Game* (New York: Simon and Schuster, 2007).

Woodward, Bob, *Bush at War* (New York: Simon and Schuster, 2003).

———, *Plan of Attack* (New York: Simon and Schuster, 2004).

———, *State of Denial* (New York: Simon and Schuster, 2006).

———, *The War Within: A Secret White House History, 2006–2008* (New York: Simon and Schuster, 2008).

Wright, Donald P., et al., *A Different Kind of War: The United States Army in Operation Enduring Freedom, October 2001–September 2005* (Fort Leavenworth, KS: Combat Studies Institute Press, 2009).

Wright, Donald P., and Timothy R. Reese, *The United States Army in Operation Iraqi Freedom, May 2003–January 2005; On Point II: Transition to the New Campaign* (Fort Leavenworth, KS: Combat Studies Institute Press, 2008).

Wright, Lawrence, *The Looming Tower: Al-Qaeda and the Road to 9/11* (New York: Knopf, 2006).

Yon, Michael, *Moment of Truth in Iraq* (Minneapolis, MN: Richard Vigilante Books, 2008).

Yoo, John, *War by Other Means: An Insider's Account of the War on Terror* (New York: Atlantic Monthly Press, 2006).

Zinni, Anthony, with Tony Koltz, *The Battle for Peace: A Frontline Vision of America's Power and Purpose* (New York: Palgrave Macmillan, 2006).

Index